# The **Pursuit**
## of **Permanence**

# Quality Matters in Children's Services

**Series Editor:** Mike Stein

**Consultant Editor:** Caroline Thomas

The provision of high quality children's services matters to those who use and provide children's services. This important series is the result of an extensive government-funded research initiative into the *Quality Protects* programme which aimed to improve outcomes for vulnerable children, as well as transform the management and delivery of children's services. Titles in the series are essential reading for all those working in the field.

*also in the series*

**Child Protection, Domestic Violence and Parental Substance Misuse**
**Family Experiences and Effective Practice**
*Hedy Cleaver, Don Nicholson, Sukey Tarr and Deborah Cleaver*
ISBN 978 1 84310 582 4

*of related interest*

**Costs and Outcomes in Children's Social Care**
**Messages from Research**
*Jennifer Beecham and Ian Sinclair*
*Foreword by Parmjit Dhanda MP, Parliamentary Under Secretary of State for Children, Young People and Families*
ISBN 978 1 84310 496 4

**Fostering Now**
**Messages from Research**
*Ian Sinclair*
*Foreword by Tom Jeffreys, Director General, Children, Families and Young People Directorate, DfES*
ISBN 978 1 84310 362 2

**Foster Placements: Why They Succeed and Why They Fail**
*Ian Sinclair, Kate Wilson and Ian Gibbs*
ISBN 978 1 84310 173 4

**Foster Children**
**Where They Go and How They Get On**
*Ian Sinclair, Claire Baker, Kate Wilson and Ian Gibbs*
ISBN 978 1 84310 278 6

**Foster Carers**
**Why They Stay and Why They Leave**
*Ian Sinclair, Ian Gibbs and Kate Wilson*
ISBN 978 1 84310 172 7

**Fostering Adolescents**
*Elaine Farmer, Sue Moyers and Jo Lipscombe*
ISBN 978 1 84310 227 4

**Leaving Care**
**Throughcare and Aftercare in Scotland**
*Jo Dixon and Mike Stein*
ISBN 978 1 84310 202 1

**Quality
Matters**
in **Children's
Services**

# The **Pursuit**
# of **Permanence**

## A Study of the English Care System

- Ian Sinclair
- Claire Baker
- Jenny Lee
- Ian Gibbs

JKP

**Changes to the structure of government departments in June 2007**

In the course of writing this book three new government departments were set up by the Prime Minister on 28 June 2007:

The Department for Children, Schools and Families (DCSF)

The Department for Innovation, Universities and Skills (DIUS)

The Department for Business, Enterprise and Regulatory Reform (DBERR)

These new departments replaced the Department for Education and Skills (DfES), which is mentioned extensively in this book, and the Department of Trade and Industry (DTI).

The Department for Children Schools and Families (DCSF) is responsible for improving the focus on all aspects of policy affecting children and young people, as part of the Government's aim to deliver educational excellence.

---

First published in 2007
by Jessica Kingsley Publishers
116 Pentonville Road
London N1 9JB, UK
and
400 Market Street, Suite 400
Philadelphia, PA 19106, USA

*www.jkp.com*

**Library of Congress Cataloging in Publication Data**

The pursuit of permanence : a study of the English child care system / Ian Sinclair ... [et al.].
    p. cm.
Includes bibliographical references and index.
ISBN 978-1-84310-595-4 (alk. paper)
1. Children--Services for--Great Britain. 2. Social service--Great Britain. 3. Foster home care--Great Britain. 4. Foster children--Great Britain. I. Sinclair, Ian, 1938-
HV245.P976 2008
362.71'20941--dc22
                        2007020374

**British Library Cataloguing in Publication Data**
A CIP catalogue record for this book is available from the British Library

ISBN 978 1 84310 595 4

Printed and bound in Great Britain by
Athenaeum Press, Gateshead, Tyne and Wear

# Contents

PREFACE     11

ACKNOWLEDGEMENTS     13

1    Introduction     15

2    Who is Looked After? The Children's Characteristics     29

3    Who is Looked After? The Children's Families, Wishes and Behaviour     43

4    Groups of Children and Their Chance of Permanence     65

5    Admissions and Discharges     85

6    The Children and Their Different Paths in Care     103

7    Going Home and Leaving Care: The Case Studies     115

8    Placements: How They are Used     133

9    Placements: How One Leads to Another     159

10    Children Based in Care     181

11    Children and Outcomes     197

12    Placements and Outcomes     207

13    Carers, Homes and Outcomes     221

14    Teams and Outcomes     235

15    Councils and Outcomes     251

16    An Overview     261

APPENDIX I: REPRESENTATIVENESS OF THE STUDY SAMPLES     277

APPENDIX II: ANALYSIS OF NATIONAL DATA     283

APPENDIX III: MONITORING AND QUALITY ASSURANCE     305

REFERENCES     309

SUBJECT INDEX     313

AUTHOR INDEX     319

# List of Figures, Tables, Boxes and Case Studies

Figure 3.1    Family difficulty score by whether child aged 11 or more at first entry    45

Figure 3.2    Challenging behaviour score by age and age at entry    46

Figure 3.3    School performance scores by age and age at entry    46

Figure 3.4    Family difficulties score by need code and age at entry    47

Figure 3.5    Challenging behaviour score by need code and age at entry    48

Figure 3.6    School performance score by need code and age at entry    49

Figure 3.7    Challenging behaviour by asylum status and whether 11 or over    50

Figure 3.8    School performance by asylum status and whether 11 or over    51

Figure 3.9    Care acceptance score by age and age at entry    54

Figure 3.10    Average length of period since last admission by social worker's view of whether child accepts care    57

Figure 4.1    Policy groups    67

Figure 4.2    Average family difficulty score by policy groups    68

Figure 4.3    Average challenging behaviour by policy groups    69

Figure 4.4    Average care acceptance score by policy groups    70

Figure 4.5    Average length of current/latest stay by policy groups    70

Figure 4.6    Average length of current/latest placement by policy groups    71

Figure 5.1    Estimated 'survival curve' for children admitted during the census year    89

Figure 5.2    Length of care careers for children still looked after at the end of the census year    91

Figure 5.3    Length of care career for children who left care during the census year    91

Figure 8.1    Placement days in the year by category of placement    139

Figure 9.1    Average length of latest placement by type of purpose    161

Figure 9.2    Length of latest placement by time since arrival    163

Figure 9.3    Average number of days in non-initial placements by number of these placements    164

Figure 9.4    Length of last or latest placement by number of non-initial placements    165

Figure 9.5     Mean challenging behaviour score by placement success          170

Figure 13.1    Relationship between fostering quality and placement quality    223
Figure 13.2    Distribution of fostering quality score                        223
Figure 13.3    Multi-level model for length of placement and fostering score  225
Figure 13.4    Rating of residential units                                    229

Figure 14.1    Social work staff establishment per team                       237
Figure 14.2    Number of FTE social work staff (including agency workers)
               per team                                                       238
Figure 14.3    Vacancy rates in teams                                         238
Figure 14.4    Adjusted cases to social workers' ratio                        240

Figure 15.1    Adjusted three placements score and type of council            255


Table 2.1      Age group of the sample at the census date                     31
Table 2.2      Age of the sample when first looked after                      31
Table 2.3      Age group at census by age group at first admission            33
Table 2.4      Ethnic origin of the total sample                              34
Table 2.5      Ethnic origin by whether seeking asylum                        36
Table 2.6      Need codes by age at entry                                     38

Table 3.1      Age group by need code of disability                           53
Table 3.2      Child accepts need to be looked after by whether voluntarily
               accommodated                                                   55
Table 3.3      Correlations: acceptance of care, behaviour and school
               performance                                                    56
Table 3.4      Logistic regression predicting rejection of care              59

Table 5.1      Time since last admission by plan at earliest recorded
               placement                                                      86
Table 5.2      Plan at first previous placement by plan at last/latest
               placement                                                      87
Table 5.3      Age distribution and length of time since last admission at
               census date                                                   92
Table 5.4      Age distribution and length of time since last admission at
               census date                                                   93
Table 5.5      Destinations by time since last admission                     94
Table 5.6      Average age at census by reason for ceasing to be looked after 95
Table 5.7      Destination on leaving the care system by time since entry    96
Table 5.8      Destination on leaving the care system by time since entry    97
Table 5.9      Destination on leaving the care system by time since entry    98

| Table 5.10 | Destination on leaving the care system by time since entry | 100 |
|---|---|---|
| Table 6.1 | Logistic regression predicting those with repeat admissions | 105 |
| Table 6.2 | Logistic regression predicting remaining when admitted in the year | 106 |
| Table 6.3 | Logistic regression predicting adoption over the course of census year | 108 |
| Table 6.4 | Need codes among 'early care leavers' | 111 |
| Table 8.1 | Placements over career histories | 134 |
| Table 8.2 | Distribution of placements on the census date | 135 |
| Table 8.3 | Completed placement lengths (in days) by type of placement | 137 |
| Table 8.4 | Average placement length in days by placement type | 138 |
| Table 8.5 | Need codes by fostered at end of year | 141 |
| Table 8.6 | Purposes of placements by fostered at end of the year | 142 |
| Table 8.7 | Need code by fostered with relatives at the census date | 144 |
| Table 8.8 | Age by type of residential unit | 149 |
| Table 8.9 | Asylum seeker status by type of residential unit | 150 |
| Table 8.10 | Need code of disability by type of residential unit | 150 |
| Table 9.1 | Purpose of placement by time since last admission | 162 |
| Table 9.2 | Purpose trajectory by placement success | 168 |
| Table 9.3 | Current age group by placement success | 169 |
| Table 9.4 | Voluntary accommodation by placement success | 170 |
| Table 9.5 | Purpose trajectory by asylum status | 171 |
| Table 9.6 | Three or more placements by placement success | 173 |
| Table 9.7 | D35 stability measure by placement success | 174 |
| Table 11.1 | Level of challenging behaviour by three or more placements by age | 200 |
| Table 11.2 | Logistic regression predicting D35 stability measure | 202 |
| Table 11.3 | Regression equation for 'doing-well' measure | 204 |
| Table 12.1 | Last completed placement by full success | 209 |
| Table 12.2 | Logistic regression predicting whether last placement a success | 210 |
| Table 12.3 | Average placement quality scores by type of placement | 211 |
| Table 12.4 | Three types of placement by quality of placement score | 212 |
| Table 12.5 | Quality of placement score by type of agency | 212 |
| Table 12.6 | Within and 'out of county' placements by quality in three types of placement | 213 |
| Table 12.7 | Quality of placement and three or more placements in a year | 215 |
| Table 12.8 | Quality of placement and D35 stability measure | 215 |
| Table 12.9 | Quality of placement by three placements by age | 216 |

Table 12.10    'Doing-well' and quality of placement score                     217
Table 12.11    Quality of placement and other predictors of 'doing-well'       218

Table 14.1     Types of social work team                                       236
Table 14.2     Resources and expected delays by age of child                   241
Table 14.3     Correlations between different measures of 'pressure'           243
Table 14.4     Factors associated with work pressure in teams                  245

Table AI.1     Demographic characteristics of 13 participating councils        278
Table AI.2     Comparison of study sample with national statistics             280
Table AI.3     Comparison of the 6-month sub-sample with the sample
               based on the social worker questionnaire returns                282

Table AII.1    Correlations between successive A1 indicators (2002–2004)        285
Table AII.2    Correlations between successive proportions of children
               fostered or adopted (Indicator B7)                              286
Table AII.3    Correlations between successive proportions of children
               fostered or adopted under the age of 10 (Indicator C22)         287
Table AII.4    Correlations between successive D35 indicators                   287
Table AII.5    Correlations between successive years on new PSA indicator       288
Table AII.6    Correlations between successive adoption performance measures
               (Indicator C23)                                                 289
Table AII.7    Correlations on education measure for 2003 and 2004
               (Indicator A2)                                                  289
Table AII.8    Education, employment and training: correlations between
               successive measures (Indicator A4)                             290
Table AII.9    Correlations between selected stability performance measures
               in 2004                                                        291
Table AII.10   Correlations between selected performance measures              292
Table AII.11   Correlations between selected performance indicators            293
Table AII.12   Correlations between performance measures and overall
               measures of performance                                        294
Table AII.13   Correlation between PAF domains and inspectors' ratings         296
Table AII.14   Regression equation predicting three placements measure         297
Table AII.15   Correlations between adoption rates (C23) and the
               D35 indicator                                                  298
Table AII.16   Correlations between the D35 measure and the measure
               of educational performance (A2)                                299
Table AII.17   Further education, training and employment measure (A4)
               with D35                                                        299

| Box 3.1 | Young people's reflections | 54 |
|---|---|---|
| Box 6.1 | Managers' reflections | 106 |
| Box 6.2 | Managers' reflections | 109 |
| Box 8.1 | Social workers' reflections | 143 |
| Box 8.2 | Manager and Team Leader reflections | 148 |

| Case study | Colin | 72 |
|---|---|---|
| Case study | Alan | 73 |
| Case study | Ifan | 74 |
| Case study | Nina | 75 |
| Case study | Ian | 76 |
| Case study | Neil | 78 |
| Case study | Joseph | 79 |
| Case study | Hannah | 81 |
| Case study | Adrienne | 117 |
| Case study | Mary | 118 |
| Case study | Connor | 119 |
| Case study | Daniel | 121 |
| Case study | Shaun | 123 |
| Case study | Eric | 124 |
| Case study | Keith | 125 |
| Case study | Angela | 126 |
| Case study | Brian | 129 |
| Case study | Hailey | 183 |
| Case study | Frances | 185 |
| Case study | Helen | 187 |
| Case study | Lewis | 190 |
| Case study | Graham | 191 |
| Case study | Sarah | 192 |

# Preface

The less one knows about 'children in care' the more similar they may appear. Many people 'know' that the outcomes of 'care' are not, on the face of it, good. Much is spoken about the poor education of those who have been looked after in this way and their high chances of becoming homeless adults or entering prison. Responses are commonly sympathetic. Some blame the care system; others the parents. Little account is taken of the great variety of the children and of their experiences, yet there is very little that is true of all the children who are looked after by the state.

This book takes this variety seriously. A number of questions arise. Consider, for example, three children who are described in more detail later in this book.

> Mary entered the care system at the age of nine, as a result of neglect by her mother. Two years later she left to live with her father. She is happy at school; happy to be with her siblings; she and her father adore each other; the result according to all concerned is a great success.

> Connor entered care at roughly the same age as Mary and also for reasons of neglect. He has been 'in care' for six months. He loves his foster carers, has grown 6 inches in six months and put on 1.5 stone, and has apparently never looked so happy or content. He wants to stay with his carers 'forever'.

> Lewis came into care at the age of six. He is now 18. In the intervening time he has had over 20 placements, interspersed with periods with his mother that did not work out. He is now in a Young Offenders' Institution. His future is uncertain and he prefers not to think about it at all.

These three stories are only three out of the great number that we collected. Even on their own, however, they suggest questions.

Some of these are about 'philosophy'. Most people assume that children want to be and should be with their families. No doubt this is generally right. But is it true in all the three cases we have just described?

Other questions are about 'need'. All these children came into the system at around the same age. Nevertheless the care system has played very different roles in their lives. What combination of characteristics may determine which role is appropriate? Which ones affect the likelihood that this role will be played successfully?

Other questions are about 'process' – what determines whether children go home like Mary or remain in the system like Connor, or whether like Lewis they have numerous placements? Is this a matter of their own characteristics, their own families, or the policies and practices of the councils that look after them?

Still other questions are about 'outcomes'. Why are two of these children happy with their current position while the third is not? How far does this depend on their council and the policies it pursues? How far does it depend on their social worker and her or his team? How far does it depend on the kind and quality of the placements they experience?

This book is centrally concerned with these questions and others related to them. Its starting point was a study of movement into, out of and within the care system. In seeking to understand this movement, it had, however, to describe the operation of the care system as a whole.

The result is a book that ranges broadly and tackles a number of very difficult questions that have practical importance. In the end our argument is that the care system has to be built around the children's relationships – not only those that they have with their own families or may have with adoptive parents but also those with their carers. We use this conclusion along with other findings to make suggestions about the way the care system should work, what it should offer, and how it should be managed and inspected.

The book is not an easy read throughout all of its sections, due to the complexity of the subject. We have tried, however, to make its outline and argument accessible to any concerned reader. In this way we have tried to repay our debt to the children and professionals on whose co-operation our research essentially depended.

# Acknowledgements

The project that led to this book was very large. Of necessity, it was above all a team effort involving three groups: the staff of the participating councils, the children and young people who took part in the study and ourselves. We want here to acknowledge our own particular debts.

The study was funded by the Department of Health (DoH) and then by the Department for Education and Skills (DfES). We are very grateful to Caroline Thomas, our liaison officer at both Departments, and to her colleague, Dr Carolyn Davies, for their steady and constructive advice.

We would also like to thank our colleagues at the Social Work Research and Development Unit for bearing with us over a long and demanding project. Dawn Rowley played a key role organising the vast numbers of questionnaires that were returned, transcribing many of the interviews, entering much of the data, and remaining calm and good humoured throughout. Rosie Gray and Alastair Gibbs also helped with these tasks. We are very grateful to them all.

Our debt to the staff in the councils is immense. In the midst of very busy lives they responded with great generosity to our questionnaires, ensuring exceptionally high response rates. Particular thanks are owed to the reviewers who undertook our case studies, the information staff who provided much of the data and the managers and liaison officers who read our reports, corrected errors and ensured that the project kept on the road. Without the co-operation of all these people the project could not have succeeded. Indeed it could not have taken place at all.

We must equally thank the children and young people in the study. Their stories were often encouraging but also painful. We did not meet them ourselves but even in the reports of others their honesty, insight and pithy turn of phrase shone through. They volunteered to take part in the study because they believed it would help other children in similar situations. We hope we have done justice to their efforts and that some change does, as a result, occur.

# Chapter 1

# Introduction

We would want our children, when they are in our care, to have a stable experience because we know that placement moves unless [they are] for positive reasons...can be highly damaging. (Social Services Manager)

## Introduction

In Britain most children stay with at least one of their parents until they are grown up. Such comparative permanence is not the lot of those looked after by the state. Their 'care careers' begin with a move from home, and usually involve one or more subsequent changes of placement. Some move many times, some less frequently, others hardly at all. This book results from research into these different patterns of movement, and the reasons for them.

The background to the research lies in the belief that most children who are looked after move too much. The children themselves complain about the moves; official indicators of performance discourage them; children who have many changes of placement do less well than those who do not. Most moves are unsettling and, for the children, 'scary'; some, such as those following the breakdown of a long-term placement, may be devastating for children and carers alike.

At the same time most agree that not all movement is bad. Moves take their meaning from a wider context: their effect on the child's chance of achieving a permanent base in which he or she can grow up, happily, attached to those looking after them and without further disruption. Some moves, for example to adoption, enable the child to gain such a base; they are seen as good. Other moves may signal the breakdown of a placement intended to be permanent; they are seen as bad. Yet other moves, for example those to allow a 'trial' of a child at home, may be needed to allow time for a permanent plan to be made or to allow a child to prepare for a more permanent solution.

The appropriateness of these moves is likely to vary with the children involved and the stage they have reached in the care process. Some children enter the system at a young age and spend a long time in it. Clearly they depend on their carers to meet their attachment needs. Their need for a permanent placement is particularly strong. Other young children move on to adoption after spending up to two or three years with the same carers; somehow they have to be enabled to transfer their attachments to someone else. Yet others enter briefly and return home; their attachment needs are not met in the system and this is not to be expected. Other children may enter the system as adolescents and at a point when foster care may feel like a threat to their loyalty to their own families or when, like some seeking asylum, their minds are focused on making a new life. Such young people may not want a permanent home in care even if it was on offer.

In the end the appropriateness or otherwise of a move has to be judged in terms of the *outcomes* achieved. Final stability is, other things being equal, an outcome of value in itself. For it can hardly be desirable that children have no base at all. Yet it is possible for children to be acutely unhappy in their long-term homes, or to have many moves but remain secure because they have a long-term base with carers they love. We need to have ways of judging whether children are settled, happy, doing well at school and so on. We also need to know how far councils, social workers and carers can influence these outcomes. Academics want to know how care works out. Practitioners want to know how to improve its results.

For these reasons a full study of movement in care has to take into account the following:

- The children – what they are like, what they need and what they want.

- Their entrances and exits – why they come in, how long they stay and why they leave.

- Their placements – what these are, what they are meant to do, how long children stay in them and how often they move between them.

- The outcomes – whether the children are settled, happy, behaving well and achieving at school.

- The reasons – why all this happens as it does and turns out as it does.

This, very broadly, constitutes the ground covered in this book. As argued later in this chapter, some of the ground covered is new – no-one, for example, has previously investigated the effects on children of social work teams or of differences between departments in quite this way. Other parts of the book add to, complement or update the work of other researchers. Although the origins of the research had to do with movement, the result is probably as broad an empirical study of the English care system as has recently been undertaken.

## Policy background

The study was commissioned as part of a research initiative stemming from the government strategy known as *Quality Protects*.[1] The strategy had a number of aims. From the point of view of this project the key one, outlined by Jacqui Smith (former Minister of State for Health), was to get 'children to live in the right place, not being moved around and settling down so that they [could] fulfil their potential' (Department for Education and Skills (DfES) 2003). This ambition was based on the views of children. It was to be advanced by improved management, in particular the development of a number of key indicators of excessive movement between placements. These ambitions in turn reflected two central concerns of the initiative: listening to children and management.

Policy has developed since *Quality Protects*. A new programme *Choice Protects*[2] has sought to increase the variety of placements, particularly foster placements, available. A series of government initiatives on Care Standards, Adoption, Leaving Care and Education[3] have all striven to improve outcomes for children who are looked after by the state. The Green Paper *Every Child Matters* (DfES 2003) has re-emphasised the importance of a positive vision of what is possible. At the same time it has widened the focus to include all children, not just those who are looked after, while stressing the need for co-operation between services and the importance of early intervention.

This new agenda does not contradict the old one. Certainly it highlights potential conflicts. The care system requires relatively costly services for a minority of children and young people. It will not be easy to marry such expenditure with the provision of an equally high quality service for larger numbers of children whose needs are less severe. Nevertheless the new Green Paper, *Care Matters* (DfES 2006), should have laid to rest any doubts about government's wish to improve the lot of children in care. This passionate document retains the ambition of prevention: early, multi-disciplinary intervention will prevent admission to care where possible. At the same time everything possible will be done to reduce the yawning gap in achievement and outcomes between those in care and other children.

The reduction of this gap is seen as requiring continuity in the form of adults who will be available throughout a child's 'care career'; better and also more specialised and differentiated placements; even more commitment from the school system (earlier policies have already given education priority); greater opportunities outside school; and a later and better supported transition to adult life. Steps to ensure greater accountability, more independent inspection and greater responsiveness to the needs of the children the system is to serve will underpin the whole.

The organisational setting for the new agendas differs from that in place at the time of *Quality Protects*. There now are or, almost certainly, will soon be Children's Trusts, Directors of Children's Services, an enhanced role for the Office for Standards in Education, Children's Services and Skills (OFSTED) and Independent Reviewing Officers, a Commissioner for England and a range of new standards. *Quality Protects* foresaw none of this.

Despite these changes the fundamental philosophy remains the same. The four abiding themes are that children should have 'permanence' (by which is meant a lasting experience of a family that gives them the opportunity to attach to adults); that this attachment should underpin better outcomes, particularly in education; that there should be a choice of high quality provision; and that both the provision and the system around it should be well managed.

Even the philosophy of management shows much continuity. There is a continuing belief in empowering children so that their views are heard and used to improve the system. And there is a continuing emphasis on accountability, the achievement of external standards and targets, and the enforcement of this regime through external inspection. In these ways the policy agenda is very similar to that of this book. There is, however, a difference in perspective. Those making policy have to believe in their prescriptions. To do any less could be a recipe for ineffectiveness. Research is allowed the luxury of doubt. For example, in this book we will not assume that the current indicators of stability are necessarily appropriate. Nor will we assume that councils can necessarily influence outcomes. Insofar as we are able to reduce doubt we will, we hope, lay the ground for surer policy and practice.

## How may research contribute to this agenda?

Research on the care system may contribute to this agenda in at least four ways.

First, it can describe what the care system is doing. This task is more complex than it seems. At the very least it covers what the system is trying to achieve for whom, how and over what length of time. So we need to know about the characteristics, needs, and lengths of stay of a representative sample of the children who are looked after. We also need to know how different groups of children get on in the system and what happens to them there. Such a description does not allow a formal evaluation – a demonstration that what is done works better or worse than possible alternatives. It does, however, allow for an appraisal – an informed assessment of what the children's needs are and how far what is done is likely to meet them.

Second, research can investigate what children and young people think. To date we know, for example, that they feel they are consulted too little, that they commonly feel they are moved around too much, that some feel that they are kept too long in places where they are unhappy, that young people hate being bullied, and dislike being made to feel the odd one out in foster homes, that most want to see more of their families, that this does not mean that they want to see more of all members of their family – and much else besides (see, for example, references in Sinclair 2005). This knowledge is also an essential part of appraising what is going on.

A third way in which research can contribute is by assessing the role and impact of placements. It is natural to think that moves occur because of poor placements. Some do. Young children may be moved from placements where they are unhappy. Older ones may prove too much for their carers. However, 'good' carers may also enable movement, for example by working with a social worker over an adoption or a return home. A child who enters the system at the age of three and is still there at the age of nine is unlikely to want a move. An adolescent who has fallen behind with their education may need a placement that helps them to catch up and move on. Research may help determine what counts as a good placement and what impact it has on movement and other outcomes.

A fourth possible research contribution lies in its implications for the use of movement as a measure of performance. Performance measurement is central to the 'New Public Management' (Strathern 2000). It may be variously justified as enabling accountability, providing feedback and focusing managers' minds on performance. It is also believed to promote informed choice, competition between agencies and attention to quality as well as cost. In these ways measurement is a central feature of current attempts to drive up performance through targets, standards and external inspection.

In practice the use of performance measurement is controversial. There are criticisms of the technical quality of the measures, the degree to which they do enable choice or competition, and the degree to which they focus on the measurable rather than the important. In addition it is hard to obtain useful feedback in a situation where managers are uncertain how to affect the measures or where the staff, on which performance depends, have a more complex agenda. In this field complexity comes with the territory. Social services pursue a variety of goals, have to satisfy a variety of audiences, and are influenced by differing professional and managerial values. They have to do this in situations where they have to account for their activities, compete for funds, and collaborate with others without whom they cannot successfully achieve their ends. In this situation neither the measurement nor the management of performance is easy (for discussion and numerous references see Paton 2003; Smith 1995).

Research may help with these measurement issues in a variety of ways. For the purposes of this study we have focused on the accuracy and meaning of the measures and on the capacity of managers to influence them. In this context research can help unravel the factors that contribute to high or low scores on the measurement of movement, assess their accuracy and explore how they relate to other measures of 'outcome'. Insofar as it turns out that the measures are valid it can explore how managers can influence these measures. For without such understanding there may be little that managers can do to improve performance, except perhaps 'game' (for example, by delaying moves until they are counted in a different year), 'give up' or resort to random action or defensive explanation.

## Earlier research

Discussions with managers in this project showed that research can influence their thinking. Usually it does this as part of a complex argument and is used along with other considerations. In this context we have argued above that research can contribute by describing the care system, reporting on the views of children, analysing the effects of placements, and assessing aspects of management and performance measurement. How far has this contribution already been made?

The key descriptive study of the care system is that by Rowe and her colleagues (1989). The researchers involved tracked all movements into, out of, and within the care systems of six local councils over a period of two years (April 1985 to March 1987). The study was concerned with placement endings and beginnings (25,000 in all).[4] In this way it cast a flood of new light on the social workers' views of the purposes of placements and on the degree to which these placements were successful on certain criteria. It showed, for example, that different kinds of children were typically using different placements, that councils differed in their use of placements, and that some kinds of placement appeared more successful than others. It also highlighted the degree to which some kinds of placement (typically residential care) were used much more often in the course of a year than a simple frequency count at a particular point would suggest.

Rowe and her colleagues also began the difficult task of explaining movement. Their study encompassed three different kinds of move: admissions and discharges, purposeful movement within the care system reflecting the aims of a particular placement (e.g. to provide temporary care), and breakdowns which they defined as placements that did not last as long as needed. They were able to relate these different sorts of move to the phase of the children's care careers (discharges were much more common in the early stages), to the children's ages and characteristics and to the types of placement. So the researchers showed, for example, that adolescents were much more likely than younger children to move for reasons connected with behaviour and that placements with short-term aims were more likely to be successful than those with longer term ones.

Rowe and her colleagues' work is complemented by official statistics and also by numerous studies of particular sub-groups in the care population. So we know much more, often from research funded by government, about the characteristics of young people in residential and foster care (Archer, Hicks and Little 1998; Sinclair 2005). Other studies have described movements in and out of the care system. In the mid 1980s these included general samples of children in care (e.g. Milham *et al.* 1986; Packman, Randall and Jacques 1986). More recently this information has come from studies of particular groups such as foster children (e.g. Sinclair *et al.* 2005b), or children accommodated under section 20 of the Children Act 1989 (Packman and Hall 1998) or particular processes such as return home (Bullock, Little and Milham 1993; Bullock, Good and Little 1998; Farmer and Parker 1991) or leaving care (Stein and Carey 1986; Biehal *et al.* 1995; Dixon and Stein 2005).

In terms of children's views there has also been much progress. Rowe and her colleagues did not include this as part of their research. Since then the Department of Health and the Department for Education and Skills (DfES) have funded a wide range of studies into the child care system. Almost all of this has included the exploration of children's views as a component (see for example, Archer *et al.* 1998 and Sinclair 2005 for summaries and references). A series of reports by the Children's Rights Director (see Office of the Children's Rights Director for England (OCRD) 2007) cover children's views on a wide variety of aspects of the care system. The problem now is not so much a lack of knowledge of what children want but a lack of action resulting from it. Here too steps are being taken (see, for example, www.anationalvoice.org).

Considerable progress has also been made on the assessment of placements. For reasons connected with the kinds of data collected Rowe and her colleagues' study could only make a limited contribution to this issue.[5] More important have been the government initiative focused specifically on residential care (Archer *et al.* 1998) and the numerous studies focused on foster care (Sinclair 2005). This work has established, more or less beyond doubt, that placements do have an immediate effect on the quality of life and behaviour of those in them. The qualities demanded from placements have similarities across settings. What is needed is warmth and concern from committed adults who are also clear about and agreed on what they expect (see for example, Archer *et al.* 1998; Berridge and Brodie 1998; Farmer, Lipscombe and Meyers 2005; Hicks *et al.* 2007; Quinton *et al.* 1998; Sinclair 1971, 1975; Sinclair and Gibbs 1998; Sinclair and Wilson 2003 and summaries in Sinclair 2005 and Sinclair 2006).

Despite this progress in knowledge there are gaps. There is some evidence that it may be 'better' for a child to be in a 'good' placement in care than a 'poor' birth family home (see for example, Dando and Minty 1987; Hensey, Williams and Rosenbloom 1983; King and Taitz 1985; Sinclair *et al.* 2005b; Taussig, Clyman and Landsverk 2001; Tizard 1975; Zimmerman 1982). There is very much less evidence on the long-term effects of a 'good placement'; indeed there is some evidence that 'good effects' may not last (Hicks *et al.* 2007).[6] Equally there are major gaps in the comparisons of different types of placement. Colton (1988) has provided the only substantial, but unfortunately inconclusive, study of the differences between residential and foster care. There have been no controlled comparisons of independent and local council fostering, little until recently on the comparative effectiveness of fostering by family and friends,[7] and little conclusive evidence on comparisons of independent and local council residential care.[8]

If the evidence on the effects of placements is patchy, solid research evidence on the effects of management in children's social care is virtually non-existent. This might matter less if conclusions from other areas could be applied uncritically to social services. This is almost certainly not the case. Modern theories of management suggest that there is no one 'right approach' that fits all situations. Instead organisations have to adapt according to their own technology and size and the nature of their environments (in particular their 'predictability'). In this context social services seem most similar to the 'professional bureaucracies' described by Mintzberg (1981) (cited in Clegg, Kornberger and Pitsis 2005). These bureaucracies, however, rely on 'standardised skills'. It is not clear that social work, foster care or residential work can lay claim to such a routine repertoire. Even if they do its successful exercise depends on personal relationships, the very antithesis of the rational machine that is the ideal model for a bureaucratic system.

In summary the situation in terms of earlier research seems to be as follows:

- *Description* – Rowe and her colleagues (1989) provided an early and wide-ranging description of the care system. This is now dated, albeit supplemented by more detailed and up to date descriptions of parts of the system and by less detailed routine statistics.

- *Listening to children* – We know a lot about what children in the care system want. In general their desires seem entirely reasonable. The problem is meeting them.

- *Analysis of placement effects* – There has been good progress on analysing the effects of placements but there are still many gaps in knowledge.

- *Analysis of management effects* – There has been virtually no systematic research in this area.

As a result those making policy on the care system face some difficulties. To a greater or less extent they may be uncertain about what they are seeking to manage, how different kinds of placements may impact on it, or what kind of management is appropriate. This book bears on these issues. Before discussing how this may be so we need to describe the research itself.

## The study

The study took place in 13 councils in England: four county councils, two unitary councils and four London and three metropolitan boroughs.

The councils were selected so that they were varied and they were keen to collaborate. Their 'star ratings' varied from 0 to 3. As outlined in Appendix I, we believe that our main sample almost exactly represents the national picture.

The research focused on all children who had been looked after at any point in a year agreed with the councils. The last day of this year (census date) varied between 31 May 2003 and 30 June 2004. The main sources of data collection were as follows:

- Client information system (CIS) sample: This yielded data on 7399 children in the 13 councils and covered their full placement careers,[9] changes of legal status, reasons for admission, age, age at first entry, types of placement and dates on which, and reasons why, placements started and ended.[10]

- Social work data: Social workers completed questionnaires on 4647 children looked after in the last six months and on up to three placements in those months.[11] The information covered care plans, purposes and perceived quality and success of the placements, services received and other information on the children's characteristics and the difficulties or otherwise of providing appropriate service.

- Questionnaires from 114 team leaders provided information on the teams that served the core sample.

- Supervising social workers provided data on 1585 foster households that looked after children in the sample year, including data on the quality of care provided, registration details and training.

- A variety of staff provided data on 315 residential units used over the year, focusing on the quality of care provided.

- There were 54 extensive telephone interviews with heads of children's services and other senior managers (four or five in each authority).

- Local council staff (usually an independent reviewing officer or children's right's officer) provided 95 case studies based on interviews with young people and their social workers.

- Additional qualitative material came from comments in the questionnaires from team leaders, social workers, and supervising social workers.

- We have used national data to place our own in context and to carry out further exploration of the relevant performance indicators (see Appendix II).

Co-operation was excellent. Social workers returned questionnaires on 71 per cent of those on whom we sought information. We covered two-thirds of the team leaders involved and that together with their teams were supervising just over two-thirds of the children in the CIS sample. We slightly exceeded our target of four interviews with managers in each authority and always interviewed the assistant director or equivalent manager responsible for children's services. We achieved 95 (73%) out of a target of 130 (10 per authority) case studies.

We set out to ensure that the study was useful to the councils as well as nationally. For this reason we gave each council an individual report on its own data of approximately 25,000 words. The councils found these helpful and some at least used them in their strategy plans and in developing their services. As a senior manager put it 'There's something in there for us'. The councils' comments about the reports were certainly very positive and the seriousness with which they treated the research was both extremely helpful and very encouraging.

## Analysis

Our strategy in analysing the data was as follows. First, we used the CIS and social work samples to describe the children and to describe and analyse the operation of the system. Second, we used the data on placements and teams to see if they helped us explain differences in movement and outcome. Third, we used the case studies and other qualitative data in two ways: as a kind of conceptual 'triangulation', namely, a set of very different data that enabled us to see whether the ideas that came from the statistical data were in any way reflected in the experience of the children, young people and social workers, but also as a set of data of value in their own right and one which had rich insights into practice. Within this general analytic strategy we used the other qualitative data more opportunistically, drawing on it to illustrate or explain points that arose in the statistical material.

How far does this strategy enable us to answer the kinds of question raised earlier? The answers to this vary with the question posed.

First, in terms of description we think we have good data and that they represent the national picture (see Appendix I).

Second, our evidence on children's views comes from the case studies (where children were interviewed) and from the social workers. Clearly this is not a consumer study. Our evidence on what children want does, however, play an important part in our analysis.

Third, we examine how far the kind and quality of placements appeared to influence the stability that children achieve and their well-being. In this way we support previous research in this area and also open up new lines of enquiry.

Finally, we provide data on the degree to which and the way in which the organisation and management of services affects stability and well-being. As far as we know, our work in this area breaks new ground, at least in relation to British research in this field.

## The write-up of the research

The book combines description, analysis and appraisal (as explained earlier, we mean by appraisal, an assessment that is less than a full evaluation but which nevertheless allows for an informed judgement).

Chapters 2, 3 and 4 deal with the characteristics of the children. They provide and illustrate a way of grouping children that puts together children with similar characteristics, likely needs and careers in care. The six groups differ in their likelihood of achieving a long-term placement and, we will argue, in the degree to which this is an appropriate aim.

Chapters 5, 6 and 7 are about process: more specifically the decisions that determine whether the aim is a long-term placement. These chapters deal with movement into and out of care. Chapter 5 is about the speed with which children are divided into those who go home and those who do not and about the destinations of those who leave the system. Chapter 6 is about the differences between children who follow different paths (for example, between those who go home or who become adopted and others). Chapter 7 is about the practice around these decisions.

Chapters 8, 9 and 10 focus on the care system itself. They are about placements, movements between them, and the degree to which long-term placements are achieved. Chapter 10 provides case studies of children who, for good or ill, are not going home. It analyses the different ways they adapt to the care system and the reasons why some seem much happier and more settled than others.

The next five chapters (11 to 15) are about outcomes and the possible reasons for them. The focus is on different measures of stability (for example, whether a child has three or more placements in a year) and on 'well-being', a measure of how far a child is settled, emotionally stable, behaving well, closely attached to at least one adult and doing well at school. Chapters 11, 12 and 13 are about the possible effects of different kinds and quality of placement on these outcomes. Chapter 14 deals with the apparent impact on outcomes of differences between social work teams. Chapter 15 does the same for differences between councils.

Our final chapter (16) provides a brief summary and then our suggestions for policy and practice.

We have three appendices. One deals with how far our samples are representative. The second uses nationally available data to explore the validity of various performance indicators. The third deals with monitoring and quality assurance.

## A note on reading the book

We have written this book with different readers in mind. Some will simply want to get the gist of what we say. They may wish to read the conclusion and skim the rest, perhaps only reading the summary boxes that are at the end of some chapters. Others may wish to skim most of the book but look in more detail at some sections, for example those that deal with adoption or with the measurement of workload and pressure in social work teams. Others may wish to read the whole.

Some of the statistics used in this book will be unfamiliar to some, or even most, readers. Faced with this possibility we have always tried to make the logic of what we are doing clear. We have also tried to bring out the main points in any table or diagram in the text and to put as much technical material as we can in footnotes where it can be safely ignored.

In these ways we have tried to serve two purposes. Readers who are simply interested in what we have to say should be able to ignore tables that seem complicated, references to statistical tests and footnotes. Readers who want to test what we say and make up their own minds should have most of what they need (for some details on how we have reported statistical results please see note 12).

## Summary points

Policy and practice discourage movement in the care system, while nevertheless acknowledging that some moves are desirable. The book describes a very large study of placement moves in 13 councils. It uses a combination of qualitative and quantitative data to:

- place movement in the context of the children involved, the stages they have reached in their care careers and the purposes of placement
- describe and as far as possible explain the reasons for movement
- assess the association between movement and other outcomes of interest

- assess the impact on movement and related outcomes of the quality of placements and the way different local councils operate and use their resources.

The data used in the book appear to be nationally representative. The description they provide of the system for looking after children is therefore of more than local interest.

## Notes

1   The *Quality Protects* programme was launched by the Department of Health in September 1998 to support local councils in transforming the management and delivery of children's social services.

2   *Choice Protects* was launched in March 2002 to improve outcomes for looked-after children through providing better placement stability, matching and choice.

3   See, for example, Care Standards Act (2000), Children (Leaving Care) Act (2000), Children Act (2004).

4   An admitted limitation was that the study did not pick up children who did not move over this period.

5   Their basic difficulty was that, for good reasons, they collected information on placements not individuals. The data included some information on, for example, the age of those placed. It was, however, too limited to allow them to control for background variables in any rigorous way.

6   Sinclair (1971, 1975) found great variations in the degree of 'delinquent behaviour' found in different probation hostels. These variations were not explained by the backgrounds of those in the hostels but did relate to the characteristics of those running them. With one exception the hostels did not differ in their impact on the behaviour of probationers who had left them. In this respect it was interesting that young males sent to the hostels to be removed from 'unsatisfactory homes' were less likely than others to be convicted while in the hostel but more likely to be so after return home. Sinclair argued that the explanations for these findings were related. If the immediate environment of the hostel could have such an impact, it was reasonable to expect that this would also be true of the homes to which the probationers returned. This point was in keeping with other research at the time but does not seem to have been subsequently confirmed or refuted. Hicks and her colleagues (2007) have, however, found that children's 'happiness scores' tend to follow this pattern. Those who have been particularly 'happy' in a residential home tend to be 'less happy' on leaving it. Conversely those who have been particularly 'unhappy' tend to become 'happier'.

7   This was covered in an *ad hoc* way in Sinclair, Wilson and Gibbs 2005a and Sinclair *et al.* 2005b. Farmer and her colleagues at the University of Bristol and Hunt and her colleagues at the University of Oxford are undertaking more substantive studies. Sinclair (2005) provides a preliminary overview of the issues.

8   Hicks *et al.* in *Managing Children's Homes: Developing Effective Leadership in Small Organizations* (2007) found that the independent sector performed, on some measures, better than the local council one. Gibbs and Sinclair (1998) found the same. It was not clear that the

independent homes recruited to these studies were a true random sample (a necessary condition for a firm conclusion that one kind of home was better than the other). Even if they were the good effects could have reflected the greater distance of the independent homes from the young people's families.

9   All councils supplied the date on which the child was first looked after, but not all had data stretching back beyond four years. One council supplied data on all the placements that occurred in the census year but not data on previous years.

10   All these data are required for the SSDA903 return to the DfES.

11   The latest three placements where there were four or more.

12   Some readers will be surprised that we often do not quote significance levels. As a rule of thumb all the associations we describe without giving a significance level are significant at a level of less than one in a hundred ($p = <.01$). Similarly we do not always give the details of particular tests (for example, the degrees of freedom and size of the relevant statistic). Usually this is because the numbers involved are so large that the level of significance is way past 1 in a 1000. Where there is room for doubt over the test we have used we have tried to give details. For example, it is not always obvious from the text how many degrees of freedom a chi square test has had. Where this is so we give the details in a bracket or a note.

# Chapter 2

# Who is Looked After? The Children's Characteristics

Social work practice is difficult to quantify and all statistics should be placed in the context of the complex and difficult work we do. (Team Leader)

## Intoduction

This book is about children who are looked after by local councils. As illustrated in our preamble their stories are individual. They are as different from each other as almost any group of children we might have selected. Nevertheless there are certain characteristics that mark out broad groups of children and which have significance for their time in care.

As we will see these characteristics are likely to influence whether placements last and the ease with which they can attach to new carers. They also partly determine the roles that the care system plays and in particular the degree to which it seeks to offer a permanent base, return children home, or 'launch' them into independent living.

## Method

We have two main samples:

1.  All the 7399 children who, according to the information system, were looked after at any point in the year before the census date. We call this the Client Information System (CIS) sample (numbers in the tables vary slightly because of missing data).

2.  All the 4647 children who were looked after at any point in the six months before the census date and on whom the social workers

returned a questionnaire. We call this the social work sample (again numbers in the tables vary slightly because of missing data).

Both these samples contain interesting sub-groups – for example those who entered during the year, those who left during it and those who were there at the end of it. The characteristics of these groups differ. To give a trivial example, those who left during the year are on average older than those who entered.

We will look at these distinctions later. This chapter uses the CIS data to describe the full sample. For this reason it is restricted to data on sex, age at census, age at entry, ethnicity, whether seeking asylum, reason for entry (need code) and legal status, all of which appear in the annual returns councils are required to make to the Department for Education and Skills (DfES).

## Age and age at entry

Age (the current age of the child at the census date) and the related concept of age at first entry to the care system are probably the most crucial variables in this study. In our qualitative data social workers and managers often talked about age when they sought to understand the reasons for movement or identify groups of children with differing needs. The children themselves referred to age and the process of growing older as helping to explain how, for example, they had come to be reconciled to being looked after or how they hoped in the not too distant future to be free of the system altogether. In some councils the age of the child was used to define the remit of social work teams, with some teams dealing specifically with children under or over a certain age.

Statistically we will see later that age influences the likelihood of movement and the reasons for which children move. It is related to other variables such as disability or being an asylum seeker that in turn influence movements and the reasons for them. It is very strongly related to the likelihood of adoption and to the reasons for admission. Age is the natural variable with which to begin any description.

Our first table (Table 2.1) gives the ages of the sample on the census date. As can be seen the largest group (38%) are aged 10–15. A fifth are under five years old. A further fifth are at least five but less than ten years old. A final fifth (22%) are aged 16 and over.

**Table 2.1** Age group of the sample at the census date

|  |  | Frequency | Percent | Valid percent | Cumulative percent |
|---|---|---|---|---|---|
| Valid | 0–1 yrs | 622 | 8.4 | 8.4 | 8.4 |
|  | 2–4 yrs | 857 | 11.6 | 11.6 | 20.0 |
|  | 5–9 yrs | 1472 | 19.9 | 19.9 | 39.9 |
|  | 10–15 yrs | 2816 | 38.1 | 38.1 | 78.0 |
|  | 16 yrs and over | 1630 | 22.0 | 22.0 | 100.0 |
|  | Total | 7397 | 100.0 | 100.0 |  |
| Missing | System | 2 | .0 |  |  |
| Total |  | 7399 | 100.0 |  |  |

Source: CIS sample.

The next table (Table 2.2) gives the ages at which the children first entered the care system. Around four out of ten were first looked after in this way when less than five years old. Just over a quarter (28%) were looked after when aged five to nine. Just under a third (31%) first entered when aged 10–15. Very few (2%) entered when aged 16 or over.

**Table 2.2** Age of the sample when first looked after

|  |  | Frequency | Percent | Valid percent | Cumulative percent |
|---|---|---|---|---|---|
| Valid | 0–1 yrs | 1520 | 20.5 | 20.6 | 20.6 |
|  | 2–4 yrs | 1342 | 18.1 | 18.1 | 38.7 |
|  | 5–9 yrs | 2064 | 27.9 | 27.9 | 66.6 |
|  | 10–15 yrs | 2328 | 31.5 | 31.5 | 98.1 |
|  | 16 yrs and over | 142 | 1.9 | 1.9 | 100.0 |
|  | Total | 7396 | 100.0 | 100.0 |  |
| Missing | System | 3 | .0 |  |  |
| Total |  | 7399 | 100.0 |  |  |

Source: CIS sample.

Table 2.3 relates the age group at which children first entered the system to their current age at the end of the census year. The table is an introduction to the subject of care careers.[1] It is, however, immediately apparent that age at entry has a major effect on the length of time a child is able to spend in care. For example, those first entering the care system at the age of 16 have to leave the system by the time they are 18 and are likely to include many of those we will later describe as using the system as a launch pad.

It is interesting that very few of those aged less than two at first entry ($n = 1520$) were actually looked after at the age of 16 or over ($n = 20$ or 1.3%). By contrast those who first entered the care system when aged two to four ($n = 1342$) were much more likely to be looked after at the age of 16 and over ($n = 81$ or 6.0%). As we will see later these contrasts have much to do with adoption. An increase in the adoption rate among those first entering aged between two and four would over time come to have a detectable impact on the care system.

The main interest in Table 2.3 is as an aid to thinking about a variety of policies. To give a further example, children entering when aged 5–9 are commonly still looked after when aged 10–15. At this age of entry those who do not leave quickly tend to stay in the system.[2] Perhaps there is a case for thinking differently about the needs of those who 'graduate' into being looked after as teenagers and those who are first looked after at this age. How many of the latter need to use the system as a permanent base?

To take this example further, 469 young people aged 16 or over had first entered the system when aged less than ten. Of these just under half (48%) had been in their latest placement for less than two years. At the other end of the spectrum nearly a third (29%) had been in the same placement for five years or more. It is worrying that both the first group have such little stability and that the second group are commonly expected to leave their placements at 18.

## Sex and ethnicity

> Young person perfectly matched in every area – ethnicity, culture, language, religion and education. (Social Worker)

A child's sex played a less crucial role in our research than we had expected. The social workers did not refer to it as a crucial variable in matching. The children did not refer to it explicitly in their interviews. We routinely included sex in our analyses of the data. In comparison with, for example, age it turned out to have rather little to do with stability.

Descriptively it is useful to know that our sample is not atypical. As in the national figures males (55.6%) outnumber females (44.4%).[3] These percentages varied slightly by age of entry but the differences are not significant. Similarly there are no significant differences in the sex of current age groups.

**Table 2.3** Age group at census by age group at first admission

| Current age group at census | | Age group at 1st admission | | | | | |
| --- | --- | --- | --- | --- | --- | --- | --- |
| | | 0–1 yrs | 2–4 yrs | 5–9 yrs | 10–15 yrs | 16 yrs and over | Total |
| 0–1 yrs | Count | 619 | | | | | 619 |
| | % within Current age group at census | 100.0% | | | | | 100.0% |
| 2–4 yrs | Count | 541 | 316 | | | | 857 |
| | % within Current age group at census | 63.1% | 36.9% | | | | 100.0% |
| 5–9 yrs | Count | 239 | 567 | 666 | | | 1472 |
| | % within Current age group at census | 16.2% | 38.5% | 45.2% | | | 100.0% |
| 10–15 yrs | Count | 101 | 378 | 1030 | 1307 | | 2816 |
| | % within Current age group at census | 3.6% | 13.4% | 36.6% | 46.4% | | 100.0% |
| 16 yrs and over | Count | 20 | 81 | 368 | 1019 | 142 | 1630 |
| | % within Current age group at census | 1.2% | 5.0% | 22.6% | 62.5% | 8.7% | 100.0% |
| Total | Count | 1520 | 1342 | 2064 | 2326 | 142 | 7394 |
| | % within Current age group at census | 20.6% | 18.1% | 27.9% | 31.5% | 1.9% | 100.0% |

Source: CIS sample.

Ethnicity seemed much more central to social work thinking about placements than gender. Table 2.4 sets out the ethnic origin of the different children in the sample using the codes first developed by the Department of Health.[4] Comparing our figures to the national picture of children who were looked after at 31 March 2004 showed an extremely close fit. Among those present on census date we had 2 per cent fewer 'white' children (78% v. 80%) but 1 per cent more Asian children (3% v. 2%) and 1 per cent more black children (9% v. 8%). The figures for children whose ethnicity was coded 'mixed' (8%) and 'other' (2%) were identical.

**Table 2.4** Ethnic origin of the total sample

| Ethnic origin | | Frequency | Percent | Valid percent | Cumulative percent |
|---|---|---|---|---|---|
| Valid | A1 – White British | 5458 | 73.8 | 75.4 | 75.4 |
| | A2 – White Irish | 23 | .3 | .3 | 75.7 |
| | A3 – White other | 164 | 2.2 | 2.3 | 77.9 |
| | B1 – White & Black Carib. | 197 | 2.7 | 2.7 | 80.7 |
| | B2 – White & Black African | 61 | .8 | .8 | 81.5 |
| | B3 – White & Asian | 134 | 1.8 | 1.9 | 83.4 |
| | B4 – Other mixed | 139 | 1.9 | 1.9 | 85.3 |
| | C1 – Indian | 40 | .5 | .6 | 85.8 |
| | C2 – Pakistani | 121 | 1.6 | 1.7 | 87.5 |
| | C3 – Bangladeshi | 20 | .3 | .3 | 87.8 |
| | C4 – Asian other | 58 | .8 | .8 | 88.6 |
| | D1 – Caribbean | 137 | 1.9 | 1.9 | 90.5 |
| | D2 – African | 470 | 6.4 | 6.5 | 97.0 |
| | D3 – Black other | 52 | .7 | .7 | 97.7 |
| | E1 – Chinese | 26 | .4 | .4 | 98.0 |
| | E2 – Other ethnic group | 142 | 1.9 | 2.0 | 100.0 |
| | Total | 7242 | 97.9 | 100.0 | |
| Missing | System | 157 | 2.1 | | |
| Total | | 7399 | 100.0 | | |

Source: CIS sample.

There were significant differences between the various ethnic groups in relation to age, age at entry and sex. Much of this was explained by the presence of asylum seekers who, as we will see shortly, had very distinctive characteristics. However, the differences remained if this group was removed. For example, there were proportionately more females among the Indian and Pakistani children. Certain groups (white and black African, white and Asian, Pakistani and Bangladeshi children) contained an unusually high percentage of children entering as babies under one year old. African children were much more likely to enter as teenagers.

Our 13 councils differed sharply in the ethnicity of their care populations. Some had virtually no ethnic groups other than white British. Some had only a minority of white British children but a very wide variety of other ethnic groupings. Some had a predominantly white British population but one or two significant sub-groups.[5] Councils with very small black and minority ethnic populations struggled to find an appropriate ethnic match for the black and minority ethnic children they had. There were similar difficulties where there were highly diverse populations including, in one or two London boroughs, difficulties in finding ethnically matched placements for white children.

These problems of matching were of concern to the social workers. They made suggestions about, for example, the need for developments in practice over assessing black and minority ethnic carers and the possibility of collaboration between neighbouring boroughs over sharing carers. Difficulties in matching led to delays in finding permanent placements and were believed by many social workers to contribute to instability. As in the case of sex we routinely included ethnicity in our analyses without, however, finding as many differences relating to it as we expected. As will be seen, perhaps the most important of the differences related to difficulties over adoption.

## Unaccompanied asylum seekers

> I think the issues that [asylum seekers] present are very different. I mean they, they come into the country having experienced, you know, really, really difficult and traumatic situations, and I think that their agenda, the young people's agenda is very different, you know, they're here, in a better place as far as they see it, and they want to make it work. So their focus is different and I think therefore their issues in terms of placement are different. (Team Manager)

One in 20 (5.3%) of the sample were unaccompanied minors seeking asylum. They came from the world's trouble spots – Somalis from the horn of Africa, Kurds and others from Iraq, Albanians from Kosovo (see Table 2.5). Their locations in different councils were partly determined by transport – the proximity of ports, airports and motorways – and partly by the wish to be with others of similar nationality. As a result of these influences young people were concentrated in three councils that together took 358 (92%) of the 391 children seeking asylum.

As a group, asylum seekers entered the care system at a much later age than others in the sample. Nearly eight out of ten (78%) entered when aged 10–15 whereas this was true of only 29 per cent of the remainder. The contrast was even more striking in relation to those entering when aged 16 or over. Sixteen per cent of the asylum seekers entered the system at this age. The comparable figure for the rest of the sample was 1 per cent.

**Table 2.5** Ethnic origin by whether seeking asylum

| Ethnic origin | | Whether asylum seeker | | |
|---|---|---|---|---|
| | | No | Yes | Total |
| A1 – White British | Count | 5438 | 3 | 5441 |
| | % within Ethnic origin | 99.9% | .1% | 100.0% |
| A2 – White Irish | Count | 23 | 0 | 23 |
| | % within Ethnic origin | 100.0% | 0% | 100.0% |
| A3 – White other | Count | 90 | 74 | 164 |
| | % within Ethnic origin | 54.9% | 45.1% | 100.0% |
| B1 – White & Black Carib. | Count | 197 | 0 | 197 |
| | % within Ethnic origin | 100.0% | 0% | 100.0% |
| B2 – White & Black African | Count | 55 | 6 | 61 |
| | % within Ethnic origin | 90.2% | 9.8% | 100.0% |
| B3 – White & Asian | Count | 133 | 1 | 134 |
| | % within Ethnic origin | 99.3% | .7% | 100.0% |
| B4 – Other mixed | Count | 136 | 3 | 139 |
| | % within Ethnic origin | 97.8% | 2.2% | 100.0% |
| C1 – Indian | Count | 35 | 5 | 40 |
| | % within Ethnic origin | 87.5% | 12.5% | 100.0% |
| C2 – Pakistani | Count | 117 | 4 | 121 |
| | % within Ethnic origin | 96.7% | 3.3% | 100.0% |
| C3 – Bangladeshi | Count | 18 | 2 | 20 |
| | % within Ethnic origin | 90.0% | 10.0% | 100.0% |
| C4 – Asian other | Count | 41 | 17 | 58 |
| | % within Ethnic origin | 70.7% | 29.3% | 100.0% |
| D1 – Caribbean | Count | 137 | 0 | 137 |
| | % within Ethnic origin | 100.0% | 0% | 100.0% |
| D2 – African | Count | 261 | 208 | 469 |
| | % within Ethnic origin | 55.7% | 44.3% | 100.0% |
| D3 – Black other | Count | 49 | 3 | 52 |
| | % within Ethnic origin | 94.2% | 5.8% | 100.0% |
| E1 – Chinese | Count | 12 | 14 | 26 |
| | % within Ethnic origin | 46.2% | 53.8% | 100.0% |
| E2 – Other ethnic group | Count | 91 | 51 | 142 |
| | % within Ethnic origin | 64.1% | 35.9% | 100.0% |
| Total | Count | 6833 | 391 | 7224 |
| | % within Ethnic origin | 94.6% | 5.4% | 100.0% |

Source: CIS sample.
Note: The three white British children apparently seeking asylum were presumably miscoded.

In other respects the asylum seekers were highly diverse. Ninety-three per cent of those who were white, 89 per cent of the 'Asians', and 83 per cent of the 'Chinese and other' were male. By contrast a slight majority (54%) of those who were black were female. The features which result in some councils but not others becoming important hosts for asylum seekers also influenced the characteristics of those asylum seekers who were looked after. In one of the three major 'host councils', for example, a high proportion of asylum seekers were white males. One of the others had hardly any such young people.

## Need codes

As is well known, children are looked after for complex reasons. Their mother may be psychiatrically ill but at the same time they themselves may be neglected, there may be domestic violence and adults in the household may be abusing alcohol.

Government statisticians require these complex reasons to be summarised under the heading of one main reason or 'need code'. These in turn can be used to provide a rough and ready description of the sample as Table 2.6 sets out.[6]

As can be seen from Table 2.6, children whose first entry was under the age of 11 were much more likely to have a need code of 'abuse or neglect' (71% v. 32%). This contrast is made starker by the presence of asylum seekers. Children in this group almost always entered the system as teenagers and were given the code 'abandoned'. If they are omitted the contrast in abuse rates becomes 72 per cent against 38 per cent. Similarly the proportion of abandoned teenagers drops to 7 per cent.

## Presence of a care order

Children and young people move into, out of and within the care system for two basic reasons: they want to move or somebody else decides that they should do so. Often, of course, these reasons coincide. However the ability to move them against their will depends to some extent on the children's legal status.[7] We divided their latest legal status into voluntary arrangements (34%) and compulsory ones (66%). In this respect there were large differences between the asylum seekers and others. Ninety-five per cent of the asylum seekers were voluntarily accommodated. The same was true of only 30 per cent of the others.

Among those who were not asylum seekers voluntary arrangements were related to age at first admission and to a need code of abuse:

**Table 2.6** Need codes by age at entry

| Reason for being looked after | | First entry when aged 11 or over | | Total |
|---|---|---|---|---|
| | | No | Yes | |
| Abuse or neglect | Count | 3743 | 676 | 4419 |
| | % within First entry when aged 11 or over | 71.2% | 32.2% | 60.1% |
| Disabled | Count | 148 | 82 | 230 |
| | % within First entry when aged 11 or over | 2.8% | 3.9% | 3.1% |
| Parent disabled | Count | 365 | 98 | 463 |
| | % within First entry when aged 11 or over | 6.9% | 4.7% | 6.3% |
| Stress | Count | 334 | 287 | 621 |
| | % within First entry when aged 11 or over | 6.4% | 13.7% | 8.4% |
| Family dysfunction | Count | 367 | 298 | 665 |
| | % within First entry when aged 11 or over | 7.0% | 14.2% | 9.0% |
| Difficult behaviour | Count | 44 | 186 | 230 |
| | % within First entry when aged 11 or over | .8% | 8.9% | 3.1% |
| Low income | Count | 10 | 10 | 20 |
| | % within First entry when aged 11 or over | .2% | .5% | .3% |
| Abandoned | Count | 247 | 461 | 708 |
| | % within First entry when aged 11 or over | 4.7% | 22.0% | 9.6% |
| Total | Count | 5258 | 2098 | 7356 |
| | % within First entry when aged 11 or over | 100.0% | 100.0% | 100.0% |

Source: CIS sample.

- Fifty-seven per cent of those who were first admitted when 11 or over were voluntarily accommodated as opposed to only 21 per cent of those who had entered at a younger age.

- Sixty-one per cent of those who did not have a need code of abuse were voluntarily accommodated as against only 16 per cent of those who had such a need code.

Age and the presence or absence of abuse combined to influence the likelihood of an order. Among those who were not seeking asylum 77 per cent of those who were aged 11 or over on first entry and who did not have a need code of abuse and neglect were voluntarily accommodated. The same was true of only 13 per cent of those who first entered under the age of 11 and who did have a need code of abuse and neglect.

There were very large variations between councils in the proportions of children who were not on an order. Two councils had fewer than a fifth of their children voluntarily accommodated. Three had 50 per cent or more similarly without an order. These variations must reflect differences in the policies of the councils and the courts. They were certainly not explained by differences in the kinds of children the councils were looking after.[8]

## Conclusion

As far as we can judge the basic characteristics of the sample are more or less identical with the national picture. This gives reason for thinking that the results are also nationally relevant.

A key variable is the age at which the child first enters the system and their current age. This is strongly related to the official reasons for which he or she first enters the system. Compared with others those first looked after under the age of 11 are more likely to be abused, more likely to be on an order, less likely to be seeking asylum and less likely to be entering for reasons connected with unacceptable behaviour. Age at entry defines the length of a child's potential care career and is strongly related to the actual length of these careers. Those whose care careers began when aged 5–9 made up a sizeable proportion of those aged 10–15 at census date.

Tentatively therefore it may be useful to think of the care system as containing four rather different groups:

1. Those who are under the age of 11.
2. Those who were under the age of 11 at first entry but are now older ('teenage graduates').
3. Those who are seeking asylum (almost all of whom first entered the care system when aged 11 or over).
4. All others first looked after over the age of 11.

This is an extremely crude grouping. As will be seen there are many other variables that influence both movement and needs. Nevertheless there are major differences between these groups. In particular, as we will see later, age is strongly related to the explanations for high and low degrees of movement in the care system, as well as to much else besides. Age and age at entry will therefore feature prominently in the rather more elaborate typology we develop in Chapter 4.

In terms of permanence it seems likely that many of those who enter under the age of 11 may need an alternative base. Most of them have been abused or neglected. It may not be safe for them to go home, so they may need a permanent base in the care system or through adoption. By contrast many of those entering over the age of 11 may, for good or ill, have decided that their own family is their base. They do not generally enter for reasons of abuse, so it may be safe for them to go home. If they cannot do so they may move from placement to placement or alternatively use the system as a launch pad. As those seeking asylum do not have their parents in this country it seems particularly likely that they will have to use the system in this way.

## Notes

1    It is, at first sight, surprising that there are more children who had entered aged 5–9 among the 10–15 year old population than are found among those aged 5–9. Two factors account for this. First, among those who stay any length of time the chance of leaving in this age group is low at this period in their care careers. Thus around 93 per cent of those present at any one point in time are looked after a year later. There were 177 children who entered at this age, were currently aged between 9 and 10 and were present on the census date. All of them would be aged 10–11 on the next census date and would be included among those present in that year. The number of 11–12 year olds counted should be around 165 (.93×177). So the number of 10–12 year olds who first entered at the relevant ages should be 177 + 165. Similar estimates can be made for the numbers of 12, 13, 14 and 15 year olds. This would yield an expectation that in subsequent years 892 children who had entered aged 5–9 would be aged 10–15 at census date. The second factor we need to take into account is that some of the children who leave the care system come back into it. There were 206 children who had entered aged 5–9, were known to have a repeat admission when they were aged 10–15 and who were looked after at some stage in the census year. Adding this number to 892 yields an expectation of 1097 children aged 10–15 who had entered when aged 5–9 and were aged 10–16 in a census year. This is comparable with the actual figure of 1066.

2    For details on the relevant figures see previous note.

3    On 31 March 2004 the national figures were males (55%) and females (45%).

4    The justification for these groupings is clearly pragmatic – the belief they will make it possible to uncover important patterns. Clearly the labels do not correspond to cultural or ethnic groupings in any precise sense. The variety of cultures, religions and languages in India or China alone clearly make this assumption absurd.

5    Two councils had proportions of white children between 33 and 36 per cent. Four had proportions between 78 and 83 per cent. Seven had proportions of between 93 and 98 per cent. The great majority of Asian children were in just two councils.

6    The proportions of children with different need codes at census date are very close to the national figures for 31 March 2004. The slight exceptions are abuse and neglect (64% sample v. 62% national), family dysfunction (8% sample v. 10% national), socially unacceptable behaviour (2% sample v. 3% national) and abandoned (9% sample v. 8% national).

7    This qualification 'to some extent' is necessary because in practice social workers have a great deal of power that stems either from their age, experience, access to resources and so on or from the implicit threat that if the child or family do not agree with the proposed plans an order will be made.

8    A logistic regression equation that used data on age (whether or not aged 11 or over), whether or not abused, whether or not seeking asylum and local council (entered as a dummy variable) successfully predicted 87 per cent of those who were voluntarily accommodated and 66 per cent of those who were not. The addition of information on local council added to the other variables added more than 1000 to the omnibus chi square test of the coefficients for the addition of only 12 degrees of freedom.

Chapter 3

# Who is Looked After?
# The Children's Families,
# Wishes and Behaviour

I think there is an issue around the nature of some of the children that we look after who come into care primarily because of neglect, [and there are] cumulative effects of neglect on some children, which means that their capacity to attach into whatever setting you might have thought was appropriate is a long time coming. (Manager)

I mean more or less everybody so far has a lot of difficulty with…teenagers, those who come in as teenagers as opposed to those who sort of, you know, have come in earlier and graduated to be, and they move around a lot and nobody quite knows what to do with them. (Manager)

## Introduction

The data from the client information systems provided the basic structure for our project. On their own, however, they could not answer all the questions we had. This chapter uses information from the social workers to describe the children's problems, behaviour and wishes.

We use this information in three ways:

1. To show how far different characteristics 'go together' – for example, how far some groups of children have, on average, more difficulties at school than others.

2. To see which children are most likely to accept care and which to reject it.

3. To see whether children looked after in different councils tend to differ in terms of their behaviour, problems and wishes.

In this way we take further the task of seeing how far the children fall into distinct groups. We also flag up the issues of the children's wishes and of differences between councils, both of which become important later in the book.

## Method

The chapter uses four main measures based on the social work data:

1. 'Family difficulties' score.

2. 'School performance' score.

3. 'Challenging behaviour' score.

4. 'Acceptance of care' score.

We describe these measures more fully in notes when we first introduce them. Their meaning is given by their names. So they are about how far the child is seen as having difficulties at home, doing well at school, behaving in a challenging way and wanting to be looked after. Both our case studies and our statistics will suggest that these variables affect the meaning of stability to the child, the case for it, and the difficulties of achieving it.

Almost all the analyses in the chapter use information from the social workers. This limits the size of the sample in two ways. First, we only sent questionnaires to the social workers when the child had been looked after at some point in the six months before the census date. We had nearly three-quarters of these back, but our sample can be no larger than the number of returned questionnaires ($n = 4647$). Second, some of the measures were clearly inappropriate for younger or much older children who, for example, did not go to school or, if they were babies, have views on the care system.

## The children's difficulties and their age at census and at entry

As we have seen, the children's ages at first entry and at the census were closely related to many of their other characteristics. Unsurprisingly they were also related to the measures we derived from the social work data.

We asked the social workers about evidence that the children had been abused and also whether they had been exposed to 'domestic violence or substance abuse' in their family. The questions asked them to grade the evidence as 'none (1), some (2) or strong (3)'.

In keeping with our findings from the last chapter young children were much more likely to have been abused. The social workers felt there was strong evidence for abuse among two-thirds (65%) of those first admitted under the age of 11. The figure for older entrants was 35 per cent.

Those entering under the age of 11 were also much more likely to be coded as coming from families where there was strong evidence of 'domestic violence or substance abuse'. This was true of 41 per cent of those who first entered when less than 11 but only 24 per cent of those first entering when aged 11 or over.

We created a family difficulty score by adding the ratings given for 'evidence of abuse' to those given for 'evidence of domestic violence or substance abuse in the family'.[1] The higher this score was the greater was the degree of family difficulty. As can be seen from Figure 3.1, the family difficulties score was higher for children whose first entry was under the age of 11. The contrast is even stronger if those seeking asylum are omitted.

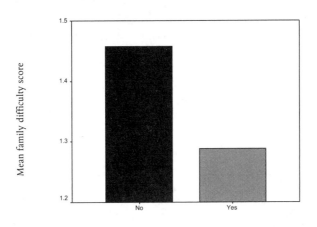

First entry when aged 11 or over

Sources: Social Worker data and CIS data. Note: The higher the score the greater the degree of reported family difficulties.

**Figure 3.1** Family difficulty score by whether child aged 11 or more at first entry

If family difficulties were more common among younger children, difficulties of behaviour were more common among older ones.[2] These older children fell into two groups. First, there were those who had started to be looked after under the age of 11 but were now aged 11 or over (adolescent graduates). Second, there were those who had first entered the system when they were 11 or over. Both groups displayed on average more challenging behaviour than younger children. The difficulties, however, were particularly severe among the children who were first looked after as adolescents (see Figure 3.2). Once again the contrast is even stronger if those who are seeking asylum are omitted.

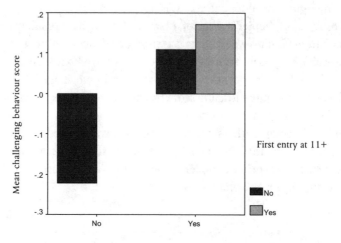

Aged 11 or over at census

Sources: Social Worker data and CIS data. Note: The higher the score the more challenging behaviour a child is said to display.

**Figure 3.2** Challenging behaviour score by age and age at entry

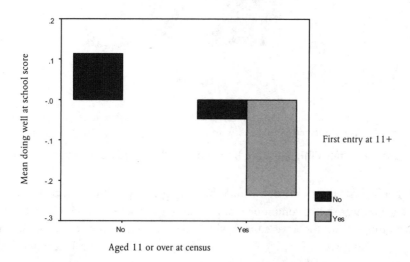

Aged 11 or over at census

Sources: Social Worker data and CIS data. Note: The higher the score the better the child is said to be doing at school.

**Figure 3.3** School performance scores by age and age at entry

We had very similar findings when we looked at how the children were doing at school. To measure this we used a school performance score.[3] Figure 3.3 suggests that many of those who have most difficulties at school have entered relatively late and at a point where their problems are likely to be very well entrenched. The care system is sometimes blamed because its children do not do well at school. Such censure must take account of the problems the system faces. Older children who are often far behind with their education on first entry must be a considerable challenge.

## The children's difficulties and their need codes

As we have seen children who were first looked after under the age of 11 were more likely to have high family difficulties scores. This contrast, however, depended on the reason the child was admitted. Where the need code was 'abuse and neglect' the average family difficulties scores were almost the same among older and younger entrants. In the case of the other need codes family difficulty scores were always on average higher among the younger entrants (see Figure 3.4).

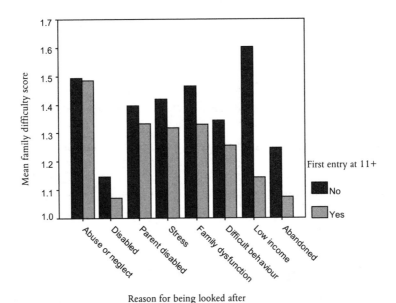

Reason for being looked after

Sources: Social Worker data and CIS data. Note: The higher the score the greater the degree of reported family difficulties.

**Figure 3.4** Family difficulties score by need code and age at entry

We had similar findings for challenging behaviour. The average scores for this reflected both need codes and age at entry. On average the highest scores (i.e. those reflecting the most challenging behaviour) were concentrated in five groups: those entering at any age with a need code of 'socially unacceptable behaviour' and those entering over the age of 11 and with need codes for abuse/neglect, disability, family stress and family dysfunction (see Figure 3.5).

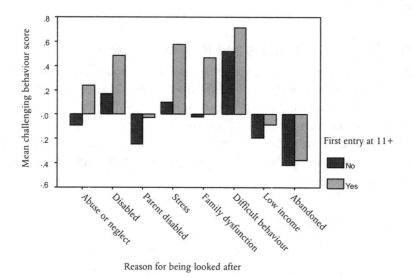

Sources: Social Worker data and CIS data. Note: The higher the score the more challenging behaviour a child is said to display.

**Figure 3.5** Challenging behaviour score by need code and age at entry

Figure 3.6 looks at how the children were doing at school.[4] Whatever their need code children were always doing better if they started to be looked after when aged less than 11.

## The children's difficulties and their sex

There were some differences on our scores between males and females. Females had, on average, slightly higher family difficulty ($p = .002$), lower challenging behaviour and better school performance scores.

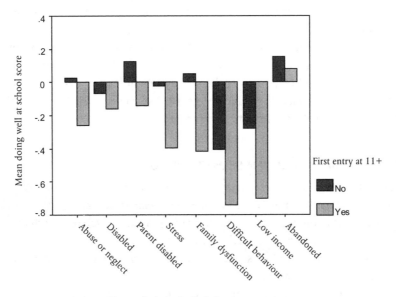

Reason for being looked after

Sources: Social Worker data and CIS data. Note: The higher the score the better the child is said to be doing at school.

**Figure 3.6** School performance score by need code and age at entry

## The children's difficulties and their ethnicity

As we saw in Chapter 2, children from minority ethnic groups were divided into two groups: those who were seeking asylum and those who had grown up in Britain. By putting these two groups together we could have obscured the distinctive needs of each. We therefore dealt with those seeking asylum as a group on their own and have omitted them from analyses in this section.

Despite this omission, children who were not white seemed in certain ways to be a less troubled group. After allowing for age at entry they had significantly lower family difficulty and challenging behaviour scores and significantly (although only just significantly) better school performance scores. Why should this be so?

It could be that children who are not white are less likely to be adopted but more likely to have 'stable, quasi-adoptions' within the care system. However, very few children get adopted if they enter over the age of five and black and minority ethnic children over this age still did better than their white British peers.

It could also be that black and minority ethnic carers are particularly success-ful. If so, it would be expected that the longer the child's care career the better the black and minority ethnic children would do – if anything the reverse seemed to hold true. Therefore, the most likely explanation may be that children who are not white are more likely to enter the care system at least in part for reasons of poverty or other social disadvantage. As a consequence their behavioural and family difficulties do not have to be as severe.

## The difficulties of those seeking asylum

Asylum seekers entered the care system because they had no one to look after them. Almost by definition their families were seen as displaying fewer difficul-ties than those of others. It is also not surprising that they were readier than others to accept their need to be looked after (see note 9).

As we have seen, asylum seekers were on average older than other children. Only 13 (3% of all asylum seekers) were aged less than 11. By contrast 3271 (47%) of the remaining children were under this age. As those seeking asylum were older than the others, they should have been doing worse at school and shown more challenging behaviour. In practice, however, this was not so – to judge from our measures they showed less challenging behaviour and did better at school.

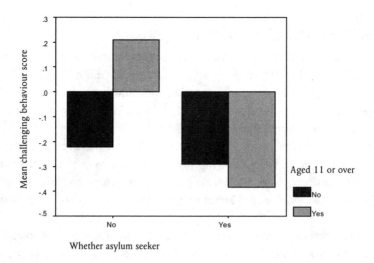

Whether asylum seeker

Sources: Social Worker data and CIS data. Note: The higher the score the more challenging behaviour a child is said to display.

**Figure 3.7** Challenging behaviour by asylum status and whether 11 or over

On average the group with the most challenging behaviour were those who were *not* asylum seekers and were over 11 (see Figure 3.7). Those with the least challenging behaviour were the older asylum seekers. Indeed on average asylum seekers over the age of 11 were better behaved than younger children who were not seeking asylum.

Figure 3.8 indicates that those seeking asylum also seemed to be doing better at school. This seemed to be mainly because they were better behaved. After allowing for age their school performance scores were much better. However the difference disappeared if allowance was made for difficult behaviour.[5] Interestingly the very small group seeking asylum under the age of 11 were doing slightly worse at school than other younger children. This difference was not significant but may be a reminder of the handicaps of language and custom that these children have to overcome.

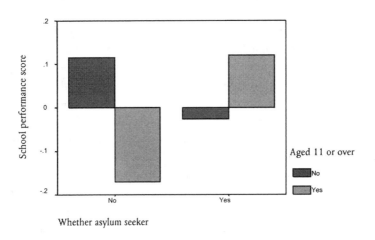

Sources: Social Worker data and CIS data. Note: The higher the score the better the child is said to be doing at school.

**Figure 3.8** School performance by asylum status and whether 11 or over

## The difficulties of disabled children

There is no agreed definition of disability. Some children are likely to be seen as disabled by everyone, so most people would call children disabled if they had profound learning difficulties or used a wheelchair. Other children have impairments that are less severe (for example, short sight corrected by glasses) or that are arguably not 'organic' (for example, ADHD) or which change over time. These make up a group that one of us has described as 'contested' (Baker 2006) where there is not clear agreement over whether the child is disabled or not.

Different views of disability produce different ways of measuring it and thus very different proportions of disabled children. This was certainly true in this study where we had three different measures of disability.

First, there was the need code. Roughly one in 29 (3.5%) of the sample had a need code of disability implying that this was the reason they were looked after. However, this can not be a full count of disabled children as some will have primary need due to 'abuse and neglect' and so this will be coded as their primary need as opposed to 'child's disability'.

Second, some councils had their own definition of disability. On their definitions (that were not necessarily the same from one council to another) roughly one in 13 (7.7%) were disabled.

Third, we asked the social workers whether in their opinion the child was disabled. This measure identified between one in six and one in five of the sample (17.7%).[6]

Clearly these data do not provide any answer to the question of how many looked after children are disabled. Similarly they cannot answer the questions of how many of these children are, for example, male or black and minority ethnic children. They do, however, provide a chance to compare those who are called 'disabled' on a given definition with others who are not. If our three definitions all suggest a similar pattern of difference between disabled children and others, we can be surer about the kinds of differences that exist irrespective of what definition is applied.

The most obvious difference was by age. Table 3.1 compares the ages at census of children with a need code of disability with the ages of other children in the sample. As can be seen older children were increasingly likely to be disabled although the chance of being so was never high. On average children with a need code of disability were nearly three years older than others (10.8 v. 13.7 years).

There were similar, albeit slightly less clear, trends with our other two measures of disability. Those described as disabled by the council were on average nearly two years older than the others (10.5 v. 12.4 years). Those described as disabled by the social workers were on average just over one year older (10.8 v. 11.8 years). Hence, the definitions that produced higher numbers of disabled children also yielded smaller differences in age between disabled children and others.

This difference in age seemed to arise for two reasons. First, on average disabled children entered the system at a slightly older age.[7] Second, disabled children stayed in the system longer than others. Whatever the definition of disability or their age of entry disabled children had on average stayed longer in their

**Table 3.1** Age group by need code of disability

| Current age group at census/end last placement | | Need code of disability | | |
|---|---|---|---|---|
| | | No | Yes | Total |
| 0–1 yrs | Count | 679 | 5 | 684 |
| | % within Current age group at census/end last placement | 99.3% | .7% | 100.0% |
| 2–4 yrs | Count | 819 | 9 | 828 |
| | % within Current age group at census/end last placement | 98.9% | 1.1% | 100.0% |
| 5–9 yrs | Count | 1424 | 37 | 1461 |
| | % within Current age group at census/end last placement | 97.5% | 2.5% | 100.0% |
| 10–15 yrs | Count | 2760 | 96 | 2856 |
| | % within Current age group at census/end last placement | 96.6% | 3.4% | 100.0% |
| 16 yrs & over | Count | 1444 | 83 | 1527 |
| | % within Current age group at census/end last placement | 94.6% | 5.4% | 100.0% |
| Total | Count | 7126 | 230 | 7356 |
| | % within Current age group at census/end last placement | 96.9% | 3.1% | 100.0% |

Source: CIS sample.

latest period in care.[8] The size of the difference varied between six months (on the need code definition), through 12 months (on the social workers' definition) to 17 months (on the councils' definitions).

There were other consistent differences between disabled children and others. They were more likely to be male, and much less likely to be seeking asylum. A striking difference on all definitions was that disabled children were much more likely to display a high level of challenging behaviour.

The findings on school performance and disability were more complicated. Children defined as disabled by the social workers were said to be doing significantly worse than others at school. This was not true of children with a need code of disability or defined as disabled by the councils. We have argued in note 7 that the social workers were probably including two groups in their definition of who was disabled: those with clear organic impairments and others with, for example, mild learning disabilities or ADHD, whose difficulties may or may not have an organic basis. It is perhaps not surprising that this second group has the greatest difficulty in living up to adult expectations.

## Motivation towards being looked after

---

**Box 3.1** Young people's reflections

I am happy. I thought [coming into care] was a good thing because I am looked after properly here. (Young Person)

I should never have been in care… Social workers should leave kids alone. They should listen to us more and give us more choices. (Young Person)

---

While the correct legal term is 'looked after', it is not a term that all key participants, especially children and their families, would use. We use both 'care' and 'looked after' in our writing, our choice determined by the need for clarity. However, where a 'care order' is involved we always refer to it as such.

Some children wanted to be looked after, others accepted it, and others resented it fiercely. We tried to measure these differences in view through the care acceptance score,[9] a rating made by the social workers rather than by the children but meant to reflect the children's views.

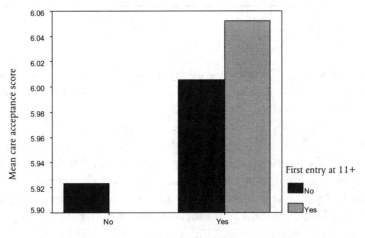

Aged 11 or over at census

Sources: Social Worker data and CIS data. Note: A higher mean care acceptance score implies child more accepting of care.

**Figure 3.9** Care acceptance score by age and age at entry

Children who were first looked after over the age of 11 were more likely to accept care than others (see Figure 3.9).

Other groups who were particularly likely to accept 'care' were:

- Children with the need code 'abandoned' (a category that included almost all asylum seekers).

- Children who were not on an order and thus 'voluntarily accommodated' (see Table 3.2).

- Children who did not have families whom the social workers saw as 'undermining the placement'.

Taken together these findings make sense. It is not surprising that children are more likely to accept the need to be looked after if they are not required to have it, have no alternative family or, although having one, do not find that their family sets them against their placement.

**Table 3.2** Child accepts need to be looked after by whether voluntarily accommodated

| Child accepts need to be looked after | | Voluntarily accommodated | | Total |
|---|---|---|---|---|
| | | No | Yes | |
| Strongly agree | Count | 626 | 268 | 894 |
| | % within Child accepts need to be looked after | 70.0% | 30.0% | 100.0% |
| Agree | Count | 1170 | 444 | 1614 |
| | % within Child accepts need to be looked after | 72.5% | 27.5% | 100.0% |
| Disagree | Count | 289 | 116 | 405 |
| | % within Child accepts need to be looked after | 71.4% | 28.6% | 100.0% |
| Strongly disagree | Count | 295 | 31 | 326 |
| | % within Child accepts need to be looked after | 90.5% | 9.5% | 100.0% |
| Total | Count | 2380 | 859 | 3239 |
| | % within Child accepts need to be looked after | 73.5% | 26.5% | 100.0% |

Source: CIS and Social Worker Data.

The groups most likely to accept the need to be looked after overlapped. For example, almost all those seeking asylum were first looked after over the age of 11 and hardly any of them were on an order or had families who were seen to be undermining the placement. As we will see below, it may be not so much age as the things that go with it that lead older children to accept the need to be looked after.

Acceptance of care was also associated with our behaviour and school performance scores. The more the child was seen as accepting care the less challenging behaviour they were likely to display and the better their school performance scores. (See Table 3.3 – those unfamiliar with correlations can read the note if they want a guide to what the table means.)[10]

**Table 3.3** Correlations: acceptance of care, behaviour and school performance

| Kendall's tau b | | Doing well at school score | Challenging behaviour score | Accepts need for care |
|---|---|---|---|---|
| Doing well at school score | Correlation coefficient | 1.000 | −.356** | .244** |
| | Sig. (2-tailed) | . | .000 | .000 |
| | N | 4061 | 4051 | 3472 |
| Challenging behaviour score | Correlation coefficient | −.356** | 1.000 | −.199** |
| | Sig. (2-tailed) | .000 | . | .000 |
| | N | 4051 | 4504 | 3534 |
| Accepts need for care | Correlation coefficient | .244** | −.199** | 1.000 |
| | Sig. (2-tailed) | .000 | .000 | . |
| | N | 3472 | 3534 | 3544 |

** Correlation is significant at the .01 level (2-tailed).
Source: Social Worker data.

As will be seen later, our case studies suggested that over time children could often become reconciled to the need for care, so they might say that they did not think it was a good idea at the time but that now they were glad they were properly looked after. Figure 3.10 sets out the relationship between perceived acceptance of care and the average length of the period since the last admission. The figure demonstrates that the average length of placement was indeed higher among those who were strongly accepting. However, those strongly opposed to care had also on average been a long time in placement, so although some children may become reconciled to care over time, this is certainly not true of all.

So which children strongly reject the need for care? Our case studies suggested that they would:

- have spent a comparatively short time in the care system

- enter the system at an older age (when they may not want another family)

- not have been abused (for abused children can be relieved)

- not be getting on well at school

- have families that were opposed to the placement

- not be living with their siblings in the care system.

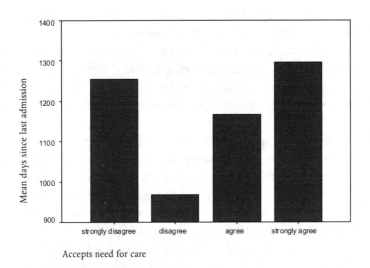

Accepts need for care

Sources: Social Worker data and CIS data. Note: A higher mean care acceptance score implies child more accepting of care.

**Figure 3.10** Average length of period since last admission by social worker's view of whether child accepts care

In addition we felt that abused children might be ambivalent on first removal and that length of time in the care system might be particularly important in enabling them to become reconciled. We also felt that children who were accommodated on a voluntary order would be more reconciled than others.

We tested these hypotheses together so that we took account of the associations between the different variables.11 Most of the hypotheses were upheld. Other things being equal children were more likely to be reconciled to being in care:

- the longer they had been looked after

- when they had a need code of abuse

- when they were not on an order
- when they were doing well at school
- when they were with their siblings (although this latter was not statistically significant $p = .12$).

They were more likely to be seen as rejecting care if:

- they entered at a relatively late age[12]
- their family was seen as disrupting the placement.

In practice the effect of age at entry was quite slight, raising the odds of rejecting care by around seven per cent for each year of age.

We found that we did not do better at predicting 'rejection of care' by taking account of whether the child was seeking asylum. Those doing so were very unlikely to be on a care order, to have severe problems at school or families who tried to undermine the placement. These characteristics made them very unlikely to reject care.

One of our hypotheses was not borne out. As we had expected, children who had been looked after for some time were less likely to reject care than those who had come in more recently. However, this was particularly so for those who did not have a need code of abuse. We had thought this would be the other way round. Why were we wrong? It may be that the explanation has to do with differences between those who stay looked after and those who go home. Children who were not abused and who did not accept care were able to go home. Abused children by contrast might be kept in care for their safety. According to this argument the abused children should, other things being equal, provide a relatively high proportion of those who stay a long time despite their wishes.

This 'selection' argument probably applies to all those in the sample, so there may be two reasons why longer-staying children may be more reconciled to being looked after. First, those who hate the system are more likely to go home early. Second, those who stay may become reconciled over time.

Table 3.4 sets out the relevant logistic regression for those who find it easier to take in information in this way. Others may be happy to accept the interpretation given above or read note 13 on how to understand tables of this kind.

## Differences between councils

There were very large differences between councils in the children they looked after. These differences applied to all the main variables discussed in the last two chapters with the exception of sex. In practice we were not interested in these differences in the children's characteristics for their own sake. We were, however,

**Table 3.4** Logistic regression predicting rejection of care

| Independent variables | B | SE | Wald | df | Sig. | Exp(b) |
|---|---|---|---|---|---|---|
| Need code of abuse | −1.960 | .644 | 9.263 | 1 | .002 | .141 |
| School performance score | −.781 | .070 | 123.298 | 1 | .000 | .458 |
| On a voluntary order | −1.983 | .245 | 65.585 | 1 | .000 | .138 |
| Age at entry | .068 | .021 | 10.903 | 1 | .001 | 1.070 |
| Family seen as undermining placement* | .649 | .075 | 75.732 | 1 | .000 | .523 |
| Time looked after (log)** | −.188 | .070 | 7.111 | 1 | .008 | .829 |
| Siblings in placement | −.251 | .159 | 2.476 | 1 | .116 | .778 |
| Abuse × time looked after (log) | .237 | .098 | 5.904 | 1 | .015 | 1.267 |
| Constant | .342 | .550 | .388 | 1 | .533 | 1.408 |

Source: CIS and Social Worker data.
Notes: *Scored from 1 (strongly agree) to 4 (strongly disagree) – hence the sign implies that family undermining is associated with rejection of placement. **This variable is the natural log of the time in days since the latest admission. Strictly speaking it is not 'length of time looked after' which would include time on previous admissions. This is therefore a convenient short-hand that we will use in this and later tables.

interested in the ability of local councils to influence other variables – for example, how well the children were doing or how many placements they had in a year. In order to estimate this influence we had to allow for differences in the children's characteristics. For example, it is of interest that in predicting 'rejection of care' knowing the child's council continues to make a very considerable difference after allowing for the variables in Table 3.4. These differences will therefore play an increasing part in the argument of our later chapters.

## Conclusion

This chapter has added to the picture that was building up in the last. Once again it suggests some reasonably distinct groups of children.

Those first entering the care system under the age of 11 were far more likely to have family difficulties than those entering over 11. Similarly far fewer of those entering over the age of 11 had need codes of abuse or neglect. The differences between those under and over 11 at entry hold irrespective of whether one uses the need code of abuse and neglect or the social workers' rating of evidence of abuse.

The children's current age was also related to their behaviour and to the way they were getting on at school. Children who were over the age of 11 had more difficulties in these respects particularly if they had also first entered over the age of 11.

These findings suggest three broad groups:

1. *Children under the age of 11* – these were the least likely to show challenging behaviour or to have difficulties at school; they were also very likely to have entered for reasons of abuse or neglect and to have families where there were problems of domestic violence or the abuse of alcohol or drugs.

2. *Young people who had entered under the age of 11 but were now 11 or older* – these were also likely to have been abused and to have difficulties at home but were more likely to be seen as 'difficult' and as not getting on at school than those who were younger.

3. *Young people who had first entered the system over the age of 11* – these had the most difficulties at school and with behaviour; some also had difficulties at home and had entered for reasons of abuse, but on average they had fewer difficulties at home than those who had come in at a younger age.

Those seeking asylum again emerged as a distinct and, on average, older group. They were in care because they had no family in England rather than because of family difficulties. They were less likely than others of similar age to display challenging behaviour or to have difficulties at school. (In practice their problems with language and a new curriculum may have given them more problems at school than their co-operative behaviour would lead one to expect.) They were much more likely than others to be seen as accepting their need for care.

Disabled children made up a further group that emerged in this chapter. Much, however, depended on the definition of disability. Those with a need code of disability made up a very small group (between three and four per cent of the sample) and they had a very distinctive profile. They seemed to enter later and stay longer than others. They were likely to be seen as displaying challenging behaviour (albeit the reasons for this may be to differ from those found in other groups). They were less likely than others to be seen by social workers as the victims of abuse or neglect.

There was a much larger group (16% of the sample) who were defined by the social workers as disabled. They almost always included those with a need code of disability whom they resembled in being older and displaying more challenging behaviour. They were, however, seen as has having more difficulties at school than those with a need code of disability and were much more likely than them to be seen as having suffered abuse. We suggested that social workers were describing two rather different groups as disabled. One group had very severe 'organic' impairments (as described by the need code). The other group may have a variety of difficulties (for example, ADHD) that may or may not have had an organic origin and were commonly associated with abuse.

The chapter also introduced a new set of considerations around what children want. There are ethical and practical reasons for considering these wishes very important. From a practical point of view children who do not wish to be in a placement may be more likely to disrupt it (Sinclair and Wilson 2003). Ethically they have a right to be consulted. For both reasons it is important to understand why they may or may not wish to be looked after 'in care'. This chapter has approached this question indirectly by looking for differences between those who did apparently accept being looked after and those who did not.

Other things being equal, the children were apparently less likely to reject care, if:

- they were not on a care order and their families were not seen as undermining the placement (family acceptance arguably made both children's acceptance and a voluntary admission easier)

- they had a need code of abuse or neglect (this may be because it came as a relief after what went before)

- they had been looked after for a relatively long time (this may be because those who did not accept care were more likely to leave earlier but also because some became reconciled to care over time)

- they were said to be doing well at school

- they were first looked after under the age of 11.

These findings on what children want are complicated. For example, children who were first looked after under the age of 11 were more likely than others to be on an order and to have families who were said to undermine their placements. Both these characteristics made these children more likely to reject care. At the same time this same group of children were more likely to have been abused, to have been looked after for a long time and to be doing well at school. All these characteristics made them more likely to accept care.

The net effect of these conflicting influences was that young children in our sample were both more likely to be seen as rejecting care and to have a need code of abuse. Therefore, need and what children want do not necessarily go hand in hand. As we will see, the challenge of dealing with some policy groups is to pay attention both to what the children want and to what they need.

## Notes

1   Strictly speaking we used the mean of the two scores added together and square rooted them to create a rather more normal distribution.

2   Our measure of behavioural difficulties was derived from two questions, one asked for a 4-point rating of whether the child had many problems (1) to no problems (4) and the other for another 4-point level of agreement over whether the child's behaviour was difficult with high agreement (1) and strong disagreement (4). We reversed this scoring, standardised the scores and calculated the mean. The school performance measure used a similar procedure and questions related to 'doing well at school', 'getting on in education/occupation' and 'placement affected by absence from school'.

3   We have chosen to present these contrasts graphically and in terms of broad groupings. We have, however, tested them using regression and allowing for age, age at entry and whether or not child was an asylum seeker. The conclusions given above still hold.

4   In this and other tables the bars relating to 'low income' are based on very low numbers of children.

5   The reverse was not true. Asylum seekers continued to score much better on the behaviour score if allowance was made for their age and for their performance at school.

6   The most 'restrictive definition' was clearly the one based on the need code. Nearly eight out of ten of those who were defined as disabled by their councils did not have a need code of disability. This was also true of eight out of ten of those seen as disabled by the social workers. By contrast eight out of ten of those with this need code were defined as disabled by their councils and nine out of ten were seen as disabled by their social workers.

7   This statement is complicated by the need to take account of asylum seekers and of the definition of disability. Asylum seekers were older and hardly any of them were disabled on any definition (none had a need code of disability, two were considered disabled by councils, and four by social workers). Those with a need code of disability entered on average at a year older if asylum seekers were included and a year and a half older if they were not. Those considered disabled by councils entered in both cases at a marginally older age but only if asylum seekers were omitted did this difference verge on significance ($p = .08$). Those considered disabled by social workers entered at a significantly younger age if asylum seekers were included ($p = .03$). If asylum seekers were excluded they entered at a marginally older age but the difference was not significant. These differences by definition of disability may have to do with abuse. Where the social worker considered the child disabled those who had a need code of disability entered the system on average nearly a year and a half later than those who did not. So the social workers' definition of impairment may well include two groups: those with clear organic impairments, many of them with a need code of abuse who enter later; and those without such clear impairments (for example, those with mild learning disabilities, ADHD or 'attachment disorders') and with difficulties that may be associated with early deprivation and abuse.

8    We tested this further through a regression equation using length of time of latest episode looked after as the dependent variable and asylum, age at entry and disability as the independent variables. In this analysis disability was associated with length of stay irrespective of its definition.

9    This was based on a question of whether the child 'accepts the need to be looked after'. This was scored from 4 (strongly disagree) to 1 (strongly agree).

10   Correlations can be positive meaning that an increase in one variable implies an increase in another (like height and age among children) or negative (like global temperature and the size of the icecaps). They can vary in size from -1 (a 'perfect' negative correlation) through 0 (no association or at least none whereby one variable consistently rises or falls with the other) to 1 (a perfect positive correlation whereby a rise in one variable always goes with a proportionate rise in the other). In the table, a minus sign means that the variable in the relevant row and column are 'negatively associated', while the following number (e.g. .356) says something about how strong the association is. The number in the 'Sig.' row gives an estimate of how likely it is that if one actually looked at the underlying population (those from whom the sample is drawn) one would find that there was no association.

11   We used a logistic regression to predict 'strongly disagree that accepts care'.

12   In practice the effect of age at entry was not marked, raising the odds of rejecting care by around 7 per cent for each year of age.

13   Each of the variables in the left hand column makes a contribution to predicting the 'odds' of a particular 'outcome' (in this case 'perceived rejection of care'). The 'odds' are the chance of having that outcome over the chance of not having it. For example, if the chance of rejecting care is 60 per cent, the chance of not doing so will be 40 per cent and the odds will be 60/40 or 1.5. (For statistical reasons what is predicted is the log of the odds but this can be easily translated into the odds.) The key columns for interpreting the table are the second (under B) and the fifth (under Sig.). The B column gives the size of the association that can run from -1 to 1. The 'Sig.' column gives the chance that an association this big would be found if one did a similar calculation in the 'underlying population' and there was really no association at all.

Chapter 4

# Groups of Children and Their Chance of Permanence

## Introduction

Chapter 3 suggested that it might be useful to think of the care system as looking after a number of quite distinct groups of children. These groups have different characteristics, and may have different needs for a long-term base or for short-term shelter. This chapter takes up and explores these ideas. It develops and illustrates a way of grouping children and relates it to the different kinds of permanence that may be possible for them.

The focus of the chapter is on how far different groups of children needed and got long-stay family placements. So we will ask of each group:

- What kind of difficulties did they have?

- When were they first looked after?

- How far did they want to be looked after?

- How long had they spent in the care system?

- Had they gone home at some point after their first admission?

- How long had their latest placement lasted and what was it meant to do?

- How far was this placement in a homely setting (foster care or placement with parents) or in some form of residential care?

Our first three questions are about needs and wishes. We have already talked about these. We now need to show how they relate to our typology. Our next questions are about the children's time in care. We assume that if children are looked after for a long time they are likely to be better off if they are in a family and if their final placement lasts.

## Method

The chapter uses data from the client information system, the social work questionnaires and the case studies. The new variables are about the children's time in 'care'. We used the information systems for data on the length of the latest placement, the length of time since the last admission, and whether the child was in residential care at the census date. The social workers told us about the child's latest placement. We counted a child as having a repeat admission if there was evidence of this from the social workers or the information system or both.

The chapter has case studies as well as statistics. For a fuller description of how we selected and used our case studies, see Chapter 7. The case studies are partly for illustration. However, they also suggest hypotheses about the difficulties children in the different groups have in achieving a stable, satisfactory base where they are able to settle. Later in the book we will argue that these hypotheses are in keeping with our statistical material and also fit our other case studies.

## A trial typology

Following our analysis at the end of Chapter 3 we identified the following six groups. (The text in brackets gives the names we used for them.)

1. Children first looked after before the age of 11 and still under ten (young entrants).

2. Children first looked after when aged less than 11 but now 11 or over (adolescent graduates).

3. Children first looked after when aged 11 or over and not abused (adolescent entrants).

4. Children first looked after when aged 11 or over and with a need code of abuse (abused adolescents).

5. Children who were seeking asylum (asylum seekers).

6. Children who had a need code of disability (disabled children).

Obviously these groups overlap. For example, some children with a need code of disability also first entered the system when aged ten or over. For these reasons we allocated children who fell into more than one group into the one that we mentioned last in the above list. For example, any child with a need code of disability was put into that group.

The results of this process formed what we have called 'Policy Groups'. Figure 4.1 gives the proportions that fell into these different groups.

Most (43% of the whole sample) were 'young entrants'. They were first looked after when less than 11 and were still under this age. They made up the

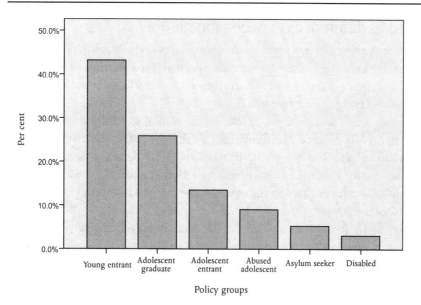

**Figure 4.1** Policy groups

largest group in the sample and for some purposes, most notably when consider-ing adoption, it was useful to divide them yet further. That said those who entered at this age had much in common. A minority (26% of the whole sample) fell into the group we called 'adolescent graduates'. They were first looked after under the age of 11 but were now over this age.

Those entering as adolescents were in many ways a more diverse group, including as they did the great majority of those seeking asylum (5% of the total sample), a group who had been abused (9% of the total sample), and others who entered for other reasons (14% of the total sample).

Finally there was the small 'disabled group'. These could enter at any age and made up between 3 and 4 per cent of the total.

Our suggestion is that the groups provide useful pointers to the different policies that may be appropriate for different sets of individuals. Obviously we are not suggesting that the same policies should be followed for all members of a group. However councils differ widely in the proportions of individuals that fall into these groups.[1] Grouping individuals in this way may prompt questions of why, for example, the numbers in a particular group are unusually high or low. Councils can also consider whether their balance of policy and provision are appropriate to the groups they have.

## Statistical differences between the groups

The various groups differed from each other in ways that are familiar from the last chapter. For example, those who were younger displayed less difficult behaviour, were much more likely to enter for reasons of abuse, and were less likely to be rated as accepting the care system.

Figure 4.2 illustrates these differences in relation to family difficulties. (To bring out the differences the figure uses a different but equivalent measure of family difficulty to that shown in Chapters 2 and 3. For details, please see note 2.) The lowest scores are among those who are seeking asylum or who are disabled. The highest scores are among the young entrants, the adolescent graduates and the abused adolescents.

Figure 4.3 (p.69) provides similar information on the difficulty behaviour score. It is now no surprise that the lowest scores were found among those seeking asylum and the young entrants. Adolescent entrants had the highest scores.

Differences between the groups in their attitudes to care were quite slight. It was striking that those seeking asylum were almost all seen as accepting care. Even without this group the differences between the others were statistically highly significant. However, this was not because of the size of the differences but because the numbers in the analysis were very large. In the social workers' view, most children were not against being looked after and this was true of all our groups (see Figure 4.4, p.70).

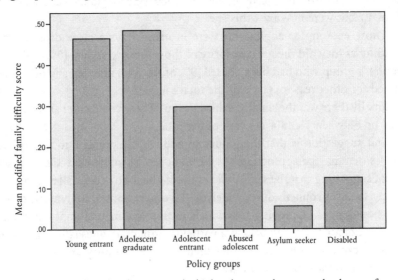

Source: Social Worker data. Note: The higher the score the greater the degree of reported family difficulties.

**Figure 4.2** Average family difficulty score by policy groups

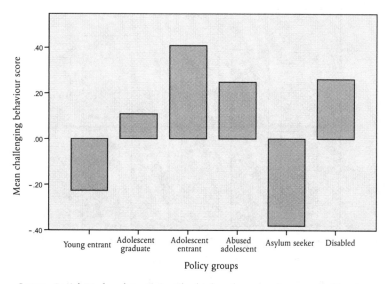

Source: Social Worker data. Note: The higher the score the more challenging behaviour a child is said to display.

**Figure 4.3** Average challenging behaviour by policy groups

The groups also differed in their care careers. The 'adolescent graduates' had had the longest length of stay – on average between five and six years (see Figure 4.5, p.70). The disabled group followed them. Other groups were limited in how long they could stay by the care system itself. Adolescent entrants, abused adolescents and the great majority of those seeking asylum could not stay a long time simply because of their age at entry. Finally the 'young entrants' had not yet had the opportunity to stay a long time.

Some of the groups were much more likely to have gone home at least once and then come back to care. Such repeat admissions were found in about a fifth (21%) of those seeking asylum and a quarter (29%) of the young entrants. They were much more common among abused adolescents (44%), disabled children (46%) and adolescent entrants (50%). They were commonest of all among the adolescent graduates (at 56%).[3] Although this last group were now based in the care system it had obviously been hoped that most of them would have been able to go home.

These differences were reflected in others. These included the length of the last/or latest placement (see Figure 4.6, p.71). The average length of the last or latest placement for disabled children and the adolescent graduates was between two and three years. The comparable figure for the adolescent entrants was less than a year.

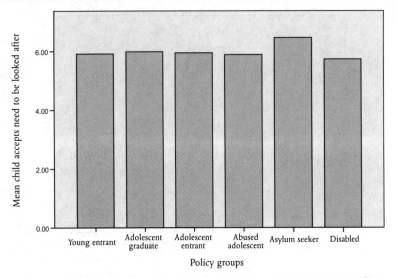

Source: Social Worker data. Note: A higher mean care acceptance score implies child more accepting of care.

**Figure 4.4** Average care acceptance score by policy groups

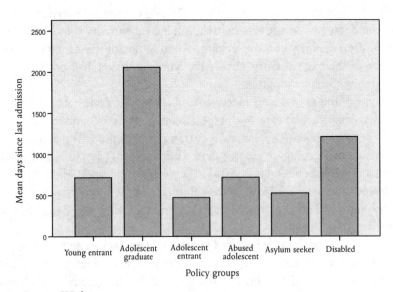

Source: CIS data.

**Figure 4.5** Average length of current/latest stay by policy groups

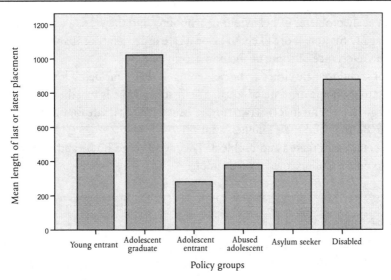

Source: CIS data.

**Figure 4.6** Average length of current/latest placement by policy groups

There were related differences over the purpose of placement as seen by the social workers. We asked them a question taken from Rowe and her colleagues (1989) about what the last or latest placement had been meant to provide. The question provided a list of ten options, two of which ('care and upbringing' and 'view to adoption') were about the offer of long-term care. Around six out of ten of the young entrants, adolescent graduates and disabled children had placements that were meant to lead to adoption or to give care and upbringing. The comparable figures for adolescent entrants (27%), asylum seekers (20%) and even abused adolescents (40%) were all much lower.

Finally, there were large differences between the groups in the use of residential care. At the end of the year one in 50 (2.3%) of the young entrants were in residential care. The same was true of nearly four in ten (37%) of the disabled children. The use of residential care for the remainder varied between 12 per cent (adolescent graduates) and 15 per cent (adolescent entrants).

Why did these differences in policy exist? How appropriate were they? In thinking about this it may be useful to look in rather more detail at each of our six groups.

## Young entrants

As we have seen young entrants share various common characteristics. Their reasons for entry almost always have to do with abuse and neglect; they rarely present acute problems of behaviour or schooling and they rarely use residential care. Legally they are more likely to be on a care order, a fact probably associated with the reluctance of some of them to accept care.

These children are either at the beginning of their time being looked after or waiting to go home or to be adopted. The first key issue is whether or not they should go home. This involves two further issues. First, is it safe for them to do so? Second, do they and their families want this?

In some cases there is no problem. They want to go home and it is safe for them to do so. Colin provides an example:

---

### Case Study: Colin

> It worked because there was a co-ordinated response. (Colin's social worker)

Colin was eight at the time of the interview and was one of a young sibling group who were found at home on their own. At first Colin went to live with his grandmother. This arrangement broke down because of ill health. The children then started to be looked after.

Following these events, matters seemed to the current social worker to have drifted. However, a new social worker found that the children wanted to return, and that the mother wanted them back and started a plan for rehabilitation. Both grandmother and mother were enormously relieved at this. The foster carer was fully committed and worked with the plan in every way.

A slight hiccup arose when the mother got a new partner. However, the mother took the relationship slowly, all concerned 'resisted her attempts to manipulate the situation' and the new boyfriend was acknowledged after police checks to be 'a genuine good guy'. In due course the children returned and the family is now living in a different local council and unsupported by social services.

Social worker and reviewer agreed in their assessment that this case was a success.

---

In other cases the child still wishes to go home, a wish often promoted by the family, but the judgement is that it is not safe for them to do so.

Alan provides an example of this dilemma. He wants to go home. It is not thought safe for him to do so. He disrupts or at best tolerates his placements. He is unlikely to have wanted to be adopted. Overall therefore Alan and other children in this group require:

> **Case Study: Alan**
>
> I would like to go back to my mum. (Alan)
>
> Alan was first looked after at the age of six. The reasons were neglect, physical abuse and his family's inability to cope with his behaviour. Following two short placements for assessment, it was decided that Alan should be adopted. After a year an adoptive placement had not been found, the carer ceased fostering and a new carer found Alan's behaviour too difficult. Alan moved to a new placement apart from his siblings. A year later the social worker said that Alan and his family had still not come to terms with his being looked after.
>
> Alan described his first placement as 'horrible'. It was too close to his family and he wanted to go home. He liked his out of county placement, said that in his third placement he had been a 'little bit naughty' and was prepared to stay with his current carers while they went on holiday but wanted to go home after a year. His main suggestion to Social Services was that he would like to go home.

- accurate assessment of what they and their family want
- accurate assessment of the risks of return home
- the ability to make return safe enough if it is possible
- the ability to offer an adequate and acceptable, long-term alternative if return is not possible.

All this is easier said than done. Fortunately most of our young entrants did not reject care. Some welcomed it from the beginning and apparently flourished from the start. Long-term adjustment and acceptance has to be judged among the adolescent graduates to whom we turn next.

## Adolescent graduates

Adolescent graduates had first entered the care system when aged less than 11. They were now aged 11 or more. They were also marked out by the likelihood that they had been abused and the frequency with which they had been tried at home (they were the most likely of all groups to have experienced more than one admission). On average their behaviour was seen as more challenging than that of the young entrants but less so than that of other adolescents other than asylum seekers.

Almost by definition this group had spent a long time in the care system. On average it was more than five and a half years since their last admission. In keeping with this their average length of stay in their latest placement was just under three years. This average, however, conceals large variations. Just under a fifth (19%) had spent less than six months in their latest placement. At the other end of the spectrum just under a fifth (19%) had spent five years or more.

---

### Case Study: Ifan

> I have had loads of placements and because of that I get really angry and frustrated when things don't work out... (Ifan)

Ifan is now 14 and living at home under placement on a care order. This follows nine years in the care system. The original need for care arose from 'neglect' 'due to mother's lifestyle, drug misuse, leaving Ifan and his siblings inappropriately cared for and unsupervised, with no guidance or boundaries.' His time looked after included both foster and residential care, some experienced as 'OK' and almost all ending in breakdowns, and a number of failed attempts at return home. In the end his mother was thought to have married a more satisfactory partner and he returned home, as he was desperate to do.

Ifan has only recently returned home and according to the social worker home is not as he imagined it. Ifan himself said that 'It's good' and he has no intention of going elsewhere. He also says that 'I'm 14 and my life is shit'. The reviewer noted that his mother seemed on first meeting quite uninterested in Ifan's well-being and future. The social worker feels that he has enough skills and a good enough relationship with his mother's partner for the placement also to be good enough. However, she also says that there is little hope for his education. His mother has failed to keep relevant appointments, the school will not have him and other schools in the area are refusing to take him either. This is something that Ifan regrets.

Faced with what appears to be a 'barely good enough' situation the social worker is determined to put in a strong support package. Some therapeutic support is currently being provided and Ifan also appears to have a Connexions adviser. A youth offending team is providing work on anger management, and offending behaviour, and also involving him in a motorcycling scheme and camping activities.

Our two case examples illustrate these differences. Ifan had definitely not achieved a satisfactory long-term placement. Both the social worker and the reviewer regretted this. The reviewer's overall view was that:

> We should not have allowed case to drift. Why was Ifan not adopted? Because of the level of contact, why did we not restore him home? If the squalid conditions he is currently living in are better than all his previous experiences what does that say? (Reviewer)

Our second case in this section provides a marked contrast:

---

### Case Study: Nina

> London was great…packed with people, people with pink hair and there are museums and the West End. (Nina)

Nina is a dual heritage child of 17. Social workers have been involved with her since birth because of concerns about neglect. Her mother's mental health was getting worse and was not helped by the use of drugs. She was erratic, became more neglectful of Nina and rejected support. Nina was removed at the age of five.

She had initial placements with her uncle and then with her grandparents. These did not work out because of their other family commitments. At that point a neighbour who had maintained contact, despite a move to London, made it clear that she was able and willing to look after Nina. The placement was ethnically matched and the offer of long-term foster care was accepted.

Nina recalls her removal from home. 'It wasn't very nice. Mum was blocking the way and I didn't know what was going on. The social worker got in and passed me over people's heads.' Nevertheless she is glad she was removed. She liked London and settled in well at school. According to the reviewer 'She views Social Services as having been helpful but is unhappy about the number of social workers she has had and not having time for getting to know them.' Apparently she has never had a black social worker but does not think that this has made a great deal of difference. The only point of criticism she raises is that unlike other looked after children in London she gets no enhanced allowance for living in a more expensive place.

In practice all seem to concur that the most important influence has been the placement. Nina is now seen as part of the family, and this, essentially, is how things should be. The reviewer felt that a residence order should be pursued more enthusiastically in such cases and that there should be no financial disincentives for carers who wish to pursue it.

---

The main point of these case examples lies in the contrast. One seems a manifest success while the other has, at best, a dubious outcome. This contrast raises questions. Were the outcomes inevitable or did other 'controllable' factors play a part? Nina seems to have benefited from an unusually good placement and, possibly, from a lack of involvement with the birth family imposed by distance. Ifan differed from her in these respects. His placements seem to have been less suited to him. The failed attempts to return him home suggest continuing uncertainty over whether long-term 'care' was for the best.

So if young entrants are to stay long enough to become teenage graduates and to flourish in 'care' what seems required is a good placement and a clear plan that this should last. We will come back to these hypotheses.

## Abused adolescents

Abused adolescents are defined by the age at which they first enter the system. Our case studies suggest that they face particular difficulties. Very often their abuse was not a new event. Repeated rejection and trauma may well have made them wary of investing in a new home while it prevented return to their old one. At the same time their behaviour was more difficult than that of the adolescent graduates. It may therefore have been difficult for new carers to invest in them. In any event the time available to them was relatively short. Any new family could end at 18.

Ian provides an example of the possibilities and difficulties of such late entrants. He had not it seems given up on the chance of a family. Nevertheless his age and behaviour threatened the placement that might have given him one. The best he can now hope for is supported lodgings.

---

**Case Study: Ian**

> Well first of all I moved to…a children's home. I stayed there for about a year. It was a dump… The people were fine, but I didn't like it, I wanted to move to live in a family. (Ian)

Ian was admitted to care when his mother 'dumped him' at the office. She then made it quite clear that she did not want him back. The history of this rejection seems to go back a long way. Ian's mother was raped at a young age and she had no attachment to him at birth. It is probable that she has rejected him from this point. Ian, for his part, has no desire to return to her. 'My mum is a no go area. I wouldn't see her, I don't see her.'

All this happened around four years ago. Ian is now 15 and has not found a home from home in the care system. It seems that his first placement broke down quickly and was followed by residential care. In time a long-term placement with loving carers was found. This lasted three or four years. Ian liked it immediately and it 'felt like having a real mum'. Unfortunately this arrangement broke down with the arrival of a 'difficult young person' who led Ian 'astray'.

After two months in a children's home Ian moved to new carers. Unfortunately 'his current carers don't trust him, they are wary of him, they can't trust him. He has stolen from them'. Ian was not committed to the placement either. 'It's not as homely as [the first carers'] though. I'll be here for about a year and move into supportive lodgings, that's what I want to do, I can't wait.'

Ian has attended a special school and has been referred to Connexions, the LAC Team (Education), consultant adolescent psychiatry, YOT, a substance misuse worker, the police and an independent visitor. This, however, is not in the reviewer's eyes adequate compensation. 'I believe the loss of the [first] foster carers for Ian has been immense. His future is in the balance.'

Difficulties of this kind combined with their late arrival meant that comparatively few of the abused adolescents had achieved a long placement. Nearly half (49%) had been in their latest placement for no more than six months. Only 18 per cent had been in it for more than two years.

As the case illustrates the issues are in many ways similar to those of the young entrants and adolescent graduates. Can the young person go home? If not, can they be offered a placement where they will feel at home? There are, however, additional issues. Their behaviour may be such that it is hard for carers to accept them. There is the chance that because of their age they will be placed in residential care. There is the certainty that care ends at 18.

## Adolescent entrants

Adolescent entrants had not, by definition, been admitted for reasons connected with abuse. Their key characteristics were their age, their often challenging behaviour and their problems over school. The case studies suggested that some were still committed to their family but this did not mean that they got on with them. Their age meant that the care system could not offer them adoption or a lengthy spell of family life. They probably did not want a 'new family'; their behaviour often made it difficult for others to commit to them.

Neil is an example of such an entrant. It may be that he has not totally given up on the chance of something like a family. Nevertheless this desire is well hidden. His overt attitude to the care system is pragmatic: he tolerates it for its practical benefits and subverts the restrictions he dislikes. His behaviour is difficult for his children's home and too much for his mother. Both he and the care system seem to be marking time until he can move on.

### Case Study: Neil

> [Care] means I have somewhere to put my clothes and stuff and can have a bath if I want one. (Neil)

Neil is now 17 and first came into the care system voluntarily at the age of 13. According to his own account he lived 'on the streets' for two months prior to entry, staying in various places including stolen cars, friends' garages, and a shop roof. The reasons for this homelessness are unclear, but according to the social worker he was not getting on with his mother who was at her wit's end with him. Neil found homelessness better than being in care 'apart from the cold'. It was also difficult to get clean. Speaking of his mother he said 'I didn't see her when I first came in and I don't see her now. I don't like her.'

Care itself, however, was not welcome. Neil thought 'it was shit'. He spent ten months in a children's home resenting the speed with which others left it, and returned home in a planned move. His attempt at rehabilitation quickly broke down and he moved to another children's home where he was living when interviewed. According to his own account he found this children's home bearable because he had made some friends there, taunted others and was, in any case, hardly ever there.

Neil praised one social worker:

> [Social workers are] always sick or on holiday or just don't bother with you... The last one was the only one that did anything. She came to court with me and she'd come into the office and give me money to get something to eat. She used to come and see me...and got me celebrating success money for going back to school.

Unfortunately reconciliation with school did not last and following an enjoyable time in a pupil referral unit he stopped attending at all. The new plan is for supported lodgings. Neil sees this as a stage he has to go through and does not expect to stay there long. Despite this he is going there more often than planned. The reviewer felt that there was the beginning of a relationship with the carers, albeit one that Neil was reluctant to acknowledge. The reviewer was hopeful that the placement might work out.

Difficulties of these kinds meant that adolescent entrants rarely had long placements. Six out of ten of them had had a latest placement that lasted for less than six months. By contrast only 12 per cent had one that exceeded two years.

Only a quarter of this group were in placements meant to give 'care and upbringing'. So the issue may be not how to provide them with a more permanent home 'in care', but rather whether this is what most of them need.

## Young people seeking asylum

Young people seeking asylum have a number of distinguishing characteristics. They do not, by definition, have parents in England; they tend to enter the system later than others; they come from minority ethnic groups; they are less likely to display behaviour that is experienced as difficult by their carers; they make comparatively good progress at school. Joseph was typical of the group in all respects except perhaps the last.

### Case Study: Joseph

A bright but shy adolescent until you ask about his football interests. (Reviewer)

Joseph, a 15 year old Rwandan, arrived by air along with his sister at the age of nine. He remembers waking up in the back of a car with people taking him somewhere. He was then placed with his sister with foster carers for two years. He then moved to the foster family with whom he now lives without his sister. He is going to a local college in a couple of years to attend a football coaching course before attempting to be a professional footballer. At present he is at school where he is in some trouble because although academically fairly able he is not academically interested.

Joseph is appreciative of his care but not overtly enthusiastic. He describes both his placements as 'OK' adding that it was 'all right how people had looked after him and his sister'. Asked if coming into care was a good idea he said that he 'supposed so'. Asked if he had stayed in his placements for too long or not long enough or about the right time, he just shrugged his shoulders. Joseph has, as it were, been posted to England. He might, perhaps, have reacted to the powerlessness of his situation with hopelessness. Instead he has got his head down and got on with it.

On the positive side the reviewer and the social worker clearly regard the foster carers as excellent. Joseph himself intends to stay with his foster carers when attending college. He has apparently found an older sister in London with whom he is emotionally close and he may then move to London. His mother has also surfaced in Sweden where she has asylum status. She does not wish to come to England for fear of losing this. Joseph has been to Sweden, but finds it cold and has no wish to go there permanently. He telephones his mother instead. He sees his future in England and says he has only dim memories of Rwanda.

To an outsider provided only with the information for which we asked on our form there is something rather enigmatic about Joseph and much that is curious about his situation. There is, however, no doubt that much that is positive has been done. He has rediscovered key members of his family, found a placement which he likes and has a plan for his future in sport. The reviewer felt that he should have been placed with a black family that might have given him more help over racism. This, however, would no doubt have been done if it had been possible.

Joseph is reasonably typical of the three young people seeking asylum on whom we had case studies. He, the care system, and the other young people are all making the best of a difficult situation. The issues he confronts are those of acquiring an education and a grasp of English that will fit him for the future, re-establishing contact with members of his family that are still alive, and establishing a base that will provide support until he has adequately launched himself.

Our case studies and our statistics suggested that the key difficulty was that of establishing a base. Those seeking asylum were more likely than others to be living in residential care (including hostel accommodation); their placements were unlikely to last longer than their eighteenth birthday (a point that Joseph appeared to have resolved but which was causing anxiety in one of the case studies of an asylum seeker); they were less likely than others to be placed for 'care and upbringing'; and there could be difficulties in achieving a 'match'. In Joseph's case he was not ethnically matched – a point that possibly caused more anxiety to the reviewer than to him. In another case the young person had been ethnically matched but resented the fact that this meant he was placed with carers he did not like. Finally, although this did not feature explicitly in the case studies, there is the issue of whether the young people will in fact achieve British citizenship after they have left care.

Statistically these difficulties meant that comparatively few of these young people had achieved long placements. Forty per cent had a current or last placement that had lasted for less than six months. Only 12 per cent had a placement that lasted for more than two years.

## Disabled children

Very few of the sample had entered care with a need code of disability. As we have seen those who did had a number of distinguishing characteristics. Typically they had longer periods of stay and were seen as displaying difficult behaviour. They were much more likely to enter residential care. In all these respects Hannah can be seen as 'typical'.

---

**Case Study: Hannah**

> I know what's happening because people talk to me about it and tell me. (Hannah)

Hannah has been voluntarily accommodated for over 12 years. She is described by her social worker as having various special needs such as epilepsy, some paralysis and moderate learning and behavioural difficulties. Hannah has had a mixed package of care including ongoing family and residential respite, and is currently a boarder at a specialist school. The family-based respite care has remained stable and constant and the aim has been to enable Hannah to stay within the foster family and to provide specialist education and preparation for semi-independent living.

Hannah's parents are signed up to the plans and have been fully involved in all decisions. The social worker said that Hannah had enjoyed the placements, developed well within the package of care and now displayed less difficult behaviour. The main concern of all involved was about the transition to adult services. Adult services are not yet involved. This is causing difficulty, as the parents are keen to be informed of the options post-18.

Hannah was approaching 18 when the reviewer met with her and was clear on what she liked about where she lived:

> I like it here – I know everybody. [One of the staff] makes me laugh, she's not my key worker but I've known her a long time. At school I like IT, cooking, PSE, swimming, textiles and woodwork. I go home most weekends and holidays. I like being at home, we've got a new car and I've got my own CD player. I've got lots of friends. Respite care – I really like it. If anything's wrong I talk to my key worker or the staff or I'd phone my mum or dad or talk to my sister or my carer… I understand what's happening. I'm 19 next year. I don't want to live at home.

---

Hannah's care clearly works for her. The issue of her family allegiance is resolved. She loves them but does not want to live with them. So too is the issue of her long-term future. She has impairments that are sufficient to guarantee her the support she needs when she leaves. With that security she seems to have a happy existence, one that combines enough family life with an enjoyable and stimulating time at school.

We will see later that these conditions are not fulfilled for all disabled young people. Some, it seems, spend all their time in residential establishments and do not, in that way, have a family life. Others (although here our evidence comes only from case studies) do not have impairments that are sufficient to ensure ongoing support on leaving care.

Statistically, young people with a need code of disability have quite a high chance of achieving a long placement. Eighteen per cent have a latest placement that has lasted for less than six months. By contrast 38 per cent have one that has lasted for two years or more. Around four out of ten of these, however, are in residential rather than family care.

## Conclusion

Everyone thinks that most looked after children are best brought up in families. The key question is whether this should be at home or elsewhere.

We have seen in this chapter that it is not easy to give the children in our sample a permanent family home. Many of them had been 'tried at home' but come back into care. Many of those in care had not yet found a placement that lasted. Difficult behaviour, problems at school, and a wish to be at home could all make it hard for them to settle.

A key issue is age. Overall only two groups, adolescent graduates and disabled children, had a reasonable chance of achieving a length of placement that might seem a prerequisite of family life. This chance was not often taken up. Four out of ten of the disabled children were in residential care. Only a fifth of the adolescent graduates were in a placement of five years or more. The current young entrants were presumably no more likely to have very long placements. Few of those entering as adolescents will have the time to do so.

Such considerations prompt two broad questions. First, how realistic is it to design the care system on the basis that all those staying in it beyond a relatively limited period of time should have a reasonable chance of family life? Second, in so far as it is realistic, what changes may need to be made to increase the chance?

These questions prompt others:

- Should social workers make fewer attempts at rehabilitation and be willing to remove some children at an earlier stage? Such changes might make it easier to provide alternative families to the abused adolescents.

- Is there a case for supporting foster placements beyond the age of 18? This might make the offer of family life more realistic, particularly for those entering as adolescents.

- Should disabled children in residential establishments be routinely provided with an experience of family life, as seems to have been the case with Hannah?

There is a further question. Insofar as permanent family care is not realistic, what alternative philosophy should inform the care of those who cannot go home?

Any answer to this question must link the care system to what follows it. It is possible, for example, to see the care system as essentially involved in 'launching' those who are seeking asylum. Its success in doing so is likely to depend on its success in enabling them to gain a good education, make links with their own communities and so on. It will also depend on the degree to which they are subsequently enabled to get jobs, find accommodation, and regularise their legal position.

Similar points could be made about adolescent entrants. Some may need to change their behaviour if they are to achieve what most would regard as a happy life. Such changes may only bear fruit if they are supported by changes outside the care system. For example, some adolescents want to go home but return will only be successful if both they and their parent(s) change. Similarly some cannot go home and do not want to attach to foster carers. Their future success is likely to depend both on changes they have made within the care system and on support they receive on discharge.

## Summary points for Chapters 2, 3 and 4

The sample contained different groups of children. These included:

- Children under the age of 11 who were looked after primarily for reasons connected with abuse and neglect and had many difficulties at home.

- Children who had entered the system under the age of 11 for similar reasons but who were now older and having more difficulties at school and with behaviour.

- Children who entered when aged 11 or over for reasons other than neglect and abuse and were more likely than others to have difficulties at school or with behaviour.

- Children who entered when aged 11 or over for reasons connected with abuse.

- Children seeking asylum who were almost invariably over the age of 11 and much less likely to be seen as displaying challenging behaviour or having difficulties at home.

- A small group of children with a need code of disability who were older than others and looked after for longer.

These groups differ in their chance of achieving a long-term placement within the care system. It seems likely that they typically have different needs and require, to some extent, different provisions and policies.

## Notes

1    The most obvious difference relates to those seeking asylum (range 0–35%). If those seeking asylum are omitted the differences are still very large. The ranges then are: young entrants 35–51%; adolescent graduate 21–35%; adolescent entrant 10–23%; abused adolescents 6–13%; disabled 1–6%.

2    The minimum score on the original measure is one and the maximum three. As everyone scored at least one we started the 'origin' at this point by subtracting 1 from the original score.

3    For a full discussion of the way we defined this variable please see Chapter 6. The figures given are based on our 'best estimate' as discussed in that chapter.

# Chapter 5

# Admissions and Discharges

The expectation is that, you know, all avenues to rehabilitate children back home within their own communities and so on are explored but, you know, you don't spend two/three years trying to achieve that...if it's not seeming like it's going to be 'doable' or manageable within it's, I think it's four months now that we're saying that, you know, we need to start to be thinking about making permanent permanency plans for those children outside of their birth families. (Manager)

## Introduction

The last three chapters have looked at the characteristics of children in 'care' and the groups into which they fall. These groups seem to be a useful way of thinking about what these children may need. They are not so helpful in thinking about how they can get this. For this purpose we need to know more about the way the care system works and about what determines its outcomes. The rest of this book is about these processes and outcomes.

This chapter is the first of three that deal with a key part of these processes: the beginnings and endings of periods of being looked after. As our case studies show, the decisions over whether or not a child should go home or continue to be looked after are crucial. They are very important to the children, some of whom want desperately to go home while others are terrified of doing so. They often carry large risks. Taken together they determine which children stay for a long time, how the care population is made up and the balance between its different roles.

The processes of admission and discharge also provide the context for other moves. Placements differ in their purposes; not all of them are meant to last. Emergency placements and placements for assessment tend to come soon after an admission. Movements from such placements are intended from the beginning.

Other placements are intended to lead up to an adoption or on to independence. Placements of these kinds are usually towards the beginning or end of a child's time in care. The endings of such placements are unlikely to have the same meaning as the endings of long-term placements in which it had been planned that a child would grow up.

## Admission: a time of decision

Our telephone interviews with senior managers made it very clear that all the councils strove to avoid using the care system if they could. This wish for a community solution did not stop when the children became looked after. There was, however, a realisation that children could not always go back home and that a decision on this needed to be made soon. The period immediately after admission was therefore often a time of exploration and assessment and one leading in some, but not all, cases to return home.

The social work data cast some light on the timing of these decisions. We asked the social workers about the overall plan at the time of the child's latest placement and at previous placements in the last six months. (We limited the questions to a maximum of three placements to avoid putting an undue burden on those answering.) Table 5.1 relates the purpose of the earliest placement on which we had information to the time since the child had been last admitted.[1]

**Table 5.1** Time since last admission by plan at earliest recorded placement

| Time since last admission | | Plan at first recorded placement | | | |
| --- | --- | --- | --- | --- | --- |
| | | Return home | Permanent substitute care | Other | Total |
| Less than 6 months | Count | 353 | 215 | 212 | 780 |
| | % within Time since last admission | 45.3% | 27.6% | 27.2% | 100.0% |
| 6 months to 1 year | Count | 133 | 245 | 119 | 497 |
| | % within Time since last admission | 26.8% | 49.3% | 23.9% | 100.0% |
| Over 1 year | Count | 375 | 2363 | 483 | 3221 |
| | % within Time since last admission | 11.6% | 73.4% | 15.0% | 100.0% |
| Total | Count | 861 | 2823 | 814 | 4498 |
| | % within Time since last admission | 19.1% | 62.8% | 18.1% | 100.0% |

Source: Social Worker data.

Table 5.1 demonstrates a very clear trend. As the time since admission increases the proportion of those with a plan for return home decreases sharply. So to a lesser extent does the proportion of those with a coding of 'other' – a code that, as seen in the footnote, is used in part for those for whom a plan has yet to be determined. Conversely the proportion of those with a plan for permanent substitute care increases sharply from 28 to 73 per cent.

This trend reflects both the fulfilment of plans and their alteration. Those for whom the plan was return home were more likely to do so. They were therefore much less likely to be found among those who had spent longer in the care system. In addition the longer a child had spent in the care system the more likely it became that a plan for return home would be given up and one for long-term care put in its stead.

Table 5.2 refers to those with more than one placement in the six-month period and compares the plan at the last of these placements with the plan at the previous one. Plans seemed to move mainly in one direction. More than four out of ten of those who had a plan for return home at their first previous placement had a different plan, most commonly for permanent substitute care at the next one. It was very rare for a plan for permanent substitute care to shift to one for return home. In a number of cases such plans shifted to 'other', probably to allow for the possibility of independent living.

**Table 5.2** Plan at first previous placement by plan at last/latest placement

| Plan 1st previous placement | | Plan last/latest placement | | | |
|---|---|---|---|---|---|
| | | Rehabilitation home | Permanent substitute care | Other | Total |
| Rehabilitation home | Count | 112 | 64 | 21 | 197 |
| | % within Plan 1st previous placement | 56.9% | 32.5% | 10.7% | 100.0% |
| Permanent substitute care | Count | 19 | 434 | 45 | 498 |
| | % within Plan 1st previous placement | 3.8% | 87.1% | 9.0% | 100.0% |
| Other | Count | 11 | 52 | 138 | 201 |
| | % within Plan 1st previous placement | 5.5% | 25.9% | 68.7% | 100.0% |
| Total | Count | 142 | 550 | 204 | 896 |
| | % within Plan 1s previous placement | 15.8% | 61.4% | 22.8% | 100.0% |

Source: Social Worker data.
Note: Table is restricted to those with more than one placement in the six months.

## The leaving care curve

> I mean what we know is that…when children are leaving care at the end of…you know, some years in care that they tend to do less well as adults and so clearly if there's a way of supporting them within their own family then that is what we'd want to do. (Manager)

As we have seen nearly half those who had been looked after for less than six months had plans envisaging a return home. This finding echoes one from Rowe and her colleagues' (1989) study. They describe a 'leaving care curve'. Basically this showed that the chance of leaving the system shortly after arrival was high. Thereafter it reduced rapidly. They used this information to argue for determined activity shortly after admission in order to prevent 'drift'. Our study took place nearly twenty years after theirs. How far do our findings still support this result?

We looked at the chance that a child who started to be looked after would continue for given periods of time.[2] We estimated that:

- 89 per cent of those entering were looked after for at least a week
- 90 per cent of those who remained a week remained for at least four
- 89 per cent of those who stayed for four weeks stayed for at least three months
- 91 per cent of those who lasted for three months lasted for at least six
- 83 per cent of those who lasted for six lasted for at least a year.

These figures show the broad pattern identified by Rowe and her colleagues (1989). The chance of leaving in the first week is roughly the same as the chance that those who survive the first week will leave in the next three. This in turn is much the same as the chance that those who survive this long will leave in the next two months.

As time goes on, the chance of leaving drops still further. At the beginning of the census years there were 3701 children who had already been looked after for at least a year. Four-fifths (79.4%) of these were still looked after a year later. Their chance of leaving the system over the year was roughly the same as the chance that new entrants would leave in the first month.

These figures can be used to estimate a 'retention rate'. If 100 children enter the care system:

- 89 will be there at the end of a week
- 80 will be there at the end of four weeks
- 71 will be there at the end of three months
- 65 will be there at the end of six months

- 54 will be there at the end of the year
- 43 will be there at the end of the following year.

Figure 5.1 provides a graph of this process using a rather different technique.[3] As can be seen there is a rapid drop in the numbers present in the first 50 days and the rate of leaving then decreases. The 'wobbles' after 300 days probably represent the small numbers and the nature of the technique used rather than any genuine effect.

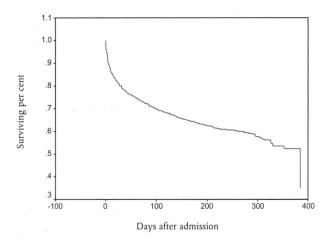

Source: CIS data. Note: * The term 'survival curve' is perhaps unfortunate but is traditional in this type of analysis. The graph describes the proportion of children who would still be retained in the system after a certain number of days (read along the bottom or x axis). For example the graph suggests that after 200 days roughly 63 per cent of the children should still be looked after.

**Figure 5.1** Estimated 'survival curve'* for children admitted during the census year

In practice the chances of leaving the care system after a year depend on the age of the child. We looked at those who had been looked after for a year at the beginning of the year. The chance of leaving in the course of the year varied with their age at the census date:

- among those under five it was 29 per cent
- among those aged 5–9 was 15 per cent
- among those aged 10–15 it was 5 per cent

- among those aged 16 and over it was 36 per cent.

As we will see later, the relatively high rate among those aged under five is influenced by adoption. The relatively high rate among the 16-year-olds and over is obviously influenced by the point at which care officially stops. If those over 17 and a half are omitted the rate is little different to that of those in their early teens. Those aged 10–16 are not adopted and they are not graduating out of care. Few of them leave the system.

In summary, the care system rapidly winnows out short-stay children. By the end of a year those who have 'survived' this process are likely to stay a relatively long time. This results in a build up of children who stay for longer periods, a process that is modified in the case of younger children by adoption and in the case of older children by the need to leave care at 18. Among those aged 10–15 the chance of going home after a year is very low.

## Length of stay of current looked after children

This pattern of entrances and exits produces the care population at any one point in time along with their age distribution and lengths of stay. We looked at those in 'care' at the census date and at the time since their latest admission (see Figure 5.2). We found that roughly:

- a quarter (26%) of the children had been looked after for less than a year
- a third (32%) had been looked after for at least one year but less than three
- a fifth (19%) had been looked after for at least three years but less than five
- 22 per cent had been looked after for at least five years.

Putting the data another way among children who were present at the end of the year:

- 91 per cent had been looked after continuously for more than three months
- 74 per cent had been continuously looked after for more than a year
- 41 per cent had been continuously looked after for three years or more
- 5 per cent had been continuously looked after for nine years or more.

Figure 5.2 can be compared with Figure 5.3 that deals with children who left care during the year.[4]

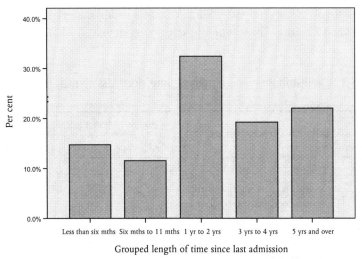

Source: CIS data.

**Figure 5.2** Length of care careers for children still looked after at the end of the census year

Half (52%) of those in this group had left within a year of arrival and the great majority of these within the first six months. A further quarter lasted for one year but left within three. The remainder had been looked after for longer than this.

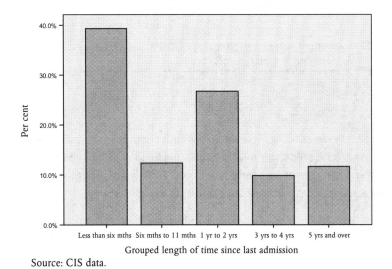

Source: CIS data.

**Figure 5.3** Length of care career for children who left care during the census year

In brief, completed care careers tended to be relatively short. Current careers, although longer, were rarely very long. Very few children had been looked after for nine years or more. Those who did stay a long time were obviously relatively old (see Table 5.3).

**Table 5.3** Age distribution and length of time since last admission at census date

| Current age group at census/end last placement | | Years since last admission | | | |
|---|---|---|---|---|---|
| | | <1 | 1–3 | 4+ | Total |
| 0–1 yrs | Count | 301 | 128 | 0 | 429 |
| | % within Current age group at census/end last placement | 70.2% | 29.8% | 0% | 100.0% |
| 2–4 yrs | Count | 179 | 353 | 11 | 543 |
| | % within Current age group at census/end last placement | 33.0% | 65.0% | 2.0% | 100.0% |
| 5–9 yrs | Count | 285 | 576 | 287 | 1148 |
| | % within Current age group at census/end last placement | 24.8% | 50.2% | 25.0% | 100.0% |
| 10–15 yrs | Count | 504 | 868 | 974 | 2346 |
| | % within Current age group at census/end last placement | 21.5% | 37.0% | 41.5% | 100.0% |
| 16 yrs and over | Count | 154 | 350 | 443 | 947 |
| | % within Current age group at census/end last placement | 16.3% | 37.0% | 46.8% | 100.0% |
| Total | Count | 1423 | 2275 | 1715 | 5413 |
| | % within Current age group at census/end last placement | 26.3% | 42.0% | 31.7% | 100.0% |

Source: CIS sample.
Note: This table only applies to children present at census date.

This pattern is even more pronounced if we omit young people who were seeking asylum. As we have seen this group is largely made up of young people who enter in their teens and cannot stay for a long time. Table 5.4 sets out the relationship between age and length of stay after omitting asylum seekers.

**Table 5.4** Age distribution and length of time since last admission at census date

| Current age group at census/end last placement | | Years since last admission | | | |
|---|---|---|---|---|---|
| | | <1 | 1–3 | 4+ | Total |
| 0–1 yrs | Count | 286 | 127 | 0 | 413 |
| | % within Current age group at census/end last placement | 69.2% | 30.8% | 0% | 100.0% |
| 2–4 yrs | Count | 171 | 341 | 11 | 523 |
| | % within Current age group at census/end last placement | 32.7% | 65.2% | 2.1% | 100.0% |
| 5–9 yrs | Count | 268 | 538 | 285 | 1091 |
| | % within Current age group at census/end last placement | 24.6% | 49.3% | 26.1% | 100.0% |
| 10–15 yrs | Count | 422 | 743 | 957 | 2122 |
| | % within Current age group at census/end last placement | 19.9% | 35.0% | 45.1% | 100.0% |
| 16 yrs and over | Count | 82 | 238 | 423 | 743 |
| | % within Current age group at census/end last placement | 11.0% | 32.0% | 56.9% | 100.0% |
| Total | Count | 1229 | 1987 | 1676 | 4892 |
| | % within Current age group at census/end last placement | 25.1% | 40.6% | 34.3% | 100.0% |

Source: CIS sample.
Note: Table excludes minors seeking asylum and those not present at census.

Around two-thirds of the children in this table share two characteristics – they are over the age of five and they have already spent a year in the system. On our data these children and young people are unlikely to go home in the next year and they have a very low chance of adoption. Unaccompanied asylum seekers are not adopted and are unlikely to return home. Therefore, with or without those seeking asylum, the care system faces the challenge of providing whatever childhood base is going to be available for a high proportion of those using it at any one time.

## Destinations on discharge: differences by age and career stage

Two characteristics were strongly related to where the children went on discharge: the time since their admission and their age.

As we have seen the chance of leaving the system drops rapidly after a year. So too does the chance of going home among those who do leave. As can be seen from Table 5.5, those going home make up nearly two-thirds of those leaving within a year of arrival but only one in five of those leaving after a year. By contrast the proportions of those going to independent living or adoption are quite large among those leaving after a year but negligible in the first year.

**Table 5.5** Destinations by time since last admission

| Why care ended | | Time since last admission | | |
| --- | --- | --- | --- | --- |
| | | 1 yr or less | Over 1 yr | Total |
| Adopted | Count | 27 | 276 | 303 |
| | % within Time since last admission | 2.6% | 28.9% | 15.3% |
| Died | Count | 4 | 2 | 6 |
| | % within Time since last admission | .4% | .2% | .3% |
| Care taken over by OLA | Count | 14 | 2 | 16 |
| | % within Time since last admission | 1.4% | .2% | .8% |
| Returned home | Count | 651 | 182 | 833 |
| | % within Time since last admission | 63.6% | 19.1% | 42.1% |
| Indep. living with support | Count | 55 | 149 | 204 |
| | % within Time since last admission | 5.4% | 15.6% | 10.3% |
| Indep. living without support | Count | 13 | 54 | 67 |
| | % within Time since last admission | 1.3% | 5.7% | 3.4% |
| Transfer to adult service | Count | 5 | 35 | 40 |
| | % within Time since last admission | .5% | 3.7% | 2.0% |
| Looked after ceased, other | Count | 254 | 255 | 509 |
| | % within Time since last admission | 24.8% | 26.7% | 25.7% |
| Total | Count | 1023 | 955 | 1978 |
| | % within Time since last admission | 100.0% | 100.0% | 100.0% |

Source: CIS sample.
Note: The table is restricted to those who ceased to be looked after in the census year. Figures are based on last time care ceased.

Table 5.6 sets out the average age at which 'care' ceased by destination. The table includes the label 'Looked after ceased, other'. Unfortunately we do not know what councils meant when using this category. Otherwise there are no surprises. Children who are adopted are young; those who go to independent living are much older. In the penultimate sections of this chapter we look at destinations within age groups, taking account of the length of time for which the child had stayed in the system.

**Table 5.6** Average age at census by reason for ceasing to be looked after

| Why care ended | Age at census (Mean) | N | Std. Deviation |
|---|---|---|---|
| Adopted | 4.83 | 304 | 3.31 |
| Died | 12.26 | 6 | 6.19 |
| Care taken over by OLA | 9.35 | 16 | 7.15 |
| Returned home | 9.69 | 834 | 5.59 |
| Indep. living with support | 18.01 | 205 | .80 |
| Indep. living without support | 17.96 | 67 | .90 |
| Transfer to adult service | 18.59 | 40 | .84 |
| Looked after ceased, other | 13.51 | 509 | 5.64 |
| Total | 11.25 | 1981 | 6.29 |

Source: CIS sample.
Note: The table is restricted to those who ceased to be looked after in the census year. Figures are based on last time care ceased.

## Destinations of children aged less than five

Table 5.7 sets out the destinations of those ceasing to be looked after when aged less than five.[5] As can be seen the great majority either returned home (47%) or were adopted (38%). Nearly three-quarters (72%) of those who left in the first year returned home. Nearly three-quarters of those who left after a year were adopted.

One point should be made strongly before we leave this group. The chances of adoption and the speed of adoption where it occurs are both very strongly related to age at entry. More than half (54%) of the 293 children adopted in the course of the year were first looked after when aged less than one. Even in this group age at entry was negatively related to the chance of being adopted, so children in the sample who first entered more or less at birth were more likely to be adopted in the census year than those who first entered later.

In this age group every year of delay decreases the chances that adoption will occur. Selwyn and her colleagues (2006) have powerfully set out the consequences of such delays. As they point out, the children may be condemned to an unstable and unhappy time and the care system may face major costs.

**Table 5.7** Destination on leaving the care system by time since entry

| Why care ended | | Time from last admission to departure | | |
| --- | --- | --- | --- | --- |
| | | Left within year | Left after a year | Total |
| Adopted | Count | 27 | 164 | 191 |
| | % within Time from last admission to departure | 9.7% | 72.2% | 37.7% |
| Died | Count | 1 | 0 | 1 |
| | % within Time from last admission to departure | .4% | 0% | .2% |
| Care taken over by OLA | Count | 6 | 0 | 6 |
| | % within Time from last admission to departure | 2.2% | 0% | 1.2% |
| Returned home | Count | 203 | 36 | 239 |
| | % within Time from last admission to departure | 72.8% | 15.9% | 47.2% |
| Looked after ceased, other | Count | 42 | 27 | 69 |
| | % within Time from last admission to departure | 15.1% | 11.9% | 13.6% |
| Total | Count | 279 | 227 | 506 |
| | % within Time from last admission to departure | 100.0% | 100.0% | 100.0% |

Source: CIS sample.

Note: This table only applies to children aged less than five at census date.

## Destinations of children aged from five to nine

As can be seen from Table 5.8, the pattern among those leaving in the age group 5–9 was similar to that we have just described. In this age group too the main destinations are home and adoption. However, the lower likelihood of adoption reduced the chance that children in this age group would leave the system after the initial flurry of activity. Adoption, however, remained the most likely 'late route' out of the system. Half those who left after a year were adopted.

A somewhat tantalising finding concerns those who are coded 'other'. Some may have been placed on residence orders, a category not recognised in the statistical coding in use at the time of our study. Others may have returned to other relatives or entered systems provided by health or education authorities. We do not know. What is certain is that in this age group they make up around a fifth of those leaving the system.

**Table 5.8** Destination on leaving the care system by time since entry

| Why care ended | | Time from last admission to departure | | |
|---|---|---|---|---|
| | | Left within year | Left after a year | Total |
| Adopted | Count | 1 | 85 | 86 |
| | % within Time from last admission to departure | .7% | 50.0% | 26.6% |
| Died | Count | 1 | 0 | 1 |
| | % within Time from last admission to departure | .7% | 0% | .3% |
| Care taken over by OLA | Count | 1 | 1 | 2 |
| | % within Time from last admission to departure | .7% | .6% | .6% |
| Returned home | Count | 122 | 47 | 169 |
| | % within Time from last admission to departure | 79.9% | 27.6% | 52.3% |
| Looked after ceased, other | Count | 28 | 37 | 65 |
| | % within Time from last admission to departure | 18.3% | 21.8% | 20.1% |
| Total | Count | 153 | 170 | 323 |
| | % within Time from last admission to departure | 100.0% | 100.0% | 100.0% |

Source: CIS sample.
Note: This table only applies to children aged five to nine at census date.

## Destinations of children aged from ten to fifteen

Our councils tried to keep children of all ages out of the care system. This was particularly so when the children were adolescents. One manager was very clear on this point:

> Yes, well we monitor our thirteen- to fifteen-year-old admissions weekly because we recognise that really, you know…sounds very draconian but, you know, letting them in you're on a hiding to nothing 'cos they don't get anything out of it and we certainly don't, you know, it's just sort of mayhem really. (Manager)

Young people aged 10–15 who were looked after for more than a year had generally entered at a younger age.

Table 5.9 sets outs the destinations of those leaving. As can be seen, there were very few adoptions – most probably by carers – and a few more went home.

**Table 5.9** Destination on leaving the care system by time since entry

| Why care ended | | Time from last admission to departure | | |
| --- | --- | --- | --- | --- |
| | | Left within year | Left after a year | Total |
| Adopted | Count | 0 | 23 | 23 |
| | % within Time from last admission to departure | 0% | 21.5% | 4.9% |
| Died | Count | 2 | 0 | 2 |
| | % within Time from last admission to departure | .6% | 0% | .4% |
| Care taken over by OLA | Count | 6 | 0 | 6 |
| | % within Time from last admission to departure | 1.7% | 0% | 1.3% |
| Returned home | Count | 246 | 55 | 301 |
| | % within Time from last admission to departure | 68.5% | 51.4% | 64.6% |
| Indep. living with support | Count | 1 | 0 | 1 |
| | % within Time from last admission to departure | .3% | 0% | .2% |
| Indep. living without support | Count | 2 | 0 | 2 |
| | % within Time from last admission to departure | .6% | 0% | .4% |
| Looked after ceased, other | Count | 102 | 29 | 131 |
| | % within Time from last admission to departure | 28.4% | 27.1% | 28.1% |
| Total | Count | 359 | 107 | 466 |
| | % within Time from last admission to departure | 100.0% | 100.0% | 100.0% |

Source: CIS sample
Note: This table only applies to children aged ten to 15 at census date who were no longer looked after on that date.

Most of those who did leave did so within the year. By contrast there were in total 1599 children aged 10–15 who were in a placement at the turn of the year and had already been looked after for a year or more. Of these only 77 (4.9%) were not there at the end of the next year.

Most of the longer staying group who were there at the beginning of the year had first entered the system at a much younger age and fell into the group we called 'adolescent graduates'. Eight out of ten (81%) of those who had spent a year or more continuously looked after at the start of the year were aged less than ten at first entry. On average they had entered the system six years previously around the age of seven. Their latest entry had been on average around five years three months earlier.

## Destinations of children aged 16 and over

Table 5.10 gives the reasons for leaving of those aged 16 or over. Around a third go to 'other' destinations. The majority of the remainder go to independent living with or without support. A sizeable minority return home. Most of these are recent arrivals. However, it was striking that even among those who have spent a relatively long time in the system the proportion returning home is higher than the equivalent figure among those aged 10–15.

At this age it is inevitable that many will leave the system. Anyone who reached the age of 18 during the year was bound to do so. Some managers were in favour of this, pointing out that carers were scarce and that they could not decrease their number by encouraging them to look after young adults. Others, however, were more critical. As one put it:

> It's harsh. I think it's very harsh… I think it's very, very unfortunate actually and I think, actually, that if children were permitted to stay later that perhaps it would help them engage perhaps in university education and things like that. (Manager)

In practice councils seem to look after long-stay children for as long as they can. We examined those who had been looked after for at least a year at the start of the census year and who had not reached 18 by the census date. Only 14 per cent of this group left during the year. The chance of leaving was strongly related to age at first entry. Twenty per cent of those who first entered when ten or over had left before the end of the year. The comparable figure for those who had first entered at a younger age was only 5 per cent.

## Conclusion

This chapter has been about entries and exits. As we have seen, the care system works as a kind of sieve, selecting those who cannot go home and returning the others as quickly as possible. A child had a relatively good chance of leaving shortly after arrival. After a year in the system the chance that he or she would leave in the next year was low.

There was a comparable change in where they went. Only a fifth (19%) of those who left the system after spending a year in it were said to return home. By contrast 61 per cent of those who did return home on leaving did so within six

**Table 5.10** Destination on leaving the care system by time since entry

| Why care ended | | Time from last admission to departure | | |
|---|---|---|---|---|
| | | Left within year | Left after a year | Total |
| Adopted | Count | 0 | 4 | 4 |
| | % within Time from last admission to departure | 0% | .9% | .6% |
| Died | Count | 0 | 2 | 2 |
| | % within Time from last admission to departure | 0% | .4% | .3% |
| Care taken over by OLA | Count | 1 | 1 | 2 |
| | % within Time from last admission to departure | .4% | .2% | .3% |
| Returned home | Count | 81 | 44 | 125 |
| | % within Time from last admission to departure | 34.5% | 9.8% | 18.2% |
| Indep. living with support | Count | 55 | 149 | 204 |
| | % within Time from last admission to departure | 23.4% | 33.0% | 29.7% |
| Indep. living without support | Count | 11 | 54 | 65 |
| | % within Time from last admission to departure | 4.7% | 12.0% | 9.5% |
| Transfer to adult service | Count | 5 | 35 | 40 |
| | % within Time from last admission to departure | 2.1% | 7.8% | 5.8% |
| Looked after ceased, other | Count | 82 | 162 | 244 |
| | % within Time from last admission to departure | 34.9% | 35.9% | 35.6% |
| Total | Count | 235 | 451 | 686 |
| | % within Time from last admission to departure | 100.0% | 100.0% | 100.0% |

Source: CIS sample.
Note: This table only applies to children aged 16 or over at census date.

months. The 'leaving care' curve highlighted by Rowe and her colleagues (1989) and illustrated in numerous other studies remains in place.

This pattern of activity was paralleled by the plans of social workers. At the beginning they planned for return in a sizeable proportion of cases. As time went on some of these plans worked out and the children left the system; other plans for return home were foregone and changed; as a result the proportion of those for whom return home was planned shrank sharply.

The exits from the system varied with the ages of the children as well as the length of time for which they stayed. There were four main groups:

1. Those of all ages who entered the system, left quickly, and in the great majority of cases went home.

2. Children who entered the system under the age of five and were adopted after a period of time. Most of these would otherwise have grown up in care, and their adoption has an important impact on the numbers looked after.

3. Young people over the age of 16 who graduated to independent living.

4. Children who were being 'brought up' in the system.

Other groups included those who went to the mysterious destination 'other' (a category that could with advantage be clarified in future statistical returns) and the trickle of those who went home after being looked after for one year (for although the chance of returning home in any one year is low, the chance of doing so within a number of years is clearly greater).

These possibilities seem potentially satisfactory to those we have called 'young entrants'. Depending on their age they may return home, be adopted or, hopefully, find a long-term family placement within the system as an 'adolescent graduate'. As we have seen, many of them do not in fact achieve such a long-term placement. This, however, is a problem of implementation rather than policy.

Our other policy groups may be less well served. The bulk of placements in the care system are taken up by children who are unlikely to return home in the near future and who are not going to be adopted. As we saw in earlier chapters their chance of achieving a foster placement that lasts for two years or more is low. In part this too is a problem of implementation. In part it reflects the length of time that they have available to them in the care system.

Any young person who does stay a long time with foster carers may have a problem when he or she reaches the age of 18. The numbers in this position are not great. Seventy-one children (on average about five or six for each of our councils) had been fostered with the same carers for more than three years when they left care at an age of 17 or over. At this point the placement, in theory, stops.

This is not the way in which ordinary families deal with their offspring. It might not cost an enormous amount to ensure that the care system does not do so either.

## Notes

1   We included the category 'other' as a kind of catchall for plans that were neither for return home nor permanent substitute care. In practice social workers seemed to use it in three sets of circumstances: (a) the child was over 16 and thus shortly destined to leave the system (40% of 'other' cases fell into this category as opposed to 16% of those in 'permanent substitute care'); (b) the child was under 16 but not in a placement they regarded as 'permanent substitute care' (16% were placed with parents as against .7% with those with plans for permanent substitute care and there was a similar contrast with residential schools – 3.5% v. 1%); (c) the child was under 16 and the current plan was uncertain (35% of placements were seen as temporary, emergency, remand or for assessment as against only 9.1% where the plan was permanent substitute care). Among those under 16, 8 per cent of the other category were destined for adoption but this reflected a fault in our questionnaire as we had intended this to be coded 'permanent substitute care'. Ninety-three per cent of those where the placement was intended for adoption were coded as having 'plans for substitute care'.

2   These figures are estimates of percentages with different bases. The base for those retained beyond a week consists of all those who were last admitted in the census year with the exception of those admitted in the week before the census date. The figure for those lasting a week and retained beyond 28 days was based on all those who had been admitted no more than a week before the beginning of the census year with the exception of those admitted no more than 28 days before the beginning of the census date. The exceptions are necessary in order to exclude 'censored cases', i.e. children who had an enhanced chance of staying because they had less than the stated 'retention period' to outlast. We included children who had entered before the census year in order to increase the numbers who had a chance of surviving for longer periods. However, we had to make sure that they were comparable to the group who survived the previous retention period. For example, if we had included children who had arrived 28 days before our census year in the base of our second percentage we would have had no knowledge of those who had left in the 28 days before the census date. This would have inflated our retention rate. To avoid double counting we looked at the latest admission. A small number of children will have had a double admission in the relevant period. The comparable table for admissions will therefore be somewhat different.

3   Cox proportional hazards model without covariates. This allowed us to use a definite sample – all those who had entered in the year – at the cost of having to allow for 'censored data'. The model assumes that if one group of cases is, say, twice as likely to remain as another over a given period this difference in likelihood is constant over preceding and subsequent periods.

4   A small number of children will have had more than one care career in this period. In this case only the last period has been counted.

5   This age is measured at the census date. Some of the children considered in older age groups may actually have ceased to be looked after when aged less than five.

# Chapter 6

# The Children and Their Different Paths in Care

[We try to] ensure that any, you know, care within the extended family or the family can be arranged very quickly if they do come in…[ and] for the young people who can't, babies or whoever, who can't go home or to anybody that you get a permanency in place for…to prevent them drifting, drifting too long. (Manager)

## Introduction

Some children go home soon after they start to be looked after; others stay on and are adopted; some have repeat admissions; others spend a long time being looked after by the state. We need to understand why some children follow one of these paths and others another. How far does this depend on the characteristics of the children and how far on the council that happens to be looking after them? If we knew this we would have a clear picture of the different policies that councils are following and how, if necessary, they might be changed.

This chapter looks at these issues. In doing so it uses multivariate statistical techniques. These are ways of exploring the apparent effects of combinations of variables. Those unfamiliar with these techniques may like to skip any notes or tables that seem hard to understand and concentrate instead on the text. Here we have tried to outline the logic of our analysis and also to repeat the main points from the tables in English that is as clear as we can make it.

## Method

The analysis in this chapter uses a standard set of data, which came both from the Client Information System (CIS) and the questionnaires to social workers.

The variables from CIS were: age at entry, age at census, need code of abuse, need code of disability, and days since last admission.[1]

The variables from the social workers were: whether the child was disabled, whether he or she was in placement with siblings, and the family difficulties, challenging behaviour, school performance and acceptance of care scores.

Typically we used variables from both sets of data. However:

- We did not use the data from social workers if analyses using the client information system could provide an equally good 'explanation' on their own.

- We did not use the family difficulties score at the same time as the variable 'need code of abuse' since in part these were measuring the same things.

- We did not use 'need code of disability' at the same time as 'social worker considers client disabled' because these variables also overlapped.

## Who has repeat admissions?

According to the information systems around a quarter (23%) of the children had been looked after more than once. A related question to the social workers showed, unsurprisingly, that the two sources of information did not always agree.[2] In the sample as a whole a third (33.4%) had experienced a previous admission according to the social workers, the information system or both. In cases where there was information from the social workers and the information system the proportion was four out of ten (40.3%). We consider this to be the best estimate.[3]

The variables in Table 6.1 are those which, taken together, were most strongly associated with whether or not a child in the sample had had a repeat admission.[4]

Many of the associations in this table are 'obvious'. A minus sign in the 'B' column means that a high value on this variable makes a readmission less likely, so older children and children first looked after at a relatively young age were more likely to have had a readmission. They had generally had a longer period in which to do so. It is not surprising that those who were not on a care order were more likely to have had repeat admissions. To some extent, they could come and go 'at will'. Asylum seekers were less likely to have repeat admissions. As they had no family in England they were unlikely to have been 'tried at home'.

**Table 6.1** Logistic regression predicting those with repeat admissions

| Independent variables | B | SE | Wald | df | Sig. | Exp(b) |
|---|---|---|---|---|---|---|
| Age | .212 | .011 | 345.781 | 1 | .000 | 1.237 |
| Age at first entry | −.183 | .013 | 205.638 | 1 | .000 | .833 |
| Social Worker sees as disabled | .407 | .074 | 20.698 | 1 | .000 | .713 |
| In placement with siblings | −.338 | .093 | 19.249 | 1 | .000 | 1.502 |
| Family Difficulty Score | .655 | .140 | 21.862 | 1 | .000 | 1.924 |
| Difficult Behaviour Score | .375 | .038 | 98.823 | 1 | .000 | 1.455 |
| Not on a care order | .627 | .086 | 52.737 | 1 | .000 | 1.872 |
| Seeking asylum | −.931 | .163 | 32.681 | 1 | .000 | .394 |
| Constant | −3.117 | .279 | 125.259 | 1 | .000 | .044 |

Source: CIS and Social Worker data.

Other things being equal children were also more likely to have repeat admissions if:

- they had severe family difficulties
- their social worker saw them as disabled[5]
- they had high scores for difficult behaviour.[6]

The families of such children may have found it harder to cope with them. We think that this is probably why more of them had had a time at home that had not worked out (see the notes for other, in our view less likely, explanations).

Other things being equal, children with repeat admissions were less likely to be placed with their siblings. It seems likely that they had often become separated from them in the course of their moves. For example, the other siblings may not have gone back into care when their brother or sister did.

The children were much more likely to have had a repeat admission in some councils than they were in others. On our 'best estimate' the chance of this varied from 27 per cent in one council to 59 per cent in another with a large 'spread' in between. As we have seen, the councils were looking after different kinds of children and young people. This, however, did not fully explain why some councils were more likely to have children with repeat admissions.[7] Our interviews showed that there was some awareness of these differences (see Box 6.1).

---

**Box 6.1** Managers' reflections

I think what we've found is that, occasionally children have been returned home or young people have been returned home, and you get the revolving door back in the system. And I think it is about, the thresholds are such that quite often now when they're coming out, the likelihood of them going back is quite high. (Manager)

It happens slightly differently here. I think we don't take them in until it's desperate and I think there aren't many cases of children coming in and coming out and coming in and coming out... So I think once they're in you've probably well sussed it that actually they're not going out again because we should have had them in a while before. (Manager from a different council)

---

## Who leaves shortly after arrival?

We looked at all those who began to be looked after (not necessarily for the first time) during the census year. We allowed for the period over which the child could leave. (Obviously those who arrived one week before the census date were very likely to be there on the census date.) Once we had done this the variables that predicted remaining (or, if the sign is negative, leaving) are given in Table 6.2.

**Table 6.2** Logistic regression predicting remaining when admitted in the year

| Independent variables | B | SE | Wald | df | Sig. | Exp(b) |
|---|---|---|---|---|---|---|
| Age | −.043 | .010 | 18.825 | 1 | .000 | .958 |
| Need code of abuse | .748 | .112 | 44.286 | 1 | .000 | 2.113 |
| Need code of disability | 1.728 | .444 | 15.130 | 1 | .000 | 5.631 |
| More than one admission | .342 | .122 | 7.860 | 1 | .005 | 1.408 |
| Not on a care order | −.777 | .111 | 48.890 | 1 | .000 | .460 |
| Asylum seeker | 1.954 | .237 | 67.985 | 1 | .000 | 7.055 |
| Days from admission to Census data (log) | −.609 | .066 | 85.251 | 1 | .000 | .544 |
| Constant | 3.941 | .363 | 117.804 | 1 | .000 | 51.462 |

Source: CIS sample.

The figures suggest a logical process. Children who appeared to be vulnerable or who had no family to which to return were more likely to stay. For this reason those seeking asylum, those with a need code of abuse, those with a need code of disability and those with more than one admission were all more likely to be looked after at the census date. Older children and those with a voluntary admission were more likely to leave. Arguably they were seen as being at less risk and as more able to look after themselves.

We compared the variables that predicted return from home with those that predicted return to it. There were some interesting differences:

- The challenging behaviour score and the family difficulties scores did not predict staying within the system but predicted repeat admissions.

- A need code of abuse predicted staying looked after but did not predict return from home.

One possibility is that social workers are clear about the problems of returning abused or neglected children to their families. They therefore only do so when a return is likely to succeed (for example, because an abusive adult has moved away). They may not be so worried about the children whose families have problems of drug abuse or domestic violence or who display challenging behaviour. These children may be more likely to fail at home and therefore more likely to be found among those with repeat admissions. This does not mean that these children should not go home. It does suggest that if they do so there needs to be a plan to deal with the risks.

Decisions to return children to their homes clearly involve risks. Some councils seemed more willing to take these risks than others.[8] There were large differences between the 13 councils in the speed at which children left. The proportion of children who started a period of being looked after during the year and were not looked after at the census date varied from 24 per cent to 49 per cent. The contrast was even starker when we looked at the variation among children with a need code of abuse. Here the proportion returning home varied from 12 per cent to 38 per cent – a more than threefold difference. The proportion leaving among the remainder varied from 29 per cent to 64 per cent.

One consequence of a willingness to take risks may be a higher proportion of 're-entrants'. The proportion of those entering in the year that had had a previous admission varied from 9 to 28 per cent between the different councils. Councils with a high proportion of 're-entrants' were more likely to discharge their new entrants within the year.[9] We cannot judge how far the greater risks run by some councils are justified. Clearly, however, it is an important issue for research.

## Who is adopted when aged less than eight?

As we have seen adoption is overwhelmingly restricted to younger children for whom it is a key route out of the system. We tried to predict which of the children under the age of eight would be adopted in the course of the year. Table 6.3 shows that the younger the age of admission the greater the chance of adoption. Children were less likely to be adopted if they were not white or if they had been 'tried at home'. After allowing for these factors children were more likely to be adopted when older – a reflection presumably of the time needed to bring about the adoption. They were also less likely to be adopted if they had been tried at home.

**Table 6.3** Logistic regression predicting adoption over the course of census year

| Independent variables | B | SE | Wald | df | Sig. | Exp(b) |
|---|---|---|---|---|---|---|
| Age | .306 | .043 | 51.738 | 1 | .000 | 1.358 |
| Age at first entry | −.696 | .066 | 109.631 | 1 | .000 | .499 |
| White | .858 | .206 | 17.265 | 1 | .000 | 2.358 |
| More than one admission | −.743 | .209 | 12.617 | 1 | .000 | .476 |
| Constant | −2.766 | .226 | 150.017 | 1 | .000 | .063 |

Source: CIS sample.
Note: Table is restricted to children under the age of eight.

Selwyn and her colleagues (2006) found that disabled children who had had a 'best interests' decision were less likely than others to achieve adoption. Other things being equal, we did not find that those with a need code of disability were less likely to be adopted. However, children who were disabled according to their social workers or on their council's definition of disability were indeed less likely to be so. We suggested earlier that those with a need code of disability probably had severe organic impairments. These may be less of a barrier to adoption than other impairments such as ADHD whose origin may not be so easily diagnosed (a conclusion also reached by Baker, 2006 in a longitudinal study of foster children).

Table 6.3 uses data from the CIS data only. If we include data from the social workers we get a slightly different picture. Age and age at entry still predict adoption. Children are also less likely to be adopted if:

- their social workers see them as disabled
- they are not white
- they are placed with their siblings.

So it seems easier to arrange adoptions for white children, who come in when very young, who are not disabled and who do not have brothers and sisters.

Among those children who were less than eight years old, the proportion adopted during the year varied between councils (less than 1% to 15%). Again some councils were aware that they were placing a particular emphasis on adoptions (see Box 6.2).

---

**Box 6.2** Managers' reflections

So we…invested in adoption, we got some very good managers in who would perform very well elsewhere and we set them high targets and high standards and I think they probably felt that they were well-supported, that they'd got enough people in the team to do a good job. We employed a half-time communication specialist with a dedicated brief around family placement and adoption and she's helped our adoption enquiries increase by 100 per cent and our fostering enquiries by 25 per cent. So you know, all of those things came together and…a lot of sweat and hard work really. (Manager)

We're very committed to achieving permanence for children quickly and I see all the papers that go to adoption panel…you can monitor the timescales through that route…good practice is around establishing clear protocols between…ourselves, the courts, around the care proceedings process… there's a big commitment around twin tracking. I do think it's an issue about the workloads of staff as well. So we not only went for an additional social worker…but also for an additional admin worker. (Manager, in another authority)

---

There was also a difference in the length of time adoption took. Children who were adopted in some councils were, after allowing for age at entry, significantly older than those adopted in others. The main reason for this seemed to be the differing effects of repeat admissions. These were much more likely to be associated with delayed adoptions in some councils than they were in others.[10]

It therefore seems that councils can influence both the likelihood of adoption and its speed. In part this may have to do with their ability to counter the effects of re-admission, perhaps because they use some kind of 'parallel planning'.

## Among those not adopted, who returns home after staying for at least a year?

Some children stay in 'care' for some time but are not adopted. In this group some cease to be looked after before reaching the age of 16. What distinguishes them from those who do not?

The answer to this question was, as far as we could see, 'rather little'. In general the longer children had been looked after the more likely they were to remain so. After allowing for this, those who had had repeat admissions were also more likely to remain. Time and the experience of failed attempts at return home presumably close options, making adoption less likely and rendering slim chances of further return home even slimmer.

Council practices may also make a difference. The group we are looking at are those who had spent a year looked after at the beginning of the year and who were not adopted. There was a significant variation between councils in the proportions of this group who had left the system by the end of the year (3–17%). In no council, however, was the proportion high. The overall proportion leaving was only seven per cent.

## Which care leavers leave before they are 18?

The arrangements that now prevail for care leavers are relatively new. More attention is now rightly concentrated on this process. There are pathway plans, leaving care teams, and much else besides. The changes had obviously not passed unnoticed. As one manager commented:

> You know, when I first came in to Social Services lots of kids just became homeless and when they left care nobody knew where they went, you know…and then we started setting up leaving care teams and of course, you know, specific grants for developing leaving care services and it's a completely different world now. (Manager)

These arrangements for leaving care assume that the young person will move on from his or her placement. Such enforced departures are not common in 'ordinary families'. How far do councils anticipate them by expecting children to move on even before they reach the age of 18? Insofar as they do, which young people seem to become 'early leavers' and which stay on till almost their eighteenth birthday?

We counted a young person as an early leaver if he or she was: (a) aged from 16 to 17.5 years on the census date; (b) looked after for at least a year at the start of the census year; and (c) no longer looked after. A young person who met all these criteria would have left the system at least six months before he or she had to and despite having spent at least a year in it. In practice relatively few (12%) of the young people who met the first two of our criteria actually left the system and were thus early leavers as we defined them.

Overall there was some variation between local councils (4–21%) in the proportion of young people who could on our definition have been early leavers who actually were. This variation was of only borderline significance ($p = .052$). The differences by need code were much more significant varying from nought per cent for those with a need code of disability to 36 per cent for those with a need code of 'acute family stress' (see Table 6.4). It seems that it is difficult to make new arrangements for disabled young people. It would be interesting to know how far they are able to remain where they are.

**Table 6.4** Need codes among 'early care leavers'

| Reason for being looked after | | Whether in placement at census | | |
|---|---|---|---|---|
| | | No | Yes | Total |
| Abuse or neglect | Count | 25 | 289 | 314 |
| | % within Reason for being looked after | 8.0% | 92.0% | 100.0% |
| Disabled | Count | 0 | 21 | 21 |
| | % within Reason for being looked after | 0% | 100.0% | 100.0% |
| Parent disabled | Count | 3 | 26 | 29 |
| | % within Reason for being looked afterr | 10.3% | 89.7% | 100.0% |
| Stress | Count | 18 | 32 | 50 |
| | % within Reason for being looked after | 36.0% | 64.0% | 100.0% |
| Family dysfunction | Count | 7 | 45 | 52 |
| | % within Reason for being looked after | 13.5% | 86.5% | 100.0% |
| Difficult behaviour | Count | 4 | 14 | 18 |
| | % within Reason for being looked after | 22.2% | 77.8% | 100.0% |
| Abandoned | Count | 8 | 39 | 47 |
| | % within Reason for being looked after | 17.0% | 83.0% | 100.0% |
| Total | Count | 65 | 466 | 531 |
| | % within Reason for being looked after | 12.2% | 87.8% | 100.0% |

Source: CIS sample.
Note: Table appplies to young people aged 16 to 17.5 years and in placement for at least one year at the beginning of the census year.

## Conclusion

This chapter has linked the characteristics of the children to certain key processes. Thus:

- Vulnerable children – those who were younger, abused, disabled or seeking asylum (typically on our classification the young entrants, disabled children and asylum seekers) – were less likely to leave the system soon after they entered it. They may have had no safe place to go.

- Children who were likely to pose challenges to their parents or whose parents had difficulties relating to alcohol, drugs or domestic violence were no less likely than others to go home quickly. They were more likely to be readmitted following a failed rehabilitation. More account should perhaps be taken of the risks they pose.

- Children who were older, harder to 'match' or considered by their social workers to be disabled were less likely to be adopted. They may thus need special efforts to ensure their adoption or a long-term base in the care system.

- Children who had a need code of disability never became 'early leavers' as we defined the term. They too may need a long-term base and one that lasts beyond 18.

The chance that a child would be discharged quickly, readmitted and so on also varied with the councils involved. Some councils were much more likely to have readmissions. Some (often the same ones) discharged much higher proportions of those who enter the care system shortly after admissions. Some placed higher proportions of young children for adoption or achieved adoption within a shorter period of time. There were similar but less stark differences over the discharge of longer-staying children and the early discharge of those who were aged over 16.

We were not able to explain these differences between councils by taking account of the children's characteristics. Almost certainly they reflected differences in policies and practice. The decisions involved have major implications for children's lives. It is clearly vital that the effects of different policies are evaluated.

## Notes

1 We took the natural log to create a more normal distribution.

2 The two sources of information agree together to a far greater degree than would occur by chance.

3 The proportion of repeat admissions in the sample as a whole was 23.2 per cent according to the information system. The client information system figure for the social work

sample was 23.8 per cent. This does not suggest that the social work sample was biased towards repeat admissions.

4   The acceptance of care and school performance score were both negatively associated with repeat admissions but did not add to the predictive power of the equation.

5   Disabled children sometimes become looked after following a series of short breaks. Although we tried to exclude children who were currently on 'an agreed series of short breaks' from the analysis we counted those who had had them previously and were now fully looked after as repeat admissions. In theory this may account for the association we found. In practice short breaks were overwhelmingly found in a small number of councils. After omitting these councils the equation described above remains much the same.

6   There are various possible explanations. The experience of repeat admissions could produce challenging behaviour. Those with challenging behaviour may be more likely to experience a repeat admission, as their families find they cannot deal with them. Those admitted as a result of difficult behaviour may be less likely to have been abused. It may therefore be easier to return them home so that they have a chance of being readmitted. As we will see later, difficult behaviour does not make the chance of return home larger or smaller so the last explanation is unlikely. It is possible that failed returns produce difficult behaviour. We prefer the second explanation because it fits the other data (e.g. the increased number of returns among disabled children or those with severe family difficulties).

7   These analyses used our 'best estimate' of repeat admissions that was based on information from the social workers and the client information systems. In this way we reduced the problems arising from the differences between councils in the response rates of social workers and the completeness of the information systems. We tested the effects of councils by first running the logistic equation given in Table 6.1 and then running a second equation into which we entered 12 councils as dummy variables. We then compared the 'omnibus chi square' for the two equations. This was 656 with 7 degrees of freedom without the councils and 809 with 19 degrees of freedom with the councils, an addition of 153 for 12 degrees of freedom. The final model correctly predicted 82 per cent of those without a repeat admission and 51 per cent of those with one.

8   The addition of information on the councils to the logistic regression in Table 6.2 adds 43.96 to the omnibus chi square with 12 degrees of freedom. This means that a knowledge of which council is looking after a child adds significantly to our ability to predict whether they will remain.

9   This proportion of entrants in the year with a repeat admission correlated significantly with the proportion of entrants with a need code of abuse who were discharged over the year (tau b = .55, $p$ = .01) and also with the proportions of other entrants discharged (tau b = .46, $p$ = .03).

10   These statements reflect the results of an analysis of variance based on children adopted under the age of eight. We used age at adoption as the dependent variable, local council and repeat admissions as main effects and age at entry as covariate. The local council effect was massively significant as was the covariate. Repeat admissions were just significant ($p$ = .041). The interaction term of local council by repeat admissions was also massively significant.

Chapter 7

# Going Home and Leaving Care: The Case Studies

> If there is a planned rehabilitation [it is essential] that everyone is clear about that prior to the placement and so there should be minimum disruption and we are all clear about why that child is there and how long for and what the plan is and how they are going to be rehabilitated. (Manager)

## Introduction

A child's entry to or exit from the care system involves key decisions. The last two chapters have identified some of the factors that may influence these decisions or determine their outcome. In this chapter we use our 95 case studies to cast light on the same processes. We want to understand how it is that some cases turn out well and others less so. If we can explain these outcomes at least partly through what the social workers and carers do, we will know more about what makes for good practice.

## Method

This is the first chapter to use the case studies as its main source. We need to say more about them.

The 13 councils were as keen as we were that the children should have a voice in our work. To this end each council asked one or more experienced professionals (social workers, children's rights officers or independent reviewing officers) to carry out the case studies. We gave these reviewers a group of cases and 'reserves' selected in order to ensure a spread of care experience and a representation of children who were disabled and who came from ethnic minorities.[1] The most important restriction was that the child had to be over the age of five, a constraint that meant, among other things, that our case studies did not include any child who was being adopted.

The councils then carried out up to ten case studies. The professionals used an interview schedule that we gave them and sought to interview the child, carer and social worker and then to sum up their own view of the case. Our judgements of 'what went well or badly' are based on the views of these three sources informed by the overall summary and analysis made by the professionals. We call the latter 'reviewers'.

Our analysis of the case studies was based on putting them into groups. These were defined by whether the child had a permanent 'base' in care. Some children were clearly not going home. We consider these in a separate chapter. In this chapter we look at children where there had not been a long-standing and clear decision that the child should stay in care.

The children studied in this chapter fell into separate sub-groups. Some had come into care and then left quickly; some had recently been given a clear decision that they were not to go home; others had returned home after some time or moved backwards and forwards between their home and the care system. Yet others came into care late and at a point when they could not remain long but were unlikely to return home. All the cases involve the issues of leaving or not leaving the system that have been the focus of the last two chapters.

Our analysis begins by distinguishing between cases that seem to go well and those that do not. We want to understand the reasons for these different outcomes. So we develop an explanation that seems to suit one case. We then try out the explanation, adapting it until it fits all cases of the same kind.[2] We repeat this process with other groups. In the end the plausibility of our explanation depends on three things: the degree to which the explanations form a coherent set; the degree of fit with our statistical results; their consistency with other research.

## Brief care leading to return home

Eight children in the case studies had had a single, relatively brief (less than two years) episode of care. These almost invariably seemed 'successful'. Where such returns home ran into trouble they will appear in our case studies under other headings.

A number of conditions seemed to determine the apparently successful outcomes of these eight cases. These involved:

- Clarity about what was planned and the conditions for its success.

- Commitment of all the key players (social workers, carers, family and child to this plan) and the consequent need for good communication and co-ordination.

- A realistic assessment of whether the conditions for return were met, together with, in some cases, a 'fall-back' plan for what should happen if they were not.

- Purposeful work by the social workers to achieve the plan at a measured but urgent pace.

---

**Case Study: Adrienne**

[Adrienne] returned due to positive work completed, co-operation and positive contact which demonstrated the warmth and emotional bond between the parents and all the children. (Reviewer)

Adrienne, aged six, is at home following four months in care. As the social services see it, she was looked after as the result of domestic violence and neglect. Her father abused amphetamines and this fuelled his violence. Adrienne sees things differently. She feels that she was looked after to give her mum a rest. Adrienne thinks it was a good idea that she came into care, and liked both her foster placements.

The plan from the beginning was that Adrienne should return home. This, however, was not to be at any price. At the time of her move to a new foster family return home was considered but not tried since it was felt that the parents had not yet changed enough. Nevertheless Adrienne's move into care seems to have given the parents a shock. The father has given up his amphetamines, the warmth between parents and daughter has shone through and Adrienne has gone home. Adrienne is on the child protection register (something she is said not to want).

Everyone agrees that the current situation is a good outcome. As the reviewer sees it, the plan proved possible because it was agreed on all sides and consistently followed. Neither the reviewer nor the social worker feels that anything else should have been done. They therefore have no recommendations to make.

---

Adrienne's case clearly fulfilled these conditions. However, examining this and other cases suggests three other conditions that could also help things to go well. These were:

- Continuity – the more the child was able to share the placement with their siblings, avoid a change of school, begin a longer term placement with known carers, and maintain contact with the relatives to whom they were to return the better.

- Quality of carers – high quality carers who were able to sympathise with the parent(s), support the child and work with the social workers were highly valuable.

- Adequate staffing to enable the purposeful social work, avoid drift and allow thorough assessment.

The eight children in this group fulfilled these conditions to varying extents. None of them had returned to overtly unsatisfactory homes, but some had experienced social work of wavering purposefulness, or foster carers who, while not overtly hindering the plan, had not furthered it either. Adrienne experienced a placement move after reporting that the carer's daughter smoked cannabis.

Mary provides an example of an apparently good outcome after an uncertain start. The key points in this case were that Mary and her father were agreed on what should happen and the conditions for return were met. For a while there was not clarity about what was planned or purposeful work to ensure it. Once these further conditions were met all seems to have gone smoothly with the additional benefit that the new placement has continuity (it keeps the siblings together).

---

**Case Study: Mary**

> [Mary's] father who was initially thought to be totally unsuitable to look after his children has proved himself to be the right answer. (Reviewer)

Mary, aged 11, spent around two years looked after following a long history of neglect at home with her mother. She has now returned to her father. Initially the department resisted this step. The father, however, passed a very rigorous assessment and repeatedly demonstrated his commitment. According to the social worker 'this man has jumped through so many hoops to get control of his own children…perhaps a woman would have not been asked to do so?'

Mary was living with her mother at the time she was first looked after but despite the difficulties at home does not remember the experience of going into care as a happy one:

> It was horrible because my sister went to school and told someone that she did not want to go home and it went all around the school that we were being taken away. A teacher talked to my brother and me, and then someone came at the end of school and took us to Maggie and Jim's place [foster carers].

After the shock of removal she remembers a sense of impermanence and powerlessness. 'We just stayed where they put us.'

Her present placement with her father could not be more of a contrast. It's home and she wants to live there 'forever'. She has 'loads of friends' at school, her brother lives with them and her elder sister lives with a foster family two streets away. 'She's here every day and weekends but stays with them the rest of the time.' According to the reviewer 'She clearly adores her father and they appear to have a close relationship'. So Mary is where she wants to be with her siblings and with a parent she loves and who is committed to her.

## Brief care leading to permanent admission

The success of return home seemed to depend on what the child and the family wanted and on the quality of care the family were able to give. Precisely similar issues arose where the decision was that the child should not go home. Connor provides an example. As can be seen his 'ace' carers have offered him love and security without attempting to cut off his relationship with his family, so Connor is happy with his placement and with his family contact. He wants to stay where he is and what he gets there is good quality care.

**Case Study: Connor**

[The foster carers] are ace. (Connor)

Connor is now 11 and has been looked after in one placement for six months. His admission was precipitated by his family's eviction from their house but followed a long period of preventive work in response to his mother's and her partners' chaotic, drug dependent life-styles fuelled by criminal activity. His mother is currently in prison and her current partner has refused to co-operate with social services. There are no plans for Connor to go home unless his mother changes her life-style 'which to date she hasn't'.

According to Connor lots of things have happened since he has been looked after by [name of foster carer]…and 'they are all good'. His placement is 'perfect'. He likes the play station, the food, his bedroom, getting to choose his own things (choosing his own bed means to him that he is staying). He has started a new school and got into the football team. He has had a birthday and got the new 'England official strip' which according to Connor is 'really dear and is his to keep'. Connor feels lucky to have been in the same placement. He talks about the other foster children and the changes they have had.

Connor is sad about what happened but glad he is safe. In an ideal world he would like his 'mum to come out of prison, stay off drugs and think of the kids first'. He might then consider living with her but would want to stay in frequent contact with [his foster carers]. Counselling with a local project is helping him to give up his feelings of responsibility for his family without losing his love for them. He likes seeing 'Nanna, Mum, Mum's boyfriend, [his sister] and [his aunt]…until I am grown up or my mum changes in lots of ways. I just want to stay with my [foster carers]'.

Since admission he has grown six inches in six months and put on 1.5 stone. It is said that he has never looked so happy or content.

There are at the moment only two threats to Connor's happiness. First, his mother wants him back. It remains to be seen how he will deal with this when she comes out of prison. Her intervention could spoil the clear plan that seems one of the key conditions for success. Second, the placement is officially short-term. The carers want to keep Connor, but whether they do or not is a decision for the fostering panel. Connor, himself, takes what comfort he can from his role in buying his bed and is said to be frightened that the placement may come to an end.

One further contributory factor may be that Connor is not only loved but also a loveable and probably an 'easy' child. Our statistics later will show that difficult behaviour, particularly in older children, is associated with having frequent placements. They also strongly suggest that the quality of the placement is even more important in determining its outcomes. Daniel provides an example of both these propositions.

Both the reviewer and the social worker think it sad that Daniel had to go through so many apparently good placements in order to reach this happy situation.

Why is Daniel's current placement apparently more successful than the others? A number of different points are made. The reviewer comments on the consistency and 'stickability' of the carers and on the active nature of the household with other foster children modelling good behaviour and stepchildren visiting. Daniel goes to counselling with a local project that he finds useful. He likes his school, and the activities in the placement (he does karate, gymnastics, and dancing). He has as much contact with his father and brother as he wants, ringing one every Friday and seeing his brother when he can. He has friends in the street. He says that the female carer has a nice house, lots of friends and 'is really nice to me'.

**Case Study: Daniel**

> [I will stay here] all my life until I get my own house, move in with my girlfriend and have babies. (Daniel)

> Do we have enough foster carers to match to difficult young people or is it just the first bed that becomes free? (Reviewer)

Daniel is 11 years old. His difficulties seem to have begun or at least got worse when his mother left home to live with a new partner. He was then nine years old and at first he moved with his mother. She, however, became tired of him and his behaviour and took him to social services. To Daniel's relief his father then turned up and took him and his siblings back home to live with him. This arrangement, however, soon broke down as the father proved unable to manage the children, his parenting was 'chaotic', and there was a Section 47 enquiry about possible physical abuse. Daniel was then fostered.

In the two years since then Daniel has had four placements and two failed attempts at rehabilitation which the social worker now sees as unrealistic. In the end it was decided that long-term foster care should be tried. Daniel says that he got tired of moving and that he was never consulted about the placements or able to visit them in advance. Nevertheless he says he liked all but one of his placements although only the recent one has been able to manage him.

Daniel has been in this recent placement for about a year and loves it there. Indeed all are agreed that it is highly satisfactory. The female carer has become very fond of Daniel, although the male one may still find him a bit of a handful. The social worker feels the placement meets all of Daniel's needs.

So, in general the explanation that fits for Connor seems to fit for Daniel:

- After some hesitation there is now a clear plan that Daniel will stay in care. This has given him security and he believes he will stay as long as he wants.

- He has high quality care. His carers are, if not ace, at least in one case 'really nice to me'. The adjuncts to the placement, friends, school, activities, and the house itself are all, from his point of view, good.

- There is continuity with as much contact with his family as he seems to want and need.

These advantages, combined perhaps with a sense that it is time he stopped moving, are all helping to overcome the challenge of his behaviour. The effect and purpose of the counselling are unknown. Presumably, however, it helps him to reflect on his situation, come to terms with it, and so move on to make the best of it.

In short, success in this group again seems to depend on two key elements: what the child wants and the quality of the placement. The problem is that what the child wants may not be same as what he or she needs. Success in dealing with this dilemma may depend on addressing the child's feelings about home so that he or she can feel happy with the amount of contact and the overall plan.

## Repeated care or late returns

A number of cases involved repeated or late attempts at rehabilitation. These arose from various reasons. In some it became obvious that care was not working. Rehabilitation was therefore tried, not because home seemed a good alternative but rather because it seemed no worse than anything else. In others the child's family was at times satisfactory but care was threatened by, for example, episodic psychiatric illness. In others there was some kind of compromise. Reasonably regular periods of care were used as an alternative to full-time care in the belief that in this way a fragile home situation could be adequately maintained.

The common thread through these different cases was that the child maintained a wish, albeit sometimes an ambivalent one, to be at home. At the same time the home situation did not improve sufficiently to support them there. This was not a promising situation. As we will see later experience of a repeat admission is very strongly associated with poor well-being.

The reasons for this unhappiness varied. Some children who were looked after periodically worried about psychiatrically ill parents. Some teenagers who had returned home hung around in an environment that was unable to support them. They were bored, did not go to school, and were of the opinion that 'life was shit'. Others returned to the care system after such experiences and were equally disaffected. One 17-year-old girl had vainly tried to make a success of life with an alcoholic mother interspersed with periods of care. Recently she has failed to make a success of living on her own and according to the reviewer her life is bleak. Shaun provides another example of these unhappy young people.

Success, in so far as it was achieved, seemed to depend partly on a match between what the children wanted and what they got. Sometimes what they wanted was to make home work. One teenager, for example, had been unhappy in care and was correspondingly pleased to be home. 'Things kept changing. I knew I had a mum and dad, but I felt not wanted. I have moved to live with my

**Case Study: Shaun**

> I was too bad for them – always getting into trouble at school and my temper – if anything would get on my nerves or I couldn't get what I wanted, I would go mental. (Shaun)

Shaun was 14 at the point he participated in the study. He had first entered the system at the age of eight, had returned home after two years, only for the attempted rehabilitation to fail. Fortunately he was able to return to carers he knew. He said that he had liked his long-term carers and was pleased to be away from his family home and the troubles there. He wished he was still at this foster placement as he liked his school and friends, but he had had to leave because of his behaviour.

Shaun then had two foster placements. He did not remember much about his placement moves and didn't feel he had had much choice about what happened. He said that he wanted to return home and had been asked about this. He is 'hoping to stay at home forever now', but he does not like his current school and does not get on with the other students. His future is uncertain.

[parent] and I feel quite happy and relieved I have got my normal life back.' Another by contrast felt that the repeated failed attempts at rehabilitation had enabled her to see that life at home could not work out. 'Before then I would have been angry if someone had told me I wasn't going home… I had to decide that myself.'

Success may also be made more likely by changes in the home environment, always provided these go with a continued wish to make home work. Eric's history provides an example. Everyone agreed that in the time Eric had been away his mother had 'matured'. This made it possible to give Eric what he wanted. Paradoxically the plan for him had probably nurtured his wish to go home while seeking to ensure that he did not. During the first five years of his time in care strenuous efforts had been made to keep Eric in touch with his mother and siblings. The delay in finding a long-term placement must have helped maintain or strengthen Eric's attachment to his then carer and to his own mother. This in turn must have made it more difficult to adopt him. His continuing attachment combined with his behaviour probably affected his time in care for the worse. It is also one of the good things about where he is now.

A further positive feature of Eric's current situation seems to be the first foster carer who lives locally and whom Eric has recently seen. Eric has been able to go back to the school he was at when first fostered and where he knows some of the

**Case Study: Eric**

> I'm even confident we have reached a point he has a permanent placement... I regret it took so long. (Eric's social worker)

Eric (13) is of dual heritage. He was first looked after at the age of three, a result of neglect and his mother's abuse of drugs. At present he is at home on a care order.

> I came into care when I was 3 years old. I don't know if it was good or not. I didn't have any favourite placement; they were all okay. I was with [foster carer] for about 4½ years. That placement was near home. I felt comfortable there. Then I was with Dot. I was supposed to be adopted but it didn't work out, I was there for about 7 months. My [time there] went okay. I liked it there. I got moved to my next placement the day before I was meant to go to Scouts; I remember that... I didn't want to get adopted because I wanted to see Mum... Then I was with Claire for more than a year. Then I was with Carla for 2–3 years. In one of the placements I got told off for climbing trees in case I hurt myself. I kept climbing trees so I kept getting grounded after that. One placement wouldn't let me watch 15–18 year old movies. I didn't see [my brother] much, I would have liked to have seen him more. Food and things were okay and they were fair in terms of what chores we had to do. In most of the placements they had their own kids. I got fed up having friends and losing them. Usually when you moved placements you had to move school; I don't think it made things harder for me – I learned teachers' names easily. It's good to be at home. Being with Mum all the time and I know I'm not going to be moved again. Now I'd like to have my Care Order removed.

The social worker and the reviewer corroborate this account, adding that the difficulties in the placements arose partly from Eric's behaviour and problems in forming relationships. Both feel that the current outcome is very satisfactory. Eric's parents split up and his mother matured and had been able to parent another child satisfactorily. Both Eric and his mother are delighted that Eric is back.

pupils. He has also been able to maintain contact with some members of his extended family. This continuity is another feature that was helpful in cases of brief care.

Lack of continuity hampered attempts to use 'revolving care' to cope with episodic crises. Keith provides an example of shared or revolving care. As can be

### Case Study: Keith

> After meeting the current foster family I hope that this will evolve into a long-term placement as Keith appears to be well supported and happy. (Keith's Reviewer)

Keith is a 15-year-old young person from a rather strict religious sect. He has moderate learning difficulties and according to the reviewer he looks like a '10- or 11-year-old boy. He has a sunny temperament but limited understanding and throughout the interview looked to his foster mother for clarification'.

Keith has very little contact with his father and sibling and his mother has recurrent psychiatric problems. The department has been involved with Keith throughout his life through the continual use of emergency foster or on occasion residential care. It is, however, only recently at the age of 14 that he has had any prolonged care. Keith himself felt that the original idea of short-term care had been a good one. However he did not like the 'smoking and drinking' he met in some of his foster homes.

The present arrangement is a compromise. Keith stays with the foster carers during the week and returns to his mother at the weekend. Keith says that he 'really likes it here' [at foster placement] and that he 'is able to do things'. He gets on with the two other foster children in the placement and he goes out with friends. According to the social worker he is doing well at school and he likes the stability. He said he would like to stay there until he is 19.

Despite this apparently satisfactory situation Keith would, according to the social worker, like to be at home all the time. There are plans for this, albeit with an extensive support package. The reviewer, however, noted that Keith's mother opposed the plan and that when talking with the social worker Keith spoke about his mother and her illness but made no mention of returning home.

seen the reviewer felt that for a long time Keith lacked the security that would have come from either a definite placement or from return to known carers. Overall, therefore, what seemed to be wanted in shared care was a structure that provided security. Within this context a child might tolerate frequent movement between known carers whose role was understood. The danger was that the child had no structure and little security as continual emergencies moved them from one unknown carer to another.

Once again the key with these cases seems to lie in:

- having a clear, realistic plan
- working with what the child wants
- providing high quality care, allied if possible with continuity.

## Care as a launch pad

My social worker has spoken to me about moving into my own place...but I opted to stay with my carers. (Adolescent graduate)

I'm not an organised person so if I live, if I start living on my own, it won't be right. I like living at home... I'm really comfortable there so I don't think I would wanna move until I'm eighteen. (Asylum-seeking child)

It was a good idea at the time. I needed space from my mum... It made it easier to stay at school, I kept it together, I got suspended a few times but have done my GCSEs and revised for them. (Adolescent entrant)

Thirteen of the young people in our case studies were preparing to live independently or, in one case, had started to do so. Four of these had spent a long time in the care system. Three were seeking asylum and had entered relatively recently. Six others had also entered the system relatively late when aged 15 or over. We selected the quotations at the head of this section to illustrate key issues facing each of these three sub-groups. We have, however, considered those seeking asylum in Chapter 4. Our examples are therefore drawn from the other two groups.

For the long-stay group the key issue was the pace at which they left the system. The proposed movement from foster care was planned to reflect the young person's change of legal status rather than their need to move out at their own pace. One felt secure enough to resist this plan. The others appear to have gone along with it, although there was no evidence that they endorsed it. Angela illustrates the situation of this long-stay group.

### Case Study: Angela

I am moving to a flat when I am 18... Probably with another girl... I don't know who. (Angela)

Upon meeting Angela she presents as a noisy young teenager. She is happy to chat casually about friends, going out and the family pets, but when asked about her life she becomes unable or unwilling to respond unless in monosyllables. According to the social worker 'She is a very young 17 and enjoys hanging out with 13 or 14 year olds.' (Reviewer)

Angela (17) is said to have 'some degree of learning difficulties' which are 'well disguised.' The reviewer felt that Angela was unwilling to do things for herself, had a limited understanding, left the initiative to others, and had a short attention span. Apparently Angela felt she had little influence on what happened to her and was somehow reluctant to engage with planning it or talking about it. She described her current placement as 'OK' and had no comments for social services. Despite her apparent passivity she has recently written to her mother saying that she wants nothing more to do with her.

Angela has been known to the department since birth, and started to be looked after when ten because of child protection issues (lifelong abuse). Angela said she supposed it was a good idea at the time but that now she does not know. After two years in her first placement 'the foster Mum died… She used to make me go to church on Sundays… But I did not want to stay with her anyway'.

The next placement was believed to be thoroughly satisfactory. There was therefore great surprise when after five years Angela ran away, an event which greatly upset the foster carers and led them to say that they did not want her back. Recently Angela had had a 'disruption' meeting with her former carers and it was hoped that she would return to them. Angela describes these events as a 'hiccup'. Nothing, however, is yet fixed. The official plan is for supported living where she can maintain contact with her aunt and brother and learn to do more for herself.

Angela's current situation is not an easy one. She has rejected her mother. Her former carers have, if perhaps temporarily, rejected her. She may move back to them although not long ago they said they did not want her. In any event she will move out from foster care very shortly although she is supposed to be very young for her age. She will then move to supported living but, according to the reviewer, does not understand what the scheme involves. She hopes to get a job in a riding stable, but she is likely to find rather stiff competition from others with a far longer experience of horses than herself. A proposed contact with her aunt is, according to the reviewer, likely to cause her further problems. In the light of this history Angela's 'passivity' is not surprising. She is not in a situation where she has much power. The actions she takes – rejecting her mother and running away from her carers – are those available to her. They are comments on her situation. They probably do not advance her cause.

Apart from our three asylum seekers, six young people had last entered the care system relatively late at the age of 15 or over. The immediate reasons for this varied. In one case the family were finding it difficult to deal with the young person's impairment(s) and need for independence. Another seemed to involve the clash of parents with strong personalities with an equally strong-willed daughter. In yet another a father who had brought his daughter up on his own was finding it difficult to relax his rules. Another followed a mother's introduction of an unwelcome partner; another, a newspaper scandal involving a regretted infatuation and another (described below) the death of a sole surviving parent.

Whatever the reasons, the young people seemed to have certain common characteristics. First, they were, in most cases, actively seeking independence and therefore accepted their need to move on. Second, their upbringing had had many redeeming features. So they were seeking more freedom from their parent(s), not a rupture with them. Third, they were aware of their need for skills and qualifications – so they accepted that school was important; two were working hard for their A levels and hoping to go on to university, and one was revising for her GCSEs. Fourth, they had requirements of their placements that were clearly analogous to those of children placed at a younger age, but which typically required sensitive negotiation.

Success in these cases seemed again to depend on the young people's motivation – specifically their determination to acquire the skills and qualifications they needed. It also depended on the ability of the carers to support and listen to them while they did this and then to support them in moving on. Brian provides an example of this situation.

In some ways Brian is not typical of this final sub-group. He has been involved with social services and the care system for a much longer period. His need to come to terms with his family is symbolic rather than real as his mother is dead; his presumed father has consistently denied all responsibility for him and seems emotionally out of the picture. We nevertheless describe his case in some detail because it picks up the themes that recur throughout both this group of cases and earlier ones.

First, there is the importance of *what the children or young people want*. This means it is important to see care in terms of what it means for the child's view of his or her family and for the skills a young person may need in future life.

Second, there is the key role that can be played by *good carers* – whether these are parents, foster carers or, in a few cases, residential staff. Many children wish that relationships with these carers lasted for longer and approximated more closely to those found with relatives in ordinary life.

Third, and in keeping with this, there is the importance of *continuity* – arrangements that allow the child to feel that relationships are not simply cut off.

**Case Study: Brian**

> [Brian] clearly adores Barbara and her family and speaks of all of them in the highest terms. The move to independent living holds no fear for him and he sees the change of living location as no bar to his continuing relationship with Barbara and family. (Reviewer)

At five Brian had a brief spell in the care system followed by around five years at home where he became the sole carer for his chronically ill mother. This caring came to involve 'inappropriate intimate' care and Brian was seen as emotionally and physically neglected and abused. He was therefore looked after again for two years around the age of 11. The carers were 'not nice'. Brian became their scapegoat, reported physical abuse and finally ran away to his mother where he remained. Brian remembers this time as a difficult one. He had around ten short respite placements including one in residential care. In retrospect, he is quite clear that 'it was best when I was at home'. Around two years ago Brian's mother's illness became terminal and she entered a nursing home.

At this point Brian moved to live with Barbara, his current carer, who regularly took him to see his mother while she was in hospital. As Brian sees it, it is really good that Barbara has met her. Barbara is 'just like a mum' to him and this is his home although he will be moving out in the next year or two. When asked if this worries him he says 'not at all', it is only fair that someone else gets to live with Barbara as she is so good and besides, he is only going to be moving down the road so will continue to pop in all the time. Brian says that Barbara has promised to buy him a washing machine for his flat. In the meantime he remains in college where he is doing well on a three-year catering course.

---

Finally, these last three elements must inform the *plans* for the child. As far as possible these should be clear and agreed. In this way they can give the child security, allowing them to trust others and in their own future.

## Conclusion

Some of the cases we have described have been clearly successful. Others have not. What is it that makes the difference? Three explanations run through these histories.

The first explanation concerns the characteristics of the child. Children who displayed challenging behaviour or had problems at school found it hard to succeed at home or in a placement. Older children about to leave the system had to have the ability to make it in the outside world.

The second explanation concerns motivation: what the children wanted and how they saw their future. Children who wanted to go home tried to make this work. Those who accepted their need for care were more willing to attach to new carers. Older children who were about to leave the system needed to see this as an appropriate step.

The third explanation concerns the quality and appropriateness of the environment. Where the child returned home the caring ability of the child's parent or parents influenced the success of return. Where he or she remained in the system the quality of the carers influenced the apparent success of care. In both cases it was probably important that the previous carer (whether parent or foster carer) endorsed the new placement. The abrupt cessation of support from carers (or in a minority of cases its continuance) seemed likely to play an important role in the outcomes of those leaving the system.

These explanations are plausible and internally coherent. They are also in keeping with previous research. There is now abundant evidence that the success of foster placements depends on the carers and also on the behaviour and motivation of the child (see, for example, Sinclair 2005) and some that similar variables influence the success of return home (Sinclair *et al.* 2005b). In this research challenging behaviour and a high level of family problems are more common among those who had a failed attempt at rehabilitation. We shall show later that motivation, behaviour and the quality of care are all strongly associated with outcomes within the care system itself.

Within this framework the case studies may provide suggestions for good practice. So there may be lessons in the chapter for:

- the importance of clear plans that are, as far as possible, agreed with all concerned

- the need to take a wide view of the potential of a child's family, including fathers, sisters and other relatives as well as mothers

- the potential of shared care arrangements and the danger that they deteriorate into a succession of unplanned placements with unknown carers

- the need to take a realistic view of the characteristics of the child (educational ability, behaviour and 'ability to cope') that are likely to influence the outcome on leaving the system and to work to ensure these are encouraged

- the need to take a realistic view of the quality of the environment to which a child may go and to counter key problems

- the need for a flexible framework so that a child does not have to leave the system before he or she has a reasonable chance of success

- the need to allow for a continuity of good relationships even if placements change.

In these ways the care system has at least three major roles. It allows time for appropriate assessments to be made so that the child can return home if possible. It offers the possibility of family life in care. It also offers a chance for both families and children to change. As we will see later the first two possibilities are certainly embraced. It is not, however, clear that practitioners see the system as being in the business of facilitating change.

## Summary points for Chapters 5, 6 and 7

These three chapters have explored the processes associated with leaving the care system or, alternatively, with relatively long stays within it. They have shown that:

- Councils are determined to keep children out of the care system or return them home quickly if they cannot.

- Those who do not go home within a year generally have a low chance of leaving the system in a given year with the exception of very young children who may be adopted and much older ones who become care leavers.

- The likelihood of repeat admissions, adoption, return home and other key processes in this system is strongly related to age and other characteristics of the children.

- In general characteristics that suggest vulnerability or likely causes of difficulty at home are associated with not going home and with repeat admissions.

- Council policies and practice seem to have a major influence on these processes even after allowing for the children's characteristics.

The success or otherwise of the decisions taken are very likely to depend on what the child and parent wants, the behaviour of the child and the quality of relevant carers. 'Continuity' between successive placements (e.g. the presence of siblings or the support of previous carers for the current ones) is also likely to be important.

## Notes

1   We set quotas for the number of case studies we wanted to include that featured children who were 'beginners', 'repeat admissions', 'long-term stable' cases and 'long-term unstable' cases. We defined these in terms of variables from the CIS and then randomly sampled within them. When this process did not produce the council quota of children who were disabled or from black and minority ethnic groups we randomly dropped cases and sampled those who fitted the criterion. The purpose was not to secure a representative sample but rather to ensure a spread of experience.

2   This approach is drawn from analytic induction, the basis for Glaser and Strauss's (1967) approach to producing grounded theory. Our categories (e.g. our groups) 'arise from the data' and we make a serious attempt to wrestle with the similarities and differences between cases. However, we make some 'epistemological assumptions', for example, that it is possible to discern the 'causes' of 'success', that others may not accept. The approach is closest to that used by Sinclair (1971) in a study of probation hostels. He selected hostels that seemed, on statistical grounds, to be doing particularly well or particularly badly and then used case studies to derive explanations for why this was. He then tested the hypotheses statistically. We do not wish to claim that our approach is original or that it is an orthodox use of the ideas of others. We suggest that readers assess the approach on its own merits.

Chapter 8

# Placements: How They are Used

We ought to have loads more placement choice and we struggle to get it.
(Manager)

## Introduction

The last three chapters have concentrated on admissions and discharges. The next
three chapters deal with the internal workings of the care system and with their
outcomes. The present chapter deals with the basic building blocks of the care
system, the placements that make it up. It asks three main questions:

1. How many children receive each kind of placement?

2. How long do these placements last?

3. Who gets what kind of placement?

These questions are essentially descriptive. We ask them for three reasons: they
provide continuity with Rowe and her colleagues' (1989) research; they help
determine the role of the care system (few children, for example, have a strong
base in a residential home); they also provide a necessary context for understanding the reasons for and significance of placement movement. In our next chapter
we will turn to movements and sequences of movements between placements.

## Method

The information used in the chapter comes from data on the placement history of
all the children in the sample. The degree to which these were complete varied by
council and depended on the date at which the council started its client information system. Some councils had data going back 18 years. Others could only
supply us with data for the past four. One council supplied complete data on the
census year but none on placements that were outside the census year.

**Table 8.1** Placements over career histories

| Placement code (numeric) | Frequency | Per cent | Valid per cent | Cumulative per cent |
|---|---|---|---|---|
| Valid  A1 – Placed for adoption | 628 | 2.5 | 2.5 | 2.5 |
| F1 – Fostered rels/friend LA | 1588 | 6.4 | 6.4 | 8.9 |
| F2 – Other foster place LA | 11804 | 47.7 | 47.7 | 56.6 |
| F3 – Agency foster place | 271 | 1.1 | 1.1 | 57.7 |
| F4 – Fostered rels/friend OLA | 384 | 1.6 | 1.6 | 59.3 |
| F5 – Other foster place OLA | 2447 | 9.9 | 9.9 | 69.1 |
| F6 – Other agency foster OLA | 1287 | 5.2 | 5.2 | 74.3 |
| H2 – Secure Unit | 122 | .5 | .5 | 74.8 |
| H3 – Home/Hostel LA | 1596 | 6.4 | 6.4 | 81.3 |
| H4 – Home/Hostel OLA | 989 | 4.0 | 4.0 | 85.3 |
| H5 – Res. accomm. not CHR | 299 | 1.2 | 1.2 | 86.5 |
| M2 – Missing not refuge | 2 | .0 | .0 | 86.5 |
| M3 – Missing: location NK | 9 | .0 | .0 | 86.5 |
| P1 – With parent/parent resp. | 1598 | 6.5 | 6.5 | 93.0 |
| P2 – Indep. no support | 520 | 2.1 | 2.1 | 95.1 |
| P3 – Res. employ. | 1 | .0 | .0 | 95.1 |
| R1 – Res. Care Home | 233 | .9 | .9 | 96.0 |
| R2 – NHS Health Trust | 150 | .6 | .6 | 96.6 |
| R3 – Family Centre | 169 | .7 | .7 | 97.3 |
| R5 – Young Offender Inst. | 69 | .3 | .3 | 97.6 |
| S1 – Res. school not dual reg. | 246 | 1.0 | 1.0 | 98.6 |
| Z1 – Other placements | 203 | .8 | .8 | 99.4 |
| M2 – Whereabouts known | 62 | .3 | .3 | 99.6 |
| M3 – Whereabouts unknown | 89 | .4 | .4 | 100.0 |
| Total | 24766 | 100.0 | 100.0 | |

Source: CIS sample.

Despite these limitations we had data on 30,421 distinct 'episodes of care'. An episode, however, was not the same as a placement. It could start or end with a change of legal status as well as with a change in the placement where the child lived. In addition some of the placements took place some considerable time ago and neither we nor the councils were certain what the numerical codes referring to them meant.[1] After taking account of these difficulties we had interpretable data on 24,766 placements.[2]

## Kinds of placement

All councils thought it important to provide a choice of placements. They differed, however, over what kinds of choice should be available and in what proportions. Taking the sample as a whole what kinds of placements were actually used? Table 8.1 refers to the approximately 25,000 distinct placements on which we had data that we were able to interpret. Obviously it gives only a very imprecise picture of the proportions of children who are in different kinds of placement at any particular point in time.

Table 8.2 brings the picture up to date and gives the type of placement used by those children who were present on census date. Unsurprisingly most children (70%) were fostered. Important minorities were in residential care of one kind or another, placed for adoption or placed with parents.

**Table 8.2** Distribution of placements on the census date

| Placement at end of year | | Frequency | Per cent | Valid per cent | Cumulative per cent |
|---|---|---|---|---|---|
| Valid | Placed for adoption | 269 | 5.0 | 5.0 | 5.0 |
| | Fostered | 3777 | 69.8 | 70.1 | 75.1 |
| | Residential care | 445 | 8.2 | 8.3 | 83.4 |
| | Residential schools | 88 | 1.6 | 1.6 | 85.0 |
| | Other residential | 161 | 3.0 | 3.0 | 88.0 |
| | Placed with parents | 437 | 8.1 | 8.1 | 96.1 |
| | Independent living | 121 | 2.2 | 2.2 | 98.3 |
| | Other | 90 | 1.7 | 1.7 | 100.0 |
| | Total | 5388 | 99.5 | 100.0 | |
| Missing | System | 25 | .5 | | |
| Total | | 5413 | 100.0 | | |

Source: CIS sample.
Note: The table is restricted to those present on the census date.

## Duration and frequency of placements

Rowe and her colleagues' (1989) research showed that the frequency with which different kinds of placements are used does not necessarily correspond with the proportion of children in those placements at a particular point in time. For example, they found that residential care was often used for short placements, so that its role in the care system over the year was much greater than figures for the yearly census suggested. For similar reasons we needed to look at the length of different placements as well as the number used on a particular day.

Table 8.3 gives a distribution of placements completed over the census year along with their average and median lengths of stay (in days) in different kinds of provision. For a rough description of median and standard deviation please see note.[3]

As can be seen the lengthier placements tended to be with adoptive parents, with the child's own parents, in residential schools or in foster placements with friends and family. Typically the mean (i.e. average) length of stay in a type of placement was much larger than the median (i.e. middle value) length. This situation arises when many children have quite short placements, while a relatively small proportion of children have very long ones.

Table 8.4 gives the means and medians (in days) for the placements that were current at the end of the year. The overall average for these 'ongoing' placements is nearly two and a half times as great as that for the completed placements shown in Table 8.3. The overall median for these placements is four times as great as that for the completed ones (384 days as against 94). So at any one time in most placement groupings there are relatively few children and young people who have stayed for a very short time.[4] The picture is rather of a much more stable group who have been joined briefly by a small number of more transient residents.

Figure 8.1 illustrates the number of placement days that different kinds of placement took up in the course of the year. For simplicity we have grouped together a number of different kinds of placement. In particular residential care includes a very wide variety of establishments – for example, family centres, residential schools and young offender institutions – as well as children's homes.

As expected the bulk of placement days (70%) are taken up by foster care. Thirteen per cent of placement days are in residential care. Placements with parents account for 9 per cent; adoption accounts for 5 per cent, and the remaining categories account for 3 per cent. These proportions differ very little from the proportions of placements that fall into these different categories at either the beginning or end of the year.

Obviously there are some variations by age. The main examples of this were placements for adoption as already discussed and residential care. Some residential placements are made when the child is very young. Examples include the

**Table 8.3** Completed placement lengths (in days) by type of placement

| Placement code (numeric) | Placement length (Mean) | N | Std. Deviation | Median |
|---|---|---|---|---|
| A1 – Placed for adoption | 373.08 | 296 | 453.451 | 250.50 |
| F1 – Fostered rels/friend LA | 461.65 | 325 | 706.846 | 168.00 |
| F2 – Other foster place LA | 267.05 | 2389 | 531.947 | 64.00 |
| F3 – Agency foster place | 161.14 | 96 | 264.931 | 67.00 |
| F4 – Fostered rels/friend OLA | 541.96 | 99 | 777.068 | 248.00 |
| F5 – Other foster place OLA | 294.14 | 600 | 499.965 | 77.50 |
| F6 – Other agency foster OLA | 253.44 | 360 | 369.732 | 119.00 |
| H2 – Secure Unit | 78.56 | 43 | 78.210 | 58.00 |
| H3 – Home/Hostel LA | 190.93 | 414 | 287.195 | 72.00 |
| H4 – Home/Hostel OLA | 237.75 | 263 | 361.677 | 108.00 |
| H5 – Res. accomm. not CHR | 157.91 | 129 | 246.587 | 53.00 |
| M2 – Missing not refuge | 2.00 | 1 | . | 2.00 |
| M3 – Missing: location NK | 121.00 | 8 | 336.988 | 2.00 |
| P1 – With parent/parent resp. | 409.54 | 388 | 610.534 | 180.00 |
| P2 – Indep. no support | 124.78 | 264 | 149.177 | 72.50 |
| R1 – Res. Care Home | 126.92 | 52 | 231.038 | 22.50 |
| R2 – NHS Health Trust | 80.94 | 32 | 279.336 | 13.50 |
| R3 – Family Centre | 247.57 | 35 | 356.807 | 112.00 |
| R5 – Young Offender Inst. | 136.76 | 29 | 181.852 | 95.00 |
| S1 – Res. school not dual reg. | 646.52 | 31 | 548.616 | 484.00 |
| Z1 – Other placements | 448.95 | 57 | 797.451 | 60.00 |
| M2 – Whereabouts known | 90.91 | 22 | 142.761 | 63.00 |
| M3 – Whereabouts unknown | 38.68 | 31 | 42.783 | 23.00 |
| Total | 279.02 | 5964 | 501.548 | 98.00 |

Source: CIS sample.
Note: The table is restricted to placements ending in census year.

**Table 8.4** Average placement length in days by placement type

| Placement code (numeric) | Placement length (Mean) | N | Std. Deviation | Median |
|---|---|---|---|---|
| A1 – Placed for adoption | 300.09 | 252 | 424.575 | 182.00 |
| F1 – Fostered rels/friend LA | 939.65 | 520 | 924.242 | 635.50 |
| F2 – Other foster place. LA | 740.69 | 1933 | 851.291 | 420.00 |
| F3 – Agency foster place | 465.18 | 93 | 491.341 | 264.00 |
| F4 – Fostered rels/friend OLA | 947.01 | 139 | 938.703 | 680.00 |
| F5 – Other foster place OLA | 708.75 | 587 | 783.376 | 460.00 |
| F6 – Other agency foster OLA | 520.15 | 456 | 522.641 | 362.00 |
| H2 – Secure Unit | 220.33 | 12 | 226.232 | 163.00 |
| H3 – Home/Hostel LA | 489.26 | 260 | 602.216 | 309.50 |
| H4 – Home/Hostel OLA | 482.90 | 174 | 472.261 | 357.00 |
| H5 – Res. accomm. not CHR | 210.47 | 74 | 206.238 | 154.00 |
| M3 – Missing: location NK | 788.00 | 1 | . | 788.00 |
| P1 – With parent/parent resp. | 766.49 | 427 | 744.560 | 560.00 |
| P2 – Indep. no support | 169.98 | 119 | 135.057 | 153.00 |
| R1 – Res. Care Home | 291.00 | 37 | 282.262 | 201.00 |
| R2 – NHS Health Trust | 742.40 | 10 | 569.684 | 670.50 |
| R3 – Family Centre | 158.44 | 27 | 196.843 | 86.00 |
| R5 – Young Offender Inst. | 254.77 | 13 | 439.019 | 86.00 |
| S1 – Res. school not dual reg. | 827.15 | 85 | 541.070 | 687.00 |
| Z1 – Other placements | 709.84 | 25 | 576.606 | 507.00 |
| M2 – Whereabouts known | 190.00 | 1 | . | 190.00 |
| M3 – Whereabouts unknown | 532.33 | 6 | 844.794 | 36.00 |
| Total | 670.10 | 5252 | 771.750 | 394.00 |

Source: CIS sample.
Note: The table is restricted to placements current at the census date.

placement of the child for residential assessment, emergency accommodation for babies, and babies placed with their young mothers in a residential unit. The great bulk of residential placements are, however, for older children. In this sample 85

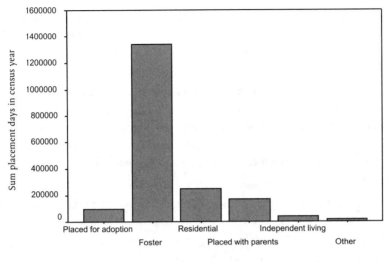

Source: CIS data.

**Figure 8.1** Placement days in the year by category of placement

per cent of the residential placement days in the year were taken up by children aged 11 or over at placement and 80 per cent by children aged 12 or over. Residential care plays a much more significant role in this older group, accounting for 28 per cent of the year placement days among those aged 12 or over at placement. The effect of age largely accounts for the differences in the use of residential care made by our different policy groups.

## Who gets what sort of placement?

There are four main types of placement: foster care, residential care, placements with parents, and adoption. Chapter 6 has already discussed the differences between those who are adopted and those who are not. This section discusses the distinguishing characteristics of those placed in the other three kinds of placement at the end of the year. Within these categories we will also look specifically at the characteristics of those placed in different kinds of foster and residential care.

## Who is placed in foster care?

> If it's becoming apparent that our care plan is for longer term care, whatever that might mean, so whether that is looking at family members, whether that's long-term fostering, you know, whether that's adoption, we quite quickly get onto that. (Manager)

Foster care is the placement of choice in all councils. Like adoption and care by relatives it fits the 'family agenda' of social services. Social workers see it as 'normal' and a placement in which children are likely to be settled and happy.

In practice some children were more likely to be fostered than others. Unsurprisingly they tended to be younger and to start being looked after at an earlier age:

- Three-quarters (76%) of those aged under the age of 11 as against 65 per cent of those over 11 were fostered at the end of the year.

- Three-quarters (73%) of those who first entered under the age of 11 were fostered at the end of the year. The proportion among older entrants was 59 per cent.

Table 8.5 relates the need codes of the sample to whether or not they were fostered at the end of the year. As can be seen children with a need code of 'disability' were less likely to be fostered. This was not true for children with this need code who were under the age of 11. These children were slightly more likely to be fostered than others of a similar age. Over the age of 11 the difference was in the other direction and pronounced. Only a quarter (26%) of these older, disabled young people were fostered, as against nearly two-thirds (65%) of the sample as a whole. On average they had been looked after for nearly four years since their last admission (3.76 years).

Why was this so? Clearly it can be become harder to look after older disabled children. Physical tasks can become more difficult because of their weight. Challenging behaviour may become harder for carers. Nevertheless there are questions about whether adequate effort is made to provide these children with a home life and whether residential care is what they want.

Children with difficult behaviour were also much less likely than others to be fostered. Again this statement should be qualified. At the end of the year there were only 13 children with the need code 'difficult behaviour' who were aged less than 11. With one exception, all of these were fostered. By contrast there were 100 young people with this need code and aged 11 or over. Fifty-five per cent of these were not fostered. Clearly specialist foster care such as remand fostering, treatment foster care and professional foster care capable of 'containing' these young people are not widely developed.

**Table 8.5** Need codes by fostered at end of year

| Reason for being looked after | | Fostered at end of year | | |
|---|---|---|---|---|
| | | No | Yes | Total |
| Abuse or neglect | Count | 1011 | 2445 | 3456 |
| | % within Reason for being looked after | 29.3% | 70.7% | 100.0% |
| Disabled | Count | 115 | 78 | 193 |
| | % within Reason for being looked after | 59.6% | 40.4% | 100.0% |
| Parent disabled | Count | 51 | 247 | 298 |
| | % within Reason for being looked after | 17.1% | 82.9% | 100.0% |
| Stress | Count | 119 | 248 | 367 |
| | % within Reason for being looked after | 32.4% | 67.6% | 100.0% |
| Family dysfunction | Coun | 130 | 317 | 447 |
| | % within Reason for being looked after | 29.1% | 70.9% | 100.0% |
| Difficult behaviour | Count | 56 | 57 | 113 |
| | % within Reason for being looked after | 49.6% | 50.4% | 100.0% |
| Low income | Count | 6 | 7 | 13 |
| | % within Reason for being looked after | 46.2% | 53.8% | 100.0% |
| Abandoned | Count | 139 | 349 | 488 |
| | % within Reason for being looked after | 28.5% | 71.5% | 100.0% |
| Total | Count | 1627 | 3748 | 5375 |
| | % within Reason for being looked after | 30.3% | 69.7% | 100.0% |

Source: CIS sample.
Note: Table restricted to children looked after at end of year.

Perhaps the most striking difference between foster children and others was in the purposes of their latest placements. Certain purposes – treatment, remand, and 'bridge to independence' – were less common in foster care than in other kinds of placement (see Table 8.6). The core business of foster care seemed to be to prepare children for a long-term placement and to give care and upbringing. Two-thirds (65%) of the foster placements but only one-third of the remainder had one or other of these purposes.

Some councils were more likely to use foster care than others. The proportions fostered ranged from 62 to 79 per cent. At first sight this range does not seem particularly striking. However, the differences remained very highly significant when we took account of background variables such as age.[5] As we will see, it

**Table 8.6** Purposes of placements by fostered at end of the year

| Aim last/latest placement | | Fostered at end of year | | |
| --- | --- | --- | --- | --- |
| | | No | Yes | Total |
| Temporary care | Count | 221 | 254 | 475 |
| | % within Aim last/latest placement | 46.5% | 53.5% | 100.0% |
| Emergency | Count | 44 | 22 | 66 |
| | % within Aim last/latest placement | 66.7% | 33.3% | 100.0% |
| Remand | Count | 20 | 0 | 20 |
| | % within Aim last/latest placement | 100.0% | 0% | 100.0% |
| Assessment | Count | 82 | 131 | 213 |
| | % within Aim last/latest placement | 38.5% | 61.5% | 100.0% |
| Treatment | Count | 30 | 3 | 33 |
| | % within Aim last/latest placement | 90.9% | 9.1% | 100.0% |
| Prep for LT placement | Count | 103 | 506 | 609 |
| | % within Aim last/latest placement | 16.9% | 83.1% | 100.0% |
| Bridge to indep. | Count | 309 | 170 | 479 |
| | % within Aim last/latest placement | 64.5% | 35.5% | 100.0% |
| Care and upbringing | Count | 500 | 1252 | 1752 |
| | % within Aim last/latest placement | 28.5% | 71.5% | 100.0% |
| View to adoption | Count | 320 | 271 | 591 |
| | % within Aim last/latest placement | 54.1% | 45.9% | 100.0% |
| Other | Count | 123 | 83 | 206 |
| | % within Aim last/latest placement | 59.7% | 40.3% | 100.0% |
| Total | Count | 1752 | 2692 | 4444 |
| | % within Aim last/latest placement | 39.4% | 60.6% | 100.0% |

Source: CIS and Social Worker data.
Note: Table restricted to those present on census date.

is also big enough to allow for much variation in the use of other kinds of placements.

These variations in the use of foster care were, however, a source of discomfort. Evidence from our telephone interviews and questionnaires showed an almost universal desire to improve the support available to foster carers and thus increase their numbers. In part this was meant to meet actual or potential competition from the independent sector and thus reduce costs. In part it was meant to back a second thrust: the development of schemes capable of coping with more challenging children and meeting a wider variety of purposes. In these ways the councils were striving to extend the benefits of foster care.

## Relative foster care

Only a minority of foster placements were with family and friends. As we will see later, some councils made much more use of these placements than others. In no council, however, did the proportion at the end of the year amount to more than a third of all foster placements.

As we will see from the case studies, some of these placements work out very well. A number of the questionnaires suggested that their use could be more widespread with social workers emphasising their positive experience of them. At the same time the placements were not seen as a 'free lunch'. Some comments from social workers in the questionnaire emphasised the difficulties carers could face: quarrels with the child's family, material hardship, the ill-health of ageing grandparents, and the problems of coping with challenging teenagers. An increased use of kin care therefore needed to be accompanied by increased support for the carers involved (see Box 8.1 for examples of comments by social workers).

---

**Box 8.1** Social workers' reflections

- Child more and more attached to carers (grandparents) who have now obtained a residence order with mother's agreement.

- Kinship carers lots of love and commitment. Some tensions [with birth family].

- Family and friends placements can offer a lot if properly assessed and supported.

- Our experience of friends and family placements is very patchy. Perhaps we do not offer enough support…often it is the guardians who force this issue.

- Placed with an older maternal family member… Children have very little if any positive adult role models who are not professional.

- Child placed with relations who have a negative view of child's mother and this has been difficult to deal with.

---

Children who were fostered with relatives and friends[6] differed from other foster children in age, age at entry, reasons for admission to the care system, and the purposes of the placement.

In terms of age they were less likely to be aged 11 or over (45% v. 55%), or to have been looked after for the first time when aged 11 or over (15% v. 21%).

**Table 8.7** Need code by fostered with relatives at the census date

| Reason for being Looked After | | Fostered with relative at end of year | | |
| --- | --- | --- | --- | --- |
| | | No | Yes | Total |
| Abuse or neglect | Count | 1950 | 495 | 2445 |
| | % within Reason for being looked after | 79.8% | 20.2% | 100.0% |
| Disabled | Count | 74 | 4 | 78 |
| | % within Reason for being looked after | 94.9% | 5.1% | 100.0% |
| Parent disabled | Count | 205 | 42 | 247 |
| | % within Reason for being looked after | 83.0% | 17.0% | 100.0% |
| Stress | Count | 228 | 20 | 248. |
| | % within Reason for being looked after | 91.9% | 8.1% | 100.0% |
| Family dysfunction | Count | 265 | 52 | 317 |
| | % within Reason for being looked after | 83.6% | 16.4% | 100.0% |
| Difficult behaviour | Count | 49 | 8 | 57 |
| | % within Reason for being looked after | 86.0% | 14.0% | 100.0% |
| Low income | Count | 7 | 0 | 7 |
| | % within Reason for being looked after | 100.0% | .0% | 100.0% |
| Abandoned | Count | 307 | 42 | 349 |
| | % within Reason for being looked after | 88.0% | 12.0% | 100.0% |
| Total | Count | 3085 | 663 | 3748 |
| | % within Reason for being looked after | 82.3% | 17.7% | 100.0% |

Source: CIS sample.

Note: The table is restricted to those who are fostered at the census date.

Despite their comparatively young age they were also less likely to have started their latest period of being looked after within the past year.[7]

The need codes of children fostered with relatives were also somewhat different, although in most cases the difference was very slight. Those fostered with relatives or friends were less likely to have need codes of disability, acute family stress, or abandonment. Conversely they were more likely to have a need code of abuse or neglect (see Table 8.7).

There were differences concerned with the purposes of placement. Two-thirds of the placements with relatives and friends were for 'care and upbringing'. This was true of only four out of ten of the remaining foster placements. By contrast preparation for a long-term placement was twice as common an aim among those who were not fostered with relatives (21% v. 11%). Placement with a view to adoption was four times as common among the non-kin placements (12% v. 3%). There was a slight contrast in the use of 'temporary care' (7% among relative placements and 10% among the rest) but none in relation to 'assessment' (5% v. 5%). The remaining purposes (emergency, treatment, assessment and 'other') were equally rare in both groups.

These differences may partly reflect the problems of kin care sketched earlier. For example, relatives may be less likely to want to take on a difficult teenager at a time when, if they are grandparents, their own energy may be less than it was. The differences may also reflect motivation – for example, it is likely that kin carers care out of family loyalty. They are therefore unlikely to take on children with a view to preparing them to be adopted outside the family altogether.

The main source of variation was the child's council. The proportion of foster placements with relatives varied from 6 per cent in one council to 32 per cent in another. The differences were massively significant and remained so in the multivariate analysis that we carried out.[8] We will argue later that councils with low rates could, with advantage, aim to increase them.

## Foster placements in the independent sector

Our questionnaires from the team leaders and social workers suggested a lot of agreement on the good and bad points of the independent sector. The leader of a team of supervising social workers put many of the points succinctly:

> Advantages? Availability of placements for children 8+. Disadvantages? Distance from area, unknown carers skills/experience etc., contact with birth family, communication between social workers. (Team Leader)

On the good side the placements were seen as well-supported, so they had more frequent visits from supervising social workers, a greater chance of 'short break'

respite, and, sometimes, additional services from play therapists, psychologists or
dedicated educational provision. Such 'packages' of support meant that these
placements could take older children whom the council found it difficult to place
in-house.

On the 'bad side' children were placed with unknown carers and children
from other councils. They could be a long way from home, making it harder for
social worker, child and family to stay in close touch with each other. Above all
the cost was high. All councils saw this as a serious disadvantage and some were
very reluctant to place or keep children in independent placements at least partly
because of the expense.

In practice some councils were much more likely to use the independent
sector than were others. One had 45 per cent of its foster children placed with
independent agencies on the census date. Another had no children placed in this
sector either at the beginning or at the end of the census year. Overall 7 of the 13
councils had fewer than 10 per cent of their foster children in this form of provision on the census date. Four were using it for between 10 and 20 per cent of their
foster children and two were using it for more than 30 per cent of theirs.

London councils made more use of the independent sector than others.[9] It is
unlikely that this represents a difference in ideology. All councils seemed reluctant to use the sector, and social workers wishing to do so commonly had to
justify the expense. In practice the needs of some London boroughs and the competition between them for foster carers may have given some little choice but to
go to independent providers for some of their placements. The growth of independent foster care in neighbouring areas, particularly Kent, was able to supply
their needs. The offer of what was thought to be better money and support in the
independent agencies may also have made it harder for the councils to recruit or
keep their own carers.

Changes in council policy could also lead to greater or lesser use of the independent sector. One council was increasing the numbers of children it looked
after believing that it had left too many children at risk in the community for too
long. As a consequence, the proportion of foster placements in the independent
sector had risen, arguably because this council was not able to meet the new
demands by increased recruitment of in-house carers. Another council had made
a substantial reduction in its use of the independent sector over the year. The
managers argued that their new policy allowed children to be placed near their
homes and accompanied it with a drive to recruit their own carers. Social workers
were less happy with the change, feeling that the policy was financially driven,
and too often removed children from independent foster placements where they
were doing well. The policy was accompanied by, and may have contributed to, a

sharp fall in the performance indicator measuring the proportion of long-stay children in the same foster placement for more than two years.

Over the sample as a whole those fostered on the census date in the independent sector were less likely to be white, more likely to be aged 11 or over, and more likely to have first entered when aged 11 or over. We found, however, that in interpreting these figures we needed to take account of differences between the London councils and the others.

Black and minority ethnic children were more commonly placed in the independent sector for two reasons. First, there were more of them in London and London made particularly high use of this sector. Second, councils outside London were more likely to use this sector for their black and minority ethnic children than for their white ones. London councils by contrast were slightly (but not significantly) more likely to use the sector for white children.[10]

We found a similar pattern for children who first entered over the age of 11. There were comparatively more of them in London councils. The London and other councils were both more likely to place these children in the independent sector but this difference in the placements used was less pronounced in London than elsewhere.[11]

Adolescents over the age of 11 were more likely to be placed in the independent sector irrespective of the council in which they were.

We had expected those in the independent sector to differ from the others in their need codes. This proved not to be the case.[12] Again contrary to our hypothesis they were not more likely to be doing worse at school.[13] They were, however, more likely to have high challenging behaviour scores. This finding held when we took account of their age and also of the local council in which they were.

Overall therefore our findings suggest that:

- Councils use the independent sector when they are finding difficulty in meeting demand from their own resources and there is a reasonably local supply of independent placements.

- This situation is particularly likely to occur in London.

- Although councils differ somewhat in the way they use the sector, they most commonly use it for children that they have difficulty in placing: those from black and ethnic minority children, older children and children who display challenging behaviour.

- This pattern is slightly different in London where councils are no more likely to use the independent sector for black and minority ethnic children than they are to use it for others.

Contrary to what we had expected councils were not more likely to use this form of placement for disabled children.

## Who uses residential care?

One particular council said that it was proudly investing in its own residential care. Almost all the others appeared to be trying to keep children out of such provision if possible. Despite this view there was a grudging acceptance that some children needed residential care either because of their impairment(s) or because this was seen as the only way to manage their behaviour. Many team leaders and social workers went along with this view but felt that the establishments available were often unsuitable. Generally they wanted a form of residential care that was based on small units with a therapeutic purpose (see Box 8.2 for examples).

---

**Box 8.2** Manager and Team Leader reflections

You get the group where the use of residential is absolutely appropriate and it's usually generally funded either bi or tripartite, because you've got Education and Health issues, and obviously some children are just in residential for the education purposes, but where it's Social Services involved we've always got that little group of children and young people who are in residential care, because it is the only way to enable them to access an education and be safe. (Manager)

There are a few children who are extremely difficult to care for – challenging behaviour, poor attachments, major control issues, dangerous behaviour. I believe we need small residential units to help them prepare to move into families. The units need to be staffed with very skilled workers. (Team leader)

---

Against this background those in residential care at the census date differed from the others who were looked after in other ways. They were more likely to be 11 or over (89% v. 51%) and to have first been looked after when aged 11 or over (50% v. 20%). They were more likely to have a need code of disability (13% v. 2%), acute family stress (11% v. 7%) or difficult behaviour (6% v. 2%). Conversely they were less likely to have a need code of abuse (49% v. 67%). Irrespective of whether they were under or over 11 they had on average worse school performance scores and higher challenging behaviour scores.

Those seeking asylum were also more likely to be in residential care. Once again, however, we need to take account of differences between councils. As will be remembered those seeking asylum were almost all in three councils. Only one out of the 33 who were seeking asylum in the other councils was in residential care. By contrast 12 per cent (15/126) of those seeking asylum in one council, 13 per cent of those seeking it in another (15/116) and 24 per cent (28/116) of those in another were looked after in this way. The reason may be that only councils with large numbers seeking asylum are in a position to plan for this kind of provision for them and that having planned for it they use it and thus have a higher proportion of asylum seeking children in residential care. There was a threefold variation (7–21%) between local councils in the proportion of looked after children placed in residential care at the end of the year. The differences remained significant when we took account of the children's background characteristics.[14]

As already pointed out, residential care covers different kinds of provision. We distinguished between children's homes, residential schools and 'other'. The latter was itself a catchall term covering establishments as diverse as care homes, residential assessment centres for families with young children and young offender institutions.

Residential schools hardly ever seemed to cater for children under the age of 11 (see Table 8.8) while residential units only did so rarely.

**Table 8.8** Age by type of residential unit

| | | Placement at end of year | | | |
|---|---|---|---|---|---|
| Aged 11 or over at census | | Residential care | Residential schools | Other residential | Total |
| No | Count | 43 | 2 | 30 | 75 |
| | % within Placement at end of year | 9.7% | 2.3% | 18.6% | 10.8% |
| Yes | Count | 402 | 86 | 131 | 619 |
| | % within Placement at end of year | 90.3% | 97.7% | 81.4% | 89.2% |
| Total | Count | 445 | 88 | 161 | 694 |
| | % within Placement at end of year | 100.0% | 100.0% | 100.0% | 100.0% |

Source: CIS sample.
Note: Table restricted to those in residential care at the census date.

There was also a difference by whether the child was an asylum seeker. None of them were in residential schools and relatively few of them in ordinary children's homes. Most of those in the Table 8.9 were probably in 'hostel style' accommodation.

Children in residential care were much more likely to have a need code of disability. Those with one formed the bulk of those in residential schools. They were very rarely found in other forms of residential provision.

**Table 8.9** Asylum seeker status by type of residential unit

| | | Placement at end of year | | | |
|---|---|---|---|---|---|
| Whether asylum seeker | | Residential care | Residential schools | Other residential | Total |
| No | Count | 428 | 87 | 117 | 632 |
| | % within Placement at end of year | 96.4% | 100.0% | 73.1% | 91.5% |
| Yes | Count | 16 | 0 | 43 | 59 |
| | % within Placement at end of year | 3.6% | 0% | 26.9% | 8.5% |
| Total | Count | 444 | 87 | 160 | 691 |
| | % within Placement at end of year | 100.0% | 100.0% | 100.0% | 100.0% |

Source: CIS sample.
Note: Table restricted to those in residential care at the census date.

**Table 8.10** Need code of disability by type of residential unit

| | | Placement at end of year | | | |
|---|---|---|---|---|---|
| Need code of disability | | Residential care | Residential schools | Other residential | Total |
| No | Count | 423 | 36 | 150 | 609 |
| | % within Placement at end of year | 95.1% | 40.9% | 93.2% | 87.8% |
| Yes | Count | 22 | 52 | 11 | 85 |
| | % within Placement at end of year | 4.9% | 59.1% | 6.8% | 12.2% |
| Total | Count | 445 | 88 | 161 | 694 |
| | % within Placement at end of year | 100.0% | 100.0% | 100.0% | 100.0% |

Source: CIS sample.
Note: Table restricted to those in residential care at the census date.

## Placements outside the council

The general assumption is that, other things being equal, looked after children should be placed near their families. Social services staff responding to our questionnaires certainly shared this view. They variously emphasised the problems distance made for contact between children and families, and the difficulties of arranging services, and, particularly, appropriate schooling, in councils that did not initially have an obligation to the children and where the social worker did not 'know the ropes'.

As we will see in Chapter 9, out of county placements may, in some circumstances, have advantages. If so, however, these features were certainly not stressed by our respondents. One manager expressed a more typical view:

> Some of our in-house foster carers actually live 20 or 30 miles away from [the council], …I sometimes struggle with this 'cos I have said to [name of social worker] who does this side of it, I'm saying, you know, 'Well when you assess them do you not ask them how they intend to take, look after children who are living in [this council] and going to [this council]'s schools but they live 30 miles away.' (Manager)

For statistical purposes the client information systems distinguish between foster children placed within and outside the council. The same distinction is made for children's homes but not for secure accommodation or other forms of placement. What distinguished those we knew to be placed outside the council from others who might be?

Unsurprisingly the major source of variation was the local council. Overall a third of those on whom the relevant information was available were outside the council's boundaries. The proportion placed outside the authority varied from 68 per cent in one London council to 11 per cent in a county council in the south. Four out of the top five percentages belonged to London councils. One reason for this may be size, allied to density of population. A child placed in a neighbouring London borough may well be far closer to her or his home than is the case with other children placed within their own larger councils. A second reason is that London councils make much use of the independent sector. The social workers reported that 83 per cent of the independent placements in their census day sample were outside the council area as opposed to only 20 per cent of the placements with in-house council carers and homes.

The characteristics of those placed outside the area were much the same as those placed in the independent sector. They were less likely to be white, more likely to be aged 11 or over, more likely to have their first admission when aged 11 or over and more likely to be an asylum seeker. Conversely they were less likely to have a need code of abuse.[15] In short they tended to be older children or children for whom the social workers may have had difficulties in finding ethnically matched placements.

## Which children are placed with their parent(s)?

> I think it showed how strong the bond with birth family remains for young people even when they have been let down by them in the past. The young person's strong commitment to making this latest placement work despite professional reservations has been shown to be paramount and a temporary stay with parent turning into a permanent placement with him has been a great success. (Social Worker)

As was clear from our telephone interviews, all councils wanted, if at all possible, to keep children with their parents or failing this to return them to their families as soon as possible. At times this led to criticism from social workers or reviewers, as it seemed that children had been kept at home too long. At other times remaining home was manifestly impossible, risky or dependent on the resolution of a crisis, for example, the successful return of a parent from psychiatric hospital. Placement with parents seems to offer a way of building on the strengths of children's relationships with their families while seeking to maintain some control over the risks.

In order to be officially placed with their parents children have to be on a care order. Unsurprisingly, therefore, they were more likely to have a need code of abuse (84% v. 63%). They were also less likely to be aged over 11 or to have first entered the system at this age.[16] Less predictably such placements were less common among those considered by their social workers to be disabled (10% v.18%) or to have a need code of disability (.2% v. 3.9%). For obvious reasons those placed with parents were not young people seeking asylum.

The proportion placed with parents at the end of the year varied by local council (from 3% to 17%), a variation that remained significant when we took account of the background variables.[17] In part this may have reflected a varying willingness to make these provisions in the first place. It also reflected variations in the speed with which they discharged the care order. We looked at the length of time for which these placements had lasted. The average was just over two years (766 days). There was, however, a substantial variation by local council from more than four years (1540 days) to a minimum of just over a year and a half (576 days).

## Placements and policy groups

As might be expected there were large differences between the policy groups. At the end of the year:

- young entrants were overwhelmingly fostered (76%), placed for adoption (11%) or placed with parents (9%)

- adolescent graduates were mostly fostered (72%), in some form of residential establishment (14%) or placed with parents (9%)

- adolescent entrants included a majority in foster care (60%) but a sizeable minority in some form of residential care (29%) or independent living (6%)

- abused adolescents included a majority in foster care (60%) and sizeable minorities in some form of residential care (21%) or placed with parents (12%)

- asylum seekers had a majority in foster care (69%) but a sizeable minority in some kind of residential care (20%) or independent living (10%)

- disabled children included minorities in some kind of residential care (42%), foster care (40%), and 'other' accommodation.

As can be seen foster care was the predominant placement for all groups except disabled children. It played, however, a more central role with young entrants and adolescent graduates than it did with the others.

## Conclusion

The care system carries out varied functions and serves varied kinds of children. These differences show up in its placements. Some are short-term; some are typically used for younger children, others for older ones and so on.

At any one point in time most kinds of placement in this study were filled with relatively long-staying children. The median length of stay in current placements was over a year. Over the course of the year, however, most kinds of placement had catered for much larger numbers of children who stayed for a short period. The median length of stay in completed placements was just over three months. Any picture of the care system obtained from a study of completed placements needs to be balanced by acknowledging the greater stability of current ones.

A second common feature was that in all councils the great majority of placements, both long and short-term, were in foster care. Residential care continued to play an important role with adolescents. The other main categories were placement with parents and placement for adoption. Entry to all these other types of placement was strongly influenced by age at first entry to the system. Adoption was virtually reserved for those who first entered when aged less than five with a strong bias towards those first looked after when less than one. Residential care was very strongly concentrated on those who entered when aged 11 or over. Placement with parents was more common among those who were aged less than 11 at entry.

Other characteristics that influenced placement choice were asylum seeker status and disability. Those with a need code of disability were less likely to be placed with parents, more likely to be placed in residential care (mainly residential schools) in their teens and, as seen earlier, were less likely to be adopted. In this sense they climb what one of us has called a 'reverse ladder of permanence' (Baker 2006), being more likely to receive the least favoured 'permanency option', residential care and less likely to receive the most favoured ones of return home or (in the case of those seen as disabled by their social workers) adoption.

A third common feature was the apparent decay of the concept of 'treatment'. Rowe and her colleagues (1989) found that one in nine (11.4%) of completed placements was intended to provide treatment. Less than 1 per cent of the placements in our study were meant to do this and almost all of these were in residential care. In part this change may reflect a change in philosophy. The care system is no longer expected to reform those who break the law. One consequence may be the increasing numbers of young people in prison. Another may be that young people whose behaviour contributes to the instability of their placements are deprived of an approach they need.

Within this context residential care, foster care in the independent sector and placements outside the local council all seemed to play a similar role. They were primarily used for children whom the local council had difficulty in looking after in its own foster placements. Therefore, foster placements in the independent sector served older children who were not white, who showed challenging behaviour, or who first entered the system over the age of 11. Children's homes served a similar purpose, while other forms of residential care provided for young people who were disabled or seeking asylum. London councils made more use of independent foster carers, partly no doubt because of difficulties in recruiting their own, but were not particularly likely to use the independent sector for black and minority ethnic children, perhaps because they were able to recruit carers for them.

These results provide the basis for some – necessarily tentative – suggestions:

- Councils that make comparatively little use of kin placements can think of using more of them provided they pay attention to the special requirements of these placements for support (see Sinclair 2005 and references therein, also later evidence in this book).

- This increase is likely to further the emphasis in 'ordinary' foster care on more specialist functions – preparation for adoption, maintenance of challenging adolescents and so on.[18]

- Councils that do not wish to sub-contract these functions to the independent sector will need to adapt their recruitment and support to carers for such groups rather than relying on generalised campaigns to recruit carers.

- Councils outside London may also need to use targeted approaches to recruit black and minority ethnic carers if fewer black and minority ethnic children are to be placed out of county and in the independent sector.

- Further research is required to see if foster care can provide 'treatment' for teenagers with challenging behaviour,[19] remand care and appropriate care for disabled teenagers, all functions that at present it seems to perform rarely.

- There are wide variations in the length of time children spend on a care order but looked after by their parents. Councils may wish to monitor this.

- It appears that some disabled children may only have residential placements. Councils may wish to ensure some family life for them through foster care in the holidays or other means.

In general these suggestions can be seen as a response to two rather general trends in the care system: the rapid reduction in the residential sector with a consequent effect on the provision of 'treatment'; and the growing demands for a better remunerated and more professional foster care service that may have difficulty in providing for long-term, quasi-adoptive placements.

## Notes

1 The relevant codes have changed over the years. So the same number could have different meanings in different years. In a small minority of cases it was not possible to determine what the equivalent of a particular code now was.

2 We combined separate episodes that were clearly part of a single placement. This accounts for the difference between the number of episodes and the number of placements. So, for example, a placement that started on a particular date and then had a change of legal status a few weeks later, before it eventually ended sometime after that, would be recorded as two episodes but would represent only one placement.

3 The median of a set of numbers is roughly the 'middle number' – for example, the median for the three numbers 1, 5, 7 is 5 whereas the average is 13/3 or 4.3. The standard deviation is a measure of 'spread' and tends to be higher relative to the average when the numbers are widely scattered.

4 This may occur in two ways. The same placement (for example, residential home) may hold both long and short-term placements. Alternatively there may be specialist placements so that some foster homes or residential homes may take short-term residents and others children who stay longer. In either event the children who stay longer predominate overall.

5　We carried out two logistic regressions predicting 'fostered' among those present at the census date. The variables in the first equation were whether aged 11 or over, whether first entered aged 11 or over, whether need codes of abuse, disability and behaviour, the interactions between being aged 11 or over and disability and behaviour, and whether last admission was more than a year ago. The second equation included the same variables as the first with the addition of 12 local councils added as dummy variables. We then compared the omnibus tests of coefficients both distributed as chi square (268.54, df = 8 and 305.61, df = 20).

6　In this section we rely on the data from the client information systems for the definition of fostered with family and friends. The social worker and CIS data agree on 76% of cases. However, there are differences between the two sources of data. For example, the social workers identified 21 children as placed with parents when the client information system had them recorded as fostered with relatives or friends. Some of the discrepancies seem to occur because of differences in coding practices, others because social workers gave answers for a later date, others because of difficulties of interpretation. For example, there may have been difficulties in deciding whether children with their mothers in their grandmothers' houses were fostered with relatives or placed with a parent.

7　There seem to be two reasons for this. First, initial placements made up a lower proportion of relative placements than they did of other foster placements. Second, relative placements lasted on average longer, so that more of them were likely to have been there for some time.

8　As before we tested the influence of local councils by carrying out two logistic regressions one with 12 of the local councils entered as dummy variables and the other without this. The variables in the first equation were age 11 or over, need codes of acute family stress, disability and abandonment, and last admission more than a year previously.

9　We carried out a Mann–Whitney U test comparing the percentages for London and the other councils. The average rank for the London councils was 10.75 and for the others 5.33. This is a significant difference ($p = .02$).

10　The difference in the placement sector of white and black and minority ethnic children is significant at .002 in the non-London councils. It is not significant in the London ones. Tarone's test of the homogeneity of the relevant odds ratios gives a chi square of 4.39, df = 1, $p = .036$.

11　The difference is significant at $p < .001$ in the non-London councils and at $p = .018$ in the London ones. Although the difference is in the same direction in both sets of councils, there is a significant difference in the strength of the effect (Tarone's test for homogeneity of odds ratios gives a chi square of 4.82, df = 1, $p = .028$).

12　They were significantly more likely to have a need code of abuse. However, the association was slight and disappeared once we had taken account of whether or not they were seeking asylum.

13　Some independent fostering agencies have their own access to education. This could neutralise the effect of their foster children's educational difficulties. We tried to test this hypothesis by comparing the independent and local council placements using age and the difficult behaviour score as covariates but the results were not significant.

14　The procedure was as before. The addition of the councils significantly improved the prediction (chi square = 32, df = 12, $p < .001$). The variables common to the two logistic regressions were: age 11 or over, age at first entry 11 or over, experienced more than one admission, need codes of disability, difficult behaviour, and acute family stress, school performance score, difficult behaviour score and being an asylum seeker.

15   Obviously some of these characteristics were more common in London councils. We checked whether these statements held if we allowed for the differences between local councils and it appeared that they did. The associations are all significant on the relevant Maentel–Haentzel test. That said, and with the exception of age, the associations are all much more pronounced outside London than they are in it.

16   The association between being aged 11 or over and placement with parents disappears if we take account of whether or not the child is an asylum seeker. The association with age at entry remains.

17   The procedure was as before. The addition of the councils significantly improved the prediction (chi square = 59.6, df = 12, $p$ < .001). The variables common to the two logistic regressions were: experience more than one admission, need codes of disability, difficult behaviour, and acute family stress, and being an asylum seeker.

18   Our questionnaires suggested considerable consensus on what a proper package of support would involve: enhanced remuneration, more frequent contact with supervising social workers, improved communication between supervising social workers, social workers and carers, dedicated support from psychologists, better educational provision, better respite and out of hours provision, improved training, practical support from assistant social workers (e.g. with children not at school), better arrangements for dealing with allegations, all underpinned by a better system of recruitment perhaps informed with public relations skills and with good administrative arrangements.

19   Scottish research (Walker, Hill and Triseliotis 2002) strongly suggests that foster care can at the least 'contain' more challenging teenagers than has commonly been thought but that it cannot completely substitute for secure provision.

Chapter 9

# Placements: How One Leads to Another

I'm not saying that all movement is bad *per se*, because obviously in relation to, you know, planning for permanence it would be unlikely that you would hit, you know, a permanent placement first time, on the basis that most young people would be placed in short-term placements first before migrating to permanent placements. (Manager)

So we have got two sorts of problems, we have got kids who are medium to long-term whose placements break down and it is a tragedy for them…and the front end of the system, where kids are rattling around between placements early on until we manage to find the right placement for them. (Manager)

## Introduction

The placements discussed in Chapter 8 had varying purposes and lasted for varying lengths of time. Their context was the overall plan for the child. As we saw in Chapter 5, these plans can change. When children are first looked after there is often the hope that they will go home. As time goes on they either do so or the hope is given up. It follows that the purposes of placement are also likely to change, as, for example, a child moves from a placement meant for assessment to one that is to look after her or him for the foreseeable future.

This chapter is about these sequences of placements and about what makes for a 'good' or 'bad' sequence. This is an important distinction. A baby admitted at birth from a hospital placement may have three placements in a year: one in hospital, one short-term placement while an adoptive home is sought, and one in that home. This sequence of three placements is very different from one whereby an adolescent in a long-term placement suffers a placement breakdown, quickly followed by a serious offence in a children's home and placement in secure provision.

We ask five questions:

1. Does the length of a placement vary with its purpose and with the time since a child was last admitted?

2. Do children with many placements have shorter placements on average and shorter 'final placements'?

3. What constitutes a successful sequence of placements?

4. Which children have successful placements and which children have sequences of placements that are less successful?

5. What is the relationship between successful and unsuccessful sequences of placements and the current indicators of stability?

## Differences in placement length and purpose

We had data on 11,385 placements in our census years. We looked at how long they lasted. Overall a quarter (24.2%) of the placements lasted throughout the year thereby accounting for half (52%) of the placement days. At the other end of the spectrum a quarter (25%) of the placements in the year lasted for no more than 33 days in the course of it.[1] This sizeable group accounted for only 1.7 per cent of the placement days.[2]

The length of a placement was logically related to its aims[3] (see Figure 9.1). We distinguished between:

- *Short-term aims* – temporary care, emergency, remand and assessment.

- *Medium-term aims* – treatment, preparation for long-term placement, bridge to independence, view to adoption.

- *Long-term aims* – care and upbringing.

- *Other* – a small miscellaneous group that made up less than five per cent of the total.

The average length of the last or latest placement rose steadily from under 200 days for short-term aims to more than 900 for the long-term aim of care and upbringing.

Children who had been looked after for some time were also much less likely to have placements with short-term aims. Nearly half (46%) of those who had been there for no more than a year had placements for essentially short-term purposes. The same was true of only 9 per cent of those who had been looked after for one or two years and only 3 per cent of those admitted earlier than that.

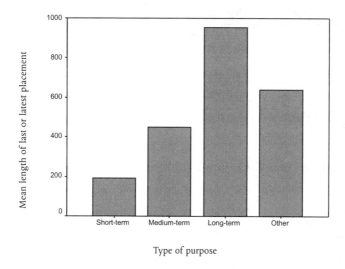

Type of purpose

Sources: Social Worker data and CIS data.

**Figure 9.1** Average length of latest placement by type of purpose

As our earlier statistics suggest the care system generally makes up its mind in the first year.

Placements with 'medium-term aims' were most common among children who had been looked after for one or two years. This had to do with placements with a view to adoption. These were most often found among those who had been looked after for one or two years (see Table 9.1 for details). By contrast children in placements with the medium-term aims of 'treatment', 'a bridge to independence', or 'preparation for a long-term placement' were equally likely to be found irrespective of how long they had been looked after.

Children who had been looked after for three years or more were much more likely than others to have placements with the long-term aim of 'care and upbringing'. Six out of ten had one (see Table 9.1) as against a third (35%) of those looked after for one or two years, and around one in six (16%) of those looked after for less than a year.

These changes in purpose over time were logically related to changes in placement length (see Figure 9.2). Obviously those who had been looked after for less than a year could not, by definition, have a placement lasting longer than this. Their average length of placement was therefore artificially depressed. This was also true of those who had been looked after for one or two years. Nevertheless Figure 9.2 usefully illustrates a truth. The care system gradually works its way towards permanence. Those in placement for three years or more are much more likely to have placements that are both intended to last and do so.

**Table 9.1** Purpose of placement by time since last admission

| Aim last/latest placement | | Time since last admitted | | | |
| --- | --- | --- | --- | --- | --- |
| | | Less than 1 year | 1 or 2 years | 3 years or more | Total |
| Temporary care | Count | 348 | 87 | 42 | 477 |
| | % within Time since last admitted | 27.3% | 6.0% | 2.4% | 10.6% |
| Emergency | Count | 46 | 7 | 13 | 66 |
| | % within Time since last admitted | 3.6% | .5% | .7% | 1.5% |
| Remand | Count | 18 | 2 | 1 | 21 |
| | % within Time since last admitted | 1.4% | .1% | .1% | .5% |
| Assessment | Count | 169 | 35 | 12 | 216 |
| | % within Time since last admitted | 13.3% | 2.4% | .7% | 4.8% |
| Treatment | Count | 9 | 8 | 16 | 33 |
| | % within Time since last admitted | .7% | .6% | .9% | .7% |
| Prep for LT placement | Count | 142 | 238 | 233 | 613 |
| | % within Time since last admitted | 11.1% | 16.4% | 13.2% | 13.7% |
| Bridge to indep. | Count | 163 | 164 | 165 | 492 |
| | % within Time since last admitted | 12.8% | 11.3% | 9.4% | 11.0% |
| Care and upbringing | Count | 198 | 503 | 1061 | 1762 |
| | % within Time since last admitted | 15.5% | 34.7% | 60.2% | 39.3% |
| View to adoption | Count | 141 | 342 | 113 | 596 |
| | % within Time since last admitted | 11.1% | 23.6% | 6.4% | 13.3% |
| Other | Count | 40 | 63 | 107 | 210 |
| | % within Time since last admitted | 3.1% | 4.3% | 6.1% | 4.7% |
| Total | Count | 1274 | 1449 | 1763 | 4486 |
| | % within Time since last admitted | 100.0% | 100.0% | 100.0% | 100.0% |

Source: CIS and Social Worker data.

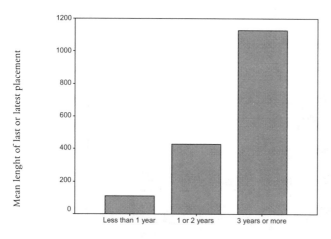

Time since last admitted

Source: CIS data.

**Figure 9.2** Length of latest placement by time since arrival

## How long had the children's placements lasted on average?

As we have seen lengths of placement reflect their purpose and their position in the child's care career. What does this mean for the average length of a child's placement? We calculated this average for each child. For example, if a child had had one placement of 100 days and another of 20 days the average of the two placements for her or him would be 60 days (120/2).

We found that:

- For a quarter of the children the average was between zero and 107 days (roughly three and a half months).

- For a further quarter the average was between 108 and 246 days (just over eight months).

- For a further quarter the average was between 247 days and 507 days (one year and four and a half months).

- The remainder had average placement lengths of 508 days or more.

These figures are for all placements. As we have seen, initial placements are often intended to be short – in many ways the quicker a child returns home or achieves a permanent base the better. We therefore analysed the average length of placements after the initial one (see Figure 9.3).[4]

In many ways what matters is not so much the length of the average placement but the length of the last or latest placement. This, after all, determines how

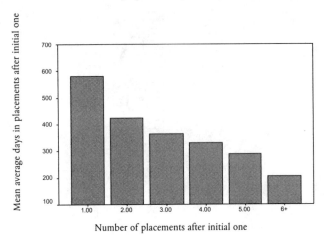

Source: CIS data.

**Figure 9.3** Average number of days in non-initial placements by number of these placements

far the child can be said to have achieved some kind of stability. A quarter of these final placements were less than 94 days (just over three months) and a quarter greater than 746 (just over two years). A sizeable number of children therefore finally achieved quite a lengthy placement.

Many of the very short last placements were in fact initial ones where the child went home. Removal of first placements means that a quarter of the placements are less than 115 days (nearly four months). At the same time it slightly reduces the number of very long last placements. Only a quarter lasted more than 704 days (just under two years). So some first placements clearly lasted for a long time.

Encouragingly it seemed that even a relatively large number of non-initial placements did not necessarily prevent a relatively lengthy last one. Figure 9.4 gives the average length of the last or latest placement by the number of placements after the first the children had had. As we have seen the average length of non-initial placements decreased steadily with the number of placements. This was not so with the average length of 'final' (i.e. current or latest) placements. Those with six or more non-initial placements did indeed have, on average, shorter final placements. In the rest of the sample there was very little relationship between the number of non-initial placements and the average length of the final one.

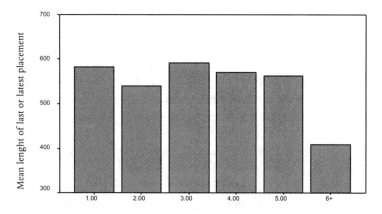

Source: CIS data.

**Figure 9.4** Length of last or latest placement by number of non-initial placements

These figures suggest that there may be some children who find it difficult to last long in placements. They are liable to have six or more placements. In our sample one in six (17%) of the sample had had six or more placements according to the client information system. (This proportion must be an underestimate, not least because some of the information systems did not cover all of the children's time in care.) Compared with others those with six placements were older, more prone to difficult behaviour, less likely to accept being looked after, doing, on average, much worse at school, and much more likely to have been admitted more than once.

That said, many children must have a number of short-term placements while nevertheless remaining capable of achieving a long one. In their case it probably matters more how their sequence of placements ends than how it begins.

## What makes for a successful sequence of placements?

The data so far suggest that the care system has to be seen as a staged process. Ideally children move from short placements to their home, adoption or long-term foster care. Such movements may be regarded as a success. Other movements may reflect individual or administrative factors. These could include for example, the breakdown of a placement because of the difficult behaviour of a foster child or a move from a long-term placement to ensure a better ethnic match. We need to explore the extent of these different kinds of movement and the reasons for them.

In this part of our analysis we used questions taken from Rowe and her colleagues (1989). They asked social workers how far placements had achieved their purposes. They also asked whether the placements had lasted as long as needed, or longer than needed. We repeated these questions with the exception that we also asked whether a placement had met the child's needs at any time. We did this because unlike Rowe and her colleagues we included current placements in our study. In our pilot study a number of social workers said that although the placement was continuing it did not meet the child's needs.

Social workers could obviously not say that a current placement had lasted for less time than needed. They were also unlikely to say that a current placement was not meeting its aims. In just over three-quarters (76%) of the cases they said that the current or latest placement fully met their aims. The comparable figure for the previous placement was only just over half (54%). Similarly a tiny proportion (3.3%) of current or latest placements were said not to meet their aims at all. The comparable figure for previous placements was three times as great.

Why were current placements seen as more satisfactory? There may be a number of reasons. Social workers were probably reluctant to criticise current placements unless they were proposing to move the child. If they had felt that the placement was very unsatisfactory they might well have moved the child already. Satisfactory placements were thus likely to last longer so that they were more likely to be current.

In keeping with the practice of Rowe and her colleagues we created a variable we called 'placement success'. This measure was concerned with *sequences of placements* rather than individual ones. Nevertheless it was based on the idea that for a placement to be *fully satisfactory* it had, in the social worker's opinion, to last as long as needed and to fully meet its aims. On these criteria an impressive 72 per cent of the current placements were seen as being fully satisfactory. The figure for the previous placements was rather less impressive at 39 per cent.[5] The figure for the second previous placement was 33 per cent.

Our measure of 'placement success' was based on all the placements on which the social workers reported. All these had necessarily taken place in the last six months and we limited the number to three. Success was 'full' where the social worker said that the child's needs had been fully met in all placements and that in each case the purpose of the placement had been completely fulfilled. Success was partial when one of these criteria was not fulfilled for at least one placement. Success was 'nil' where each of these criteria had not been fully met in at least one (not necessarily the same) placement.

Placement success was related to the characteristics of the last or latest placement. Where this was for care and upbringing eight out of ten children were seen as having had full placement success. The comparable figures for temporary care (32%), treatment (36%) or bridge to independence (45%) were much lower.[6] Similarly placements in children's homes (42%) or secure units (26%) were much less likely to be associated with placement success than placements in 'relative' (85%) or unrelated (68%) foster care. These figures relate to sequences of placements. So the implication is not, for example, that secure provision is in itself unsatisfactory but rather that it tends to occur following a placement that has not worked out well.

The successive placement outcomes were strongly related to one another. Where the second previous placement was fully satisfactory 92 per cent of the next ones were seen as fully satisfactory. Where it was not successful 90 per cent of the next ones were also seen as unsuccessful. There was a similar, if less pronounced, relationship between the previous placement and the current one. When the previous placement was seen as successful, 91 per cent of the current ones were also seen as successful. When the previous placement was not seen as successful, only 46 per cent of the current ones were seen as successful. Such continuity could occur in different ways – because some individual children render all their placements successful or unsuccessful, because placements that form part of a coherent development are seen as successful or, conversely, because one unsatisfactory placement tends to lead to another (e.g. through one emergency placement leading to another).

In the light of these findings we looked at children who had had two placements in the last six months and at their placement trajectory. Our hypothesis was that much would depend on whether a trajectory was from 'homely to homely', 'homely to unhomely', 'unhomely to homely' or 'unhomely to unhomely'. We defined homely placements as those with families (birth parents, foster carers or adoptive parents). Placements with 'homely purposes' were those that aimed at adoption or care and upbringing. Our hypothesis was that full placement success would be most commonly found where the final placement was with a family or had homely purposes.

Our hypothesis was broadly confirmed. 'Unhomely' placements or purposes only worked against a successful sequence of placements if they did not lead on to homely ones. Indeed the most successful group were those where placements with 'unhomely purposes' led on to those with homely ones. 'Homely to unhomely' or 'unhomely to unhomely' transitions were in the great majority of cases seen as less than fully successful.

**Table 9.2** Purpose trajectory by placement success

| Purpose trajectory | | Placement Success | | | Total |
| --- | --- | --- | --- | --- | --- |
| | | None | Partial | Full | |
| Homely to homely | Count | 29 | 30 | 44 | 103 |
| | % within Purpose trajectory | 28.2% | 29.1% | 42.7% | 100.0% |
| Homely to unhomely | Count | 28 | 13 | 12 | 53 |
| | % within Purpose trajectory | 52.8% | 24.5% | 22.6% | 100.0% |
| Unhomely to homely | Count | 10 | 21 | 84 | 115 |
| | % within Purpose trajectory | 8.7% | 18.3% | 73.0% | 100.0% |
| Unhomely to unhomely | Count | 91 | 61 | 47 | 199 |
| | % within Purpose trajectory | 45.7% | 30.7% | 23.6% | 100.0% |
| Total | Count | 158 | 125 | 187 | 470 |
| | % within Purpose trajectory | 33.6% | 26.6% | 39.8% | 100.0% |

Source: Social Worker data. Note: Those with two placements in last six months only.

Overall therefore the social workers want children to be with their families, adoptive parents or long-term foster carers. Individual placements need not themselves offer such permanence but do need to be a step on the road towards it.

## Variables associated with placement success

We explored the factors associated with placement success. In doing so we looked at a familiar list of variables. These related to the child's:

- *basic characteristics* – age at entry, current age, sex, ethnicity, legal status, need code, whether seeking asylum
- *scores for challenging behaviour,* school adjustment, family difficulties and acceptance of the need for care
- *care career* – whether experienced a repeat admission and time since admission.

All these variables except sex were significantly related to perceived placement success.

The likelihood of placement success was lower among recent admissions and those who had a repeat admission. It fell steadily with age and age at entry (see Table 9.3 for current age). It was also lower with the need codes that were relatively more common among adolescents – family stress, family dysfunction and socially unacceptable behaviour.

**Table 9.3** Current age group by placement success

| Current age group at census/end last placement | | Placement Success | | | |
|---|---|---|---|---|---|
| | | None | Partial | Full | Total |
| 0–1 yrs | Count | 20 | 70 | 288 | 378 |
| | % within Current age group at census/end last placement | 5.3% | 18.5% | 76.2% | 100.0% |
| 2–4 yrs | Count | 28 | 96 | 330 | 454 |
| | % within Current age group at census/end last placement | 6.2% | 21.1% | 72.7% | 100.0% |
| 5–9 yrs | Count | 57 | 196 | 635 | 888 |
| | % within Current age group at census/end last placement | 6.4% | 22.1% | 71.5% | 100.0% |
| 10–15 yrs | Count | 232 | 418 | 1226 | 1876 |
| | % within Current age group at census/end last placement | 12.4% | 22.3% | 65.4% | 100.0% |
| 16 yrs and over | Count | 120 | 236 | 548 | 904 |
| | % within Current age group at census/end last placement | 13.3% | 26.1% | 60.6% | 100.0% |
| Total | Count | 457 | 1016 | 3027 | 4500 |
| | % within Current age group at census/end last placement | 10.2% | 22.6% | 67.3% | 100.0% |

Source: Social Worker data.

In keeping with these findings, children without full placement success were more likely to show challenging behaviour, more likely to have difficulties at school, more likely to have high family difficulty scores, more likely to have a family seen as disrupting the placement and less likely to be seen as accepting the need for care.[7] Figure 9.5 can stand as an example of the association between the other scores and placement success.

Other associations were harder to explain. Children who were voluntarily accommodated were less likely to do well on this measure (see Table 9.4). These children tended to have other characteristics associated with perceived poor success. They were on average older and more likely to be asylum seekers, more likely to show challenging behaviour and more likely to have the need codes associated with poor success. Surprisingly no combination of these characteristics was able to explain the association between being voluntarily accommodated and lack of full success.[8]

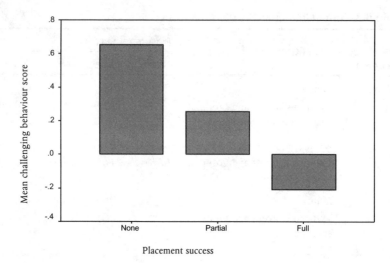

Source: Social Worker data. Note: The higher the score the more challenging behaviour a child is said to display.

**Figure 9.5** Mean challenging behaviour score by placement success

**Table 9.4** Voluntary accommodation by placement success

| Voluntarily accommodated | | Placement success | | | |
| | | None | Partial | Full | Total |
|---|---|---|---|---|---|
| No | Count | 266 | 633 | 2176 | 3075 |
| | % within Voluntarily accommodated | 8.7% | 20.6% | 70.8% | 100.0% |
| Yes | Count | 191 | 383 | 851 | 1425 |
| | % within Voluntarily accommodated | 13.4% | 26.9% | 59.7% | 100.0% |
| Total | Count | 457 | 1016 | 3027 | 4500 |
| | % within Voluntarily accommodated | 10.2% | 22.6% | 67.3% | 100.0% |

Source: CIS and Social Worker data.

Those who were voluntarily accommodated differed from others in that:

- they were far more likely to have unhomely to unhomely transitions
- they were far less likely to have homely to homely or unhomely to homely transitions.

Arguably their lack of success stems from a lack of commitment from a care system which accepts less responsibility for them than for those on a care order and is correspondingly less willing to work towards a long-term placement.

Another puzzling set of findings concerned the apparent influence of ethnicity and asylum status. Children were less likely to be perceived as having placement success if they were not white and if they were seeking asylum.

The association with ethnicity was in practice weak, and arose because more of those who were not white were seen as having their needs only partly met. These may have been children in placements that were not ethnically matched but were satisfactory in other ways.

Asylum seekers may also suffer from a lack of commitment. They rarely move to placements with homely intentions. Instead their transitions are from foster care to the bleaker worlds of lodgings and hostels and from placements intended to prepare for independence to independence itself. And what is true of those who make transitions is also true, albeit to a lesser extent, of those who had had only one placement. Both those seeking asylum and those who were voluntarily admitted were less likely to have homely placements or placements with 'homely' purposes.

**Table 9.5** Purpose trajectory by asylum status

| Purpose trajectory | | Whether asylum seeker | | Total |
|---|---|---|---|---|
| | | No | Yes | |
| Homely to homely | Count | 104 | 3 | 107 |
| | % within Whether asylum seeker | 23.1% | 8.1% | 21.9% |
| Homely to unhomely | Count | 46 | 8 | 54 |
| | % within Whether asylum seeker | 10.2% | 21.6% | 11.1% |
| Unhomely to homely | Count | 123 | 0 | 123 |
| | % within Whether asylum seeker | 27.3% | 0% | 25.2% |
| Unhomely to unhomely | Count | 178 | 26 | 204 |
| | % within Whether asylum seeker | 39.5% | 70.3% | 41.8% |
| Total | Count | 451 | 37 | 488 |
| | % within Whether asylum seeker | 100.0% | 100.0% | 100.0% |

Source: Social Worker data.
Note: The table is restricted to those said by the social workers to have had two placements in the last six months.

In general these findings suggest that social workers assess placements in terms of their relevance to the provision of a lasting homely environment. Various factors may help or hinder the achievement of this end. Primarily these concern the 'difficulty' of the child. Some children may also suffer from a lack of commitment on the part of the system or the problems of achieving an ethnic match.

## Placement success and policy groups

Unsurprisingly our six policy groups differed in the likelihood of achieving placement success. The most successful groups were the young entrants (74% full success), the adolescent graduates (71% full success) and the disabled children (78% full success). The least successful were the adolescent entrants (50% full success), abused adolescents (57%) and asylum seekers (57%).

## Placement success and measures of stability

So how far did placement success relate to the measures of stability? We calculated three measures of stability. These were 'the three placements measure' (related to but not identical with the Performance Assessment Framework (PAF) A1 measure), the 'new indicator' (identical with the corresponding DfES Public Service Agreement (PSA) target) and 'the long-term stability' measure (identical with the PAF D35 indicator).

The three placements measure differed slightly from the DfES A1 indicator that inspired it. According to the client information systems rather more than one in seven (13.4%) of those present on the census date had had three or more placements in the year. According to the social workers one in ten (10%) had had three or more placements in the past six months. The two sources of information were not completely consistent. So 8 per cent of those who did not, according to the client information system, have three or more placements in the year had had this number of placements according to the social workers in the previous six months. We combined these two sources of information counting a child as having three or more placements if:

- he or she was present at the end of the year

- he or she had had three or more placements in the year according to the client information system or in the past six months according to the social workers or both.

On these criteria nearly one in five (18.6%) of the relevant sub-group had had three or more placements. (The information systems on their own gave a figure of 13.4% that compares with a national figure of 12.9% for the year ending on 31 March 2004.)

Our 'new indicator' was also concerned with those who were in placement at the census date but was restricted to those under 16. It focused on those who had been looked after for 2.5 years. The measure of stability was the proportion of this group who had been in the same placement for the past two years or who been placed for adoption in the course of the year. Two-thirds (65.6% as against a national figure of 65.5%) of the relevant sub-group had positive outcomes on this measure.

Finally, we calculated a measure of long-term stability. This was based on those present on the census date and continuously looked after for the previous four years. Following government guidelines we looked at the D35 measure, that is the proportion of this group that had been continuously fostered with the same carer for the previous two years. This was true of 50.1 per cent of this group. This compares with a national figure of 50.5 per cent for the year ending 31 March 2004.

Children with three or more placements were less likely to have 'placement success' (see Table 9.6). This is not surprising. As we have seen, social workers rarely said that current placements were not meeting needs or fulfilling purposes. They were, however, ready to say that past placements had not done so, so children who had had more than one placement were less likely to do well on our measure. In any event a child who had had three placements was clearly more likely to have at least one that did not meet his or her needs than a child who had only one.[9]

**Table 9.6** Three or more placements by placement success

|  |  | Placement success | | | |
|---|---|---|---|---|---|
| Three or more placements in year | | None | Partial | Full | Total |
| No | Count | 164 | 677 | 2155 | 2996 |
|  | % within Three or more placements in year | 5.5% | 22.6% | 71.9% | 100.0% |
| Yes | Count | 224 | 209 | 308 | 741 |
|  | % within Three or more placements in year | 30.2% | 28.2% | 41.6% | 100.0% |
| Total | Count | 388 | 886 | 2463 | 3737 |
|  | % within Three or more placements in year | 10.4% | 23.7% | 65.9% | 100.0% |

Source: CIS and Social Worker data.

Note: Table restricted to those present on census date.

In many ways the surprising feature of Table 9.6 is the relatively high proportion of cases with three or more placements in a year that were apparently successful. In more than four out of ten of these cases the social worker felt that all the placements in the last six months met the child's needs and fulfilled their purposes.[10] This would certainly not be the case if almost all of the cases with three or more placements occurred because of placement breakdowns. In keeping with this, more detailed analysis showed that these 'surprising successes' were in many ways less 'difficult' than others with three or more placements and much more likely to end up in 'homely' placements.

We also looked at the association of our measure of placement success with the new indicator (the proportion of those under 16 who at a given point in time have been looked after for two and a half years continuously and either fostered for two years or placed for adoption in the last year) and with the D35 long-term stability measure (the proportion of children at a given point in time who have been looked after continuously for four years and fostered with the same carer for the last two). The association with our measure of placement success was strong in each case. So 82 per cent of those who were positive on the new indicator were 'fully successful' and only 3 per cent were 'not successful'. The comparable figures for those who were not positive on the new indicator were 59 per cent and 16 per cent. Table 9.7 gives the figures for the D35 measure.

**Table 9.7** D35 stability measure by placement success

| D35 stability measure | | Placement success | | | |
| --- | --- | --- | --- | --- | --- |
| | | None | Partial | Full | Total |
| Not positive | Count | 82 | 148 | 380 | 610 |
| | % within D35 stability measure | 13.4% | 24.3% | 62.3% | 100.0% |
| Positive | Count | 13 | 64 | 535 | 612 |
| | % within D35 stability measure | 2.1% | 10.5% | 87.4% | 100.0% |
| Total | Count | 95 | 212 | 915 | 1222 |
| | % within D35 stability measure | 7.8% | 17.3% | 74.9% | 100.0% |

Source: Social Worker data.
Note: Table is restricted to those looked after continuously for four years or more.

Most social workers would agree that after four years a stable foster placement is probably the 'best bet' for a child who is looked after. So those who succeed on the D35 measure are understandably very likely to be seen as successfully placed. It is surprising that nearly two-thirds of those who are not stably fostered are nevertheless seen as having full placement success. Arguably this arises because of the apparent success of the latest placement.

## Conclusion

As we saw earlier, the care system acts partly as a sieve. If the child returns home, he or she usually does so quickly. Where this does not happen the system provides a sequence of placements. Children move through one or more short-term placements into those with longer term aims. Examination of the length of final placements gives a much more stable picture than is found among those who have recently arrived.

Perhaps the most striking finding is that most placements are not intended to last. Broadly, placements can be divided into those with essentially short-term aims, those that are intended to end in the medium term (for example, those with a view to adoption) and those that are intended to provide long-term care. There is also a small residual category of 'other'. Nearly half those in the social work sample who had arrived within the last year had essentially short-term placements. Half of those in their second or third year of being looked after had placements with medium term aims. Only among those who had been looked after for more than three years were long-term placements in the majority.

Why was so much movement intended? The reasons probably include:

- *Logistical necessity* – there is a need for emergency and short-term provision at the beginning of a child's care career in order to allow stock to be taken and plans made. Similar considerations apply following a breakdown.

- *Difficulties in matching* – these are likely to occur at the beginning of a period of being looked after (or indeed following an unexpected breakdown) and it may also be true of siblings[11] and children from black and minority ethnic groups.

- *The time taken to arrange adoption* – some children have been looked after for two or three years and have not yet achieved their final adoptive placement.

- *Other practice considerations* – some plans require a series of placements for their fulfilment. For example, it may be necessary to try a child with its parents in a residential assessment centre before proceeding to adoption.

- *Reactions to events* – breakdowns may lead to plans for placement in residential care or to 'prepare for a long-term placement' in the hope that eventually the child may be able to settle down.

- *Implicit policies* – it is possible that councils do not really wish to provide a home from home for asylum seekers or for voluntary admissions. Similarly they may be reluctant to treat expensive out of county accommodation as long-term.

A surprisingly high proportion of those with three or more placements seem to move for reasons of this kind. Obviously, however, not all children moved for defensible reasons. Some had placement trajectories that the social worker did not want. Similarly some children did not achieve a long-term placement even if they were looked after for three years or more.

The main reason for unexpected and unintended placement endings was almost certainly breakdowns. Children and young people with six or more placements clearly had more difficulties of behaviour and background than others. These made up just under a fifth of the sample and may well have had more placement breakdowns than others.

We deal later with the issues raised by unintended placement endings. What might be done about intended ones? In some respects it is important to ask how far this is a desirable aim. Difficulties in matching are partly inevitable – for it is never possible to be certain that a placement will work out – and also partly a matter of resources. If all children are to be immediately offered a placement that is clearly suitable for them there will need to be a massive pool of vacancies. This in turn will cost money. It is also true that some short-term and medium-term aims may be desirable. We believe, for example, that there is a need for some form of treatment foster care. This has medium-term aims and may also require some form of 'holding placement' as children wait for a vacancy.

That said, children do not like moves. Other things being equal they find them unsettling reminders of the transience of their attachments and the powerlessness of their position. Changes of placement may mean changes of school and therefore the need to make new friends. At the minimum entering an unknown placement is for many 'scary'. So there remains a case for reducing intended movement. In this respect the possibilities are likely to vary with whether the placement has short-term or medium-term aims.

In relation to short-term aims it is possible to ask whether movement or at the least the bad effects of movement would be reduced if:

- the role of short-term foster carers were widened so that they were expected to take a wider variety of children for more varying lengths of time, thus reducing the need for emergency placements and moves from one short-term placement to another
- foster carers who took young children were prepared for enabling them either to be placed for adoption or to be returned home, thus minimising

the need to move children to special placements that are 'good at preparation for adoption'

- foster carers whose foster children returned home or moved to placements for assessment more often retained a place for them and perhaps continued to provide support, thus enabling a smooth transition if the child returned to the care system

- the definitions of the performance indicators were changed in order to encourage such arrangements

- councils were more willing to consider converting short-term placements into long-term ones in cases where child and carers wanted this.

In relation to medium-term aims it might be desirable to:

- increase the number of children for whom the aim is that they should stay on with their carers beyond the age of 18 rather than move into lodgings and other insecure forms of accommodation

- consider treating some carers with whom the children have a bond in the same way as parents, in others words expecting that the children would return from residential or other placements to these carers rather than treating the end of a placement as final

- use some carers to support children who return on a care order to their parents thus enabling them to return to the same placement if the attempt at rehabilitation does not work out

- change the definition of the stability indicators in order to encourage the above.

One of us has argued a fuller case for some of these changes elsewhere (Sinclair 2005). While they are certainly suggested by our findings in this study we cannot say how far they would work. Obviously they would take up resources and would not dispose of the need for all movement.

In the last respect one lesson of this chapter is that much of the movement captured by the A1 indicator ('the proportion with three or more placements in a year') is intended and quite possibly desirable. And this in turn is part of a wider truth. What matters is not so much the initial placements as the final result. We have seen that a number of short-term placements can be followed by one that lasts. Similarly a series of placements can be intended and can work out for good.

## Summary points for Chapters 8 and 9

Social workers generally seek lasting, homely placements with parents or foster carers close to the child's own home and provided by their own council. Movements tend to be seen as successful when they are to homely placements and unsuccessful in other cases. Difficulties in achieving such placements include:

- The shortage of placements for certain groups with the result that adolescents and black and minority ethnic children tend to be placed in the independent sector and 'out of county'.

- The use of residential care for adolescents with difficult behaviour and disabled children.

- The lack of foster placements for children with challenging behaviour.

- Arguably a lack of commitment to provide long-stay foster care for those who are admitted on a voluntary basis or are seeking asylum.

In general most movement is intended. Much of it occurs in the 'early days' as decisions are being taken about more long-term arrangements. Some occurs through the ending of placements with medium-term aims; some (almost certainly a relatively small part) through breakdowns. The number of moves may possibly be minimised by broadening the roles of short-term carers. Fortunately children who have had a number of placements often achieve a longer term one in the end.

## Notes

1    A small number of these started in the previous year and so lasted for more than 33 days in total. However, 86 per cent of them last no longer than 33 days in total and none lasted for more than 33 days in the course of the census year.

2    One in ten (9.9%) of the placements lasted for no more than seven days. The proportion is essentially unchanged if those entering in the last week who could not have stayed longer are omitted. Around half (53%) of these very short placements were initial ones and of these six out of ten (61%) resulted in the child or young person going home. The group contained a much higher proportion of adolescents than the sample of initial placements as a whole (57% v. 36%) and a rather higher proportion of children under the age of two (19% v. 15%). Some of the latter had their initial placement in hospital. The short placements that were not initial ones were presumably responses to unexpected breakdowns in the family.

3    The interpretation of this figure is complicated by the association between time since arrival and placement purpose. Those present for less than a year could not have a placement lasting longer than a year. This fact will artificially lower the average length of time in short-term placements. That said the figure does not really mislead. An analysis of variance showed that purpose is strongly associated with length of placement after taking into account time since arrival.

4    Strictly speaking the figure relates to the average of the clients' average number of placement days.

5   This definition is the same as that used by Rowe *et al.* (1989) with the exception that we required a placement to fully meet its aims whereas they allowed partial fulfilment. Rowe *et al.* found a 'success rate' among completed placements (the only ones they studied) of 49 per cent. Using their definition we found a success rate of 53 per cent among the immediately previous placements and 55 per cent among those preceding that. Their percentage will, however, have included some placements that were part of a rapid consecutive series and would be expected to be somewhat worse than ours.

6   Short-term purposes are more common among placements made shortly after admission. In keeping with this the chance of placement success rises steadily but not dramatically with length of care career and most sharply with the length of the latest placement. Those with relatively long latest placements have obviously had fewer placements that could go wrong in the six months. They are also more likely to be in placements intended for care and upbringing and these are more likely than others to be seen as meeting needs and achieving purposes.

7   Only one of these differences – that relating to family difficulty – was not significant at a level way past one in a thousand. The family difficulty score was also unusual in that only those with 'no success' stood out as having unusually high scores.

8   This conclusion is based on a series of logistic regressions with full success as the dependent variable.

9   A person who buys three apples is more likely to have at least one apple with a bruise than a person who buys only one.

10  Some of the 'three placements' will have been prior to the 6 month period about which we asked the social workers. This could affect the validity of the argument we are putting forward here. For this reason we repeated the analysis given in the table using 'Three placements in the last six months according to the social worker' instead of our usual 'Three or more placements in a year'. The pattern remains the same although the association is stronger, so only a third of those with three or more placements in the last six months have complete success while four out of ten have 'none'. There are probably two reasons for this. First, associations within data collected from a single source are typically stronger than associations between data from different sources. Second, it may well be the case that three or more placements in six months are a stronger indicator that something has gone wrong than are three or more placements in a year. In our view it still remains surprising that as many as a third of these cases were apparently fully successful. It is also surprising that on this analysis only 75 per cent of those with no more than one placement were 'fully successful'. If the chance that one placement was fully successful was independent of the chance that the next one was, a child with three placements would have a 42 per cent chance of being fully successful. This is higher than the observed 33 per cent implying that the assumption of independence is incorrect. However the difference is not as great as we would have expected. Like much of our other evidence this suggests that the individual child does have an influence on the amount of movement but that this influence is not pronounced.

11  Children with siblings were much more likely than other children in the relevant group to have homely transitions. Ninety per cent of them did so as opposed to 54 per cent of the others.

Chapter 10

# Children Based in Care

I want my children to feel settled and I want them to feel that this is, you know, where they're going to be and this is working out and they like it there. (Manager)

The children we don't have such a good record with...if I start with the younger ones first, the younger children I am talking about are probably around eight, nine, ten, who come from very abusive backgrounds, very traumatised, very damaged[1]... [The problem with some of those who enter as adolescents is that you have a] young person who quite often is violent, has been by this time excluded from school, who is into substances, who is either totally into or on the periphery of criminal activities...and you have a family who are not interested in effect and...either throw them out or they say 'over to you' basically. (Manager)

## Introduction

The experience of care is formed of different elements. There are the placements and all that goes with them; there is the child's school; there are the moves between placements that often involve a change of school as well; there is the meaning the children give to care in the context of their relationship with their family.

In this chapter we use our case studies to cast light on this experience. The chapter picks up the issues of placement and movement that have figured in our earlier chapters. At the same time it looks forward to our next chapters that are about outcomes. We use the chapter to try to understand what constitutes a good or bad outcome and also what leads to it.

The chapter concentrates on children whose current base was in care. For good or ill their own families generally remained very important to them. However, they themselves did not return home frequently or for long. Some seemed firmly based in the care system, committed to their current carers and expecting to stay with them 'forever'; others were less securely and happily placed but still expected to remain in the system; some were placed with family and friends; a final group appeared to lack any base with either their family or within the care system. This chapter deals with these four groups and with why children fall into one or other of the groups.

## Care as a strong base

> The foster mother clearly adores Leila and says that she will stay forever. (Leila's reviewer)

> I like us all being together…there's my sister and the twins… It's really nice here… We have a budgerigar, two dogs, tortoises and a rabbit. We are staying here forever…and I have an elder brother as well… His mummy and daddy did not want him so he doesn't want to see them either… It's lovely… I go to Brownies and to a dance class each week and I go to my friends on a Thursday for tea. We are all staying forever. (Leila)

Twenty-three of the children were, as we saw it, strongly committed to their current foster families. All agreed (or at least no one disagreed) that they were happy where they were. Generally they understood why they were looked after, and accepted the reasons for it. They felt they belonged in the foster family, that they were cared for and often that they were loved. They had varying attitudes to their own families but did not feel torn between conflicting loyalties. They wanted to stay 'forever'.

Many of these children were quite young. However, there were also older children in our case studies who have had longer settled histories. Hailey provides an example of one of these. The reviewer saw the apparent success of Hailey's placement as reflecting the skill and creativity of the social worker, the excellence of the foster carers and the degree of partnership developed between the grandparents, social worker and foster family. The lessons she drew concerned the need to support such placements by providing positive feedback and appropriate training, not overloading them and honouring commitments (the carers had been promised short breaks four years earlier, but had only just been given one and felt under-valued as a result).

Essentially then what seems to be required is simple: committed, sensitive carers able to handle the child's behaviour, a level of contact with the family that the child can accept and a clear permanent plan for the future that gives the child security. Nothing in the remaining cases in this group suggests that this explanation does not apply to all of them.

**Case Study: Hailey**

> Hailey has a superb foster carer; superb relationship between the families, foster carer and grandparents, school is brilliant, fabulous. (Social Worker)

Hailey entered the care system at the age of about nine and is now nearly 15. Her family history was very sad. Her mother had committed suicide when she was less than one. Her father was killed in an accident shortly after. Her grandparents then looked after her for six years but they were elderly and found it increasingly difficult to cope, managing initially on their own and then with the aid of short breaks. Finally, when they were in their eighties and one of them was ill, Hailey started to be looked after by the carers who had provided short breaks.

Hailey has learning difficulties and an 'autistic disorder', something that was originally missed in the concerns over her grief. This, however, has not prevented what seems to be generally regarded as a truly successful placement. This is seen as offering 'permanent substitute care' with the plan that the carers continue to care for Hailey when she is an adult. According to the social worker Hailey has a 'superb foster carer' and a 'brilliant school'; a small class with an approach geared to autistic children and a very committed teacher. There is a support package with an excellent community nurse and short breaks with a school support worker and there is further support from the carers' daughters who spend a lot of time with Hailey.

A key feature of this situation is that the grandparents are still in the picture:

> Foster care family and grandparents are really close. They are on the phone regularly. Foster carers show grandparents all Hailey's school books and send them mother's day cards and involve them in everything. Grandmother is given the biggest and best photos of Hailey by her foster carers.

Hailey's cousins are also in touch, although they are now at university so that contact is less frequent.

The reviewer commented that Hailey appeared extremely happy in the placement and is clearly loved by her carers. Hailey herself has difficulty in expressing her feelings but all concerned seemed to concur with this judgement, which was further supported by the reviewers' observations of the interaction between Hailey and her foster carers.

The cases do, however, illustrate the variety of factors that may help or hinder this situation coming about. The presence of siblings seemed particularly important. We placed one case dubiously in this group because he still could not see why he and his sibling had been separated. His commitment to the placement was somewhat muted. Another child was glad to be living with one sibling but happy not be with others so that 'we can have our own lives and stuff'. Generally, however, siblings wanted to be together.

Other factors also seemed to play a part in settling the children. Hence, they might accept their current situation because their parents had died, because living at home was so manifestly awful, because they had decided that their mother did not love them and transferred their love elsewhere, or because as in the previous case studies they had the contact they wanted. The presence of siblings helped provide a sense of continuity; but so too did cultural and ethnic matching (e.g. a Muslim as opposed to a Christian household), or living in the same neighbourhood. School could be a decided asset, but it was possible to survive hating school if the carers were good. The key role played by good carers ran like a golden thread through all these cases.

This group of cases also raised a question about the importance of the child's previous life. Some children in this group had been previously loved, albeit in a chaotic situation. Another child, Ellen, had not obviously been loved at all. For nine years her mother had been unable to tolerate her enuresis, allegedly made her sleep on the kitchen floor, and at other times stuffed paper in her mouth, made her the scapegoat and subjected her to unrealistic expectations. Ellen was now happy and settled in a foster placement where she was 'treated properly'. Her response, however, was rather more muted and her commitment less wholehearted than those of others. The issue of previous treatment returns in the next section.

## Care as a weak base

We thought that 19 of the children in these cases were 'not going home' but nevertheless had only a weak base in their current placement. We classified the reasons for the lack of commitment in these placements into four groups.

First, some children were in placements to which they could not be expected to make an emotional commitment. Some were in placements they knew to be short-term, others were in residential care or supported lodgings. One or two were in placements where the carers seemed unable to make an emotional commitment to them.

Second, some children appeared unable to commit to a placement because they were still emotionally invested in another one. Usually this was a commitment to their own parent or parents, although it could be to previous adoptive parents or foster carers.

Third, some children had suffered the breakdown of placements. Some had lost placements in which they had invested a great deal. As the reviewer commented of one case, 'I believe the loss of the [first] foster carers for Ian has been immense. His future is in the balance'. Others had been actively maltreated in placements that had gone on for a number of years. Either of these earlier experiences appeared able to leave the child wary and unable to commit to a new family.

Fourth, some children had had prolonged periods without any settled placement at all. This often arose from a number of reasons. Sometimes it had not become apparent that placement at home was simply not going to work. The child then shuffled between home and placement. Sometimes the child had been under some kind of 'planning blight' – the social workers' understandable determination to find an ethnic match, to have the child adopted, or to keep children with their siblings meant that the decision to go for a permanent placement was postponed. Commonly these difficulties were accompanied by somewhat challenging behaviour that only added to the problems.

These problems were not mutually exclusive. Frances exemplifies a number of them. She was emotionally committed to her own family, she had had many placements and she was currently in one that was short-term. She had not experienced the breakdown of a placement in which she had invested a great deal. It is understandable that she should be reluctant to risk such investment or that she should want more control over placement choice than she felt she got.

### Case Study: Frances

> I want carers to remember that the children are angry about moving away from their parents and then say things that they don't mean...
> I feel like I have been dumped on doorsteps... I have been to seven schools and three since I came into care. (Frances)

Frances is ten years old. She was first removed from her mother about five years ago, when the local council became concerned about her mother's drug use, chaotic way of life, lack of parenting capacity and choice of partners. One of these injured Frances and there was a belief that her mother might not be able to protect her.

At first Frances lived with her grandmother, who sadly then died. Since that time she has had seven placements in the past five years. Four of these placements have ended because of Frances's behaviour and two of them because of unfounded allegations she has made. The plan throughout has been to find a long-term placement but so far none has been found and lasted. Frances likes her present placement, but it is a short-term one and her carers have said that they cannot keep her long-term. Her social worker feels that Frances's unstable life has made it difficult for her to form relationships with her carers. In addition, other professionals are not prepared to provide psychological support until she is in a long-term placement.

Given these difficulties Frances is surprisingly philosophic. Whereas she has apparently made allegations both during and after placements, she had good things to say about almost all her placements and described one as 'absolutely perfect'. She says she is happy where she is and likes her social worker because 'he is not frightened to tell me off'. That said she still feels that social services need to think more about what children need and that children should have more choice about long-term placements, being able to visit first and sleep over so that they could get a feel for the place.

## Family and friends care

This is my home and this is my family. I think I'll be here until I'm 19 or so. (Young person in a kin placement)

Many of the children in our case studies had placements with relatives or friends that for one reason or another did not last. Sometimes grandparents were too ill to manage or even died. Aunts and uncles could also find that alternative responsibilities were too much. Statistically, however, placements with family and friends had advantages, although, on average, as we will see later, these placements were seen as of less high quality by social workers. Nevertheless, they lasted longer and were more likely to be seen as meeting their purposes. Children in these placements also did better on a measure of 'well-being'.

The advantages and disadvantages of such placements have been well documented – most recently by Farmer and her colleagues (2005) and Hunt and hers (2007). They benefit from their origin in the choice of children and carers, the commitment of the latter and maintenance of family identity and ties. On the negative side, carers may lack skill in parenting challenging children, they are often poor and ill-housed, and often fall out with the birth parents, a result either of pre-existing quarrels or of conflicts introduced by the placement (see also Sinclair, Gibbs and Wilson 2004; Sinclair 2005).

There were eight cases in our case studies where the aim was to provide a long-term placement with family or kin. Taken together they illustrated both the advantages and the potential drawbacks of this form of placement.

Helen's case illustrates the advantages. Both sides know each other and want the placement. There is some continuity. The arrangement is 'normal' whereas, as we will see in some other cases, issues of family loyalty are not necessarily resolved. At the same time, Helen's sister (the carer) has herself recently been looked after. This may give her empathy with Helen's situation, but it is unlikely to have left her financially well off. She may also have issues of her own. In these ways she may fit the picture of kin carers in other research in that she may be more disadvantaged than other carers and whereas highly committed may not have excellent parenting skills.

---

**Case Study: Helen**

> I didn't know what to do if the carers had a family event and were taking family photos. (Helen)

Helen is 14 and placed on a care order with her elder sister. The placement has so far lasted two months so it is early days. Before this Helen has had a rather turbulent history that included her becoming looked after at the age of nine because of neglect and a poor relationship with her mother. The problems at that time seem to have been long-standing and the standard of care was getting worse not better. The aim therefore was for a permanent foster placement.

This aim proved hard to achieve. Over the past four and a half years Helen has had seven placements. Three of these were short-term. Three, however, were intended to be long-term. These three all broke down because of Helen's attitude and behaviour. She herself was initially opposed to the idea of coming into care. Now, however, she is reconciled to it. She is, however, critical of the number of carers she has had. She also feels that carers should not be registered with the council if they cannot cope with difficult teenagers, 'all children in care have problems'.

Helen is now pleased to be back with her sister. Both she and her sister are critical of the fact that a family placement was not explored earlier. Both hope that the current placement will last until Helen is able to cope on her own. As for the lessons that might be learnt, the reviewer agrees with Helen that it is a matter for concern that many carers are unable to cope with difficult behaviour and that this is perhaps an issue for training. The reviewer also thinks that a family placement might have been provided earlier.

---

Like Helen, Grace (seven years old) illustrates both the strengths and potential difficulties of these kinds of placements. She started to be looked after when she was just over one and she has lived with her aunt and siblings for four years. Grace told the reviewer 'I can't remember living anywhere else – I've always lived here'. She remains on a full care order. There is currently no contact with either parent though the plan is to reassess this in the future. The plan remains to support the kinship arrangement long term. Grace is apparently happy. She told the reviewer 'I like my school and my toys… I've got lots of friends to play with'. She wants to live with her aunt 'forever'.

Despite this apparently smooth progress, the social worker reported some concerns by professionals about the placement. These focused on the possible risks of breakdown, the carer's ability to meet the emotional needs of the children or manage their behaviour, her reluctance to attend foster carer training and 'lack of openness' with the department, and the older sibling's behaviour towards Grace. The carer was wary of the social worker's role and Grace herself was reluctant to talk for fear of being removed. However, additional support services from a family centre worker (including life story work), after-school club and holiday schemes had been helpful in stabilising the situation.

The issue of relationships between families in such placements occurs in this sample also. Karen provides an example. On the one hand she says that she remembers little about moving to her grandfather's house permanently as she used to spend a lot of time there anyway. She told the reviewer she was happy about being with her grandfather: 'it's nicer than living with a stranger' and her grandfather 'encourages her to go out and also with her school work'. She wants to return to live with her mum full time, but understands this will happen 'when the time is right'.

The social worker believed that if Karen had been in foster care rather than kinship care then she might have been able to return to her mother's care earlier. The grandfather and the mother were not on good terms. The reviewer highlighted the potential dilemma for children in kinship care who may 'feel torn between relatives' and questioned how social workers could best work with children over this division of loyalties. However she also felt that Karen has received a good upbringing from her grandfather and that this would help her to make a success of returning home.

In other cases this issue of family relationships was, at least temporarily, resolved by the fact that there was no contact with birth parents. Two young people (Paula and Grace) had no contact. Another (Nina) lived a long way away and almost certainly had no contact with her parents. A fourth (Carl) had moved from his parents two years previously. He spoke a lot of his grandparents, aunts, uncles, pets, computer and school, but the reviewer noted that he made no reference to either parent. Surprisingly he said that he could not remember living in any house other than that in which he now was.

The need for support, highlighted in the case of Grace, also occurred elsewhere. One reviewer commented:

> The kinship arrangement is working out well for the children. However the impact on the grandparents is probably underestimated by the department. There are some key issues to address – finance, overcrowding and the carer not feeling well-supported. (Reviewer)

These issues were not inevitable. Councils could be generous. Placements with family could allow more frequent contact with birth parents (indeed the evidence is that on average this is what they do (Sinclair *et al.* 2005a)). In these circumstances an advantage was that the situation was 'natural', the child could return when the time felt right and the placement did not automatically end at a fixed date. In these ways a placement could achieve the elusive combination of stability and a capacity to take advantage of a change in the situation at home.

Despite the difficulties, the cases give a stronger impression of the strengths of these placements than of their difficulties. Grace's is the only case about which serious difficulties were being raised and these seemed to be being resolved.

## No place to be

> Mum couldn't handle me and Dad said he didn't want me anymore. (Looked after young person)

The aim in the cases described so far was that the child should have a long-term placement. In 14 cases this aim had apparently been given up. In general these children and young people were older than those so far discussed. Their problems were in some respects similar to those of the children we have already described as having a weak base; a refusal to accept admission to care, challenging behaviour, a high degree of movement. Their behavioural problems were, however, more severe; almost all were in lodgings, Institutions for Young Offenders, or, most common of all, in children's homes. While some were, indeed, committed to their establishments, this commitment did not seem to be the same as that of some foster children to their long-term placement. Unable to return home and without a base in care they had, in effect, no place to be.

Lewis provides an example of a young person in this position. Things did not work out at home and they did not work out in care. He had no base. In practice Lewis seems to have had some commitment to his home – at the least he returned there often. He shared this preference with a number of the young people in this group of whom Graham was the youngest. In this situation, care, it seemed, was used as an alternative to living at home, rather than, as Graham wished, a method of 'getting your head together' as a condition of and prior to return home. This,

---

**Case Study: Lewis**

> I'm not even thinking about my future, not now anyway. I'd rather do my time then think about it. (Lewis)

Lewis (18) came into care approximately 12 years ago, at the age of six, following physical and emotional abuse by his mother. Since then he has had a very turbulent care career with well over 20 placements, predominantly in residential units as a child, and in bed and breakfast accommodation, with key worker support, as a teenager. He has interspersed these placements with periods at home with his mother, while still being on a care order. The social worker said that the change of placements had been due to Lewis' difficult behaviour (including criminal activity) and that the placements with his mother had had a bad effect and were often ended by arguments. His siblings are also in care and he has very little contact with them.

Recently Lewis has had an unsuccessful placement in a supported flat, spells in bed and breakfast, and a brief period with his mother. He wants his own flat and is currently in a Young Offenders' Institution. Lewis was quite positive about care 'better than other places, put it that way…different, like more freedom'. Unlike most children in this group he felt he exercised some control over his placements, 'they just asked me like and I told them where I wanna go and that's it'. He does not feel particularly in control at the moment.

---

however, seemed to be, in effect, a necessary requirement. If the young people were unable to modify their behaviour, they seemed to have no chance of being able to make a success of going home.

Like Graham, some of these young people were against the idea of foster care. Denise maintained quite close contact with her family from her residential home. She had not been too bothered about leaving home at 15 '…they only tried to move me [into care] 'cos of me doing drugs and living all over the place'. She had, however, strong feelings about her first placement in foster care. She said that this was 'horrible, like jumping into another person's family', so she 'told the social worker she was going'. As she saw it, residential homes were not much better. Denise called them 'shit holes'.

The objection to foster care was based on a loyalty to family. Others, however, had no desire to go home. In practice, some of these seem to have had at least a hidden desire for an alternative base. Sometimes this was apparent in their use of residential care. One, for example, saw the children in her residential home

**Case Study: Graham**

No one can tell me what to do. (Graham)

Graham is now 11 years old. His school had reported problems since the age of six, when he began assaulting staff and pupils. He was first looked after at the age of eight following a particularly violent assault on someone of his own age. Neither parent acknowledged any responsibility for him. All his elder siblings had been in trouble with the law. Both parents had been in custody for drug misuse and assaults. His primary caregiver was his grandmother who felt she could not manage him. For the first three years, intensive attempts were made to help with his behaviour, and enable his mother and his grandmother to respond appropriately to him.

Graham's first placement was in a children's home with education on the premises. Unfortunately his difficulties escalated and included the use of ecstasy, cannabis and amphetamines, offending and periods of going missing, during which he was thought to place himself at risk. After this an attempt was made to manage him through foster care and through placement with his grandmother. With the failure of these placements he was again tried in various residential establishments that could not contain his violent assaults. He is at present in secure accommodation. The plan is still to help him with his behaviour.

Graham himself is very dissatisfied with the moves and where he is. He is bored in secure accommodation and resents not being able to smoke. The only redeeming features are the food, the DVDs, and TV. As for the earlier placements he liked his foster carers whom he saw as down to earth. However, he feels that he should not be in foster care as he has his own family. In this respect a children's home is better. Basically, he wants to be with his grandmother, 'where he can do what he likes'. He also wants everyone to stay out of his business. Failing this, he wants to go to a particular children's home, where they were 'real nice' and helped him 'sort out his head'.

as surrogate siblings and was grateful for the stability that they and the staff had provided. Others were grateful for the willingness of residential homes to stick with them and take them back. Education was also a source of stability and self-esteem for some of these young people.

Laura, for example, said her current children's home was the best placement because 'you don't get wrong as much and that...there's nothing about here I don't like, except half the staff'. She said she had settled in well, had remained at the same school and was able to see old friends. She said the plan was for her to stay at the children's home until she was 'old enough to leave'.

A difficulty with the use of residential care as a base was that it was, almost by definition, a somewhat impermanent one. Staff left. Young people came and went. The local council was not keen to incur the expense of residential care, particularly if 'out of county' and for prolonged periods. Voluntary agencies closed residential homes as they sought to redirect their resources to what they considered more appropriate ends. Many of these young people had rejected foster care. Nevertheless some seemed to have a latent desire for the kind of lasting relationships that foster care can provide.

In general the young people voiced two desires. First, others should listen to them, and give them a chance to select their placements. Second, they themselves should not be moved around so much. What seemed to be difficult was to amalgamate these requirements. The young people generally found their frequent movements inexplicable, thus failing to make a connection between their behaviour and their changes of placement that seemed obvious enough to an outsider. At the same time placements in the care system proved more fragile than those with the child's own family. Behaviour threatens but rarely finally ruptures the ties between family members. Foster and residential placements are less robust. Sarah illustrates the feelings that may arise.

---

### Case Study: Sarah

> They don't understand the effect it has keeping moving you; they should've worked with me. I used to think it must be me, I thought everyone must hate me, move her on. I lost loads of friends. I had loads of social workers too. I know I done wrong but it makes you feel so bad about yourself. You wouldn't do it to a normal kid so why should I be any different? (Sarah)

Sarah felt that her social workers should have asked her what she wanted. She hated the fact that everything was written down and thought workers spent more time doing paperwork rather than getting to know children and only listened when she 'kicked off':

> They don't take time to get to know you; they just read about you and assume. If people bother to get to know me they find I'm not all bad, if you're in care people assume it's your fault.

Sarah was hurt and angry about the way moves between placements had been organised. In the past she was not told what was happening face-to-face, 'social workers don't have the guts to tell you – I was told

> about moves through letters, telephone calls, care staff' and there had been a lack of warning and preparation, 'another time I woke up one morning and they said "get your things packed – they're coming for you in 5 minutes" – I was very angry'.
>
> Sarah said she was happy for the first time in her present residential placement because 'they're honest with me, not doing things behind my back'. Sarah has aspirations to go to university to study law. 'I'm determined to prove everyone wrong. So much that's happened to me is unfair. I want to put it right'.

By definition care for this group of young people had not 'worked'. For this reason it is hard to say what would make things better. Our suggestion is that whatever is done has to meet two criteria:

1.  It has to make 'sense' to the young person in terms of the way they want their life to go and the relationships they want to have.

2.  It has to involve excellent placements that address the problems that the young people have.

## Conclusion

For good or ill some children have to use the care system as a permanent base. 'Objectively' this can be defined as continuing to be looked after for a reasonable length of time, without a plan for return, and without an undue number of placements. Subjectively, some children use this opportunity to become attached to their carers. Others do not. Our case studies suggest that the chance of either outcome depends on a number of factors. These include:

- the children's behavioural difficulties
- whether the carer is known or related to them
- the effect of their earlier experience at home or 'in care' on their ability to make new attachments
- their view of care and of whether they want to go home
- the quality of their carers
- school and friends.

This means that steps to give more security to these children must take into account their behaviour and their relationships with their family, their carers and their school.

In terms of behaviour it may be important to:

- equip carers to deal with challenging behaviour (some carers seemed much better able to do this than others)

- work with young people to enable them to modify their behaviour in situations where they wish to return home or to a particular carer but are unlikely to do so successfully unless they change (as in Treatment Foster Care) (a suggestion that arises from the situation of those with 'no place to be').

In terms of the children's view of their family it may be important to work with the children's view of the situation, meeting those wishes that can be met (e.g. over contact) and enabling them to come to terms with those that cannot. This may mean:

- always considering placements with relatives (something also supported by our later statistics) but keeping a wary eye for their difficulties

- placing siblings together unless there are strong reasons against this (the absence of siblings was one of the reasons that some children appeared less happy with their placements than they might have been)

- taking a wide view of family contact and always considering contact with grandparents and siblings as well as parents (contact with grandparents was clearly a strength in some of our cases)

- counselling the child to enable them to relinquish feelings of responsibility for family (one project seemed to be having success with this)

- negotiating contact with family and siblings of a kind and frequency with which the child is comfortable (frequent contact was clearly a strength in some cases while it was not in others).

Excellent carers and good relationships between carers and children are clearly a jewel beyond price. It is important to value and nurture them where they are found. This may mean:

- avoiding leaving children too long in placements if it is clear that these arrangements are damaging and are not going to work out (some young children had clearly stayed a long time in placements where they were very unhappy)

- being prepared to change a short-stay placement into a long-stay one if the placement 'works' and all concerned want this (some children were afraid they were going to have to leave placements in which they were happy, whereas others were 'marking time' with short-term carers)

- being careful about creating threats to placements that are going well (e.g. through the introduction of new foster children)

- working with foster families to which the child is committed but where there are difficulties, as would be done with the children's own families if their base was there (some children were still mourning the loss of valued placements)

- enabling those young people who do not feel ready to move on at 18 to remain with their carers (a suggestion that arises from our earlier chapter).

Finally, some young people were clearly drawing strength from their achievements at school. This suggests a need to do everything possible to ensure that a child is happy at school. It is possible to make suggestions as to how this should be done (see for example the account of foster carer practice in Walker *et al.* 2002). These suggestions, however, would not come from our case studies.

## Summary points for Chapter 10

The significance and, to some extent, likelihood of movement depend on whether a child needs to use their family as their base, find a new base within the care system, or use the system as a springboard to a new life. A successful base within the care system seems likely to depend on:

- the child's acceptance or otherwise of their need to be looked after

- the degree to which the child's previous experience is such that they find it easy to trust a new relationship

- the quality of the child's current carers (including parents where applicable) and how s/he gets on with them

- the degree to which the child is comfortable about the amount and nature of the contact s/he has with siblings and other family members

- how the child is getting on at school

- the child's behaviour and the capacity of the carers to cope with it

- the current stage in the child's care career and their view of their future.

The success of social work seems to depend partly on the ability of social workers to make realistic assessments of these factors, to influence them and to work, as far as possible, with the grain of what the child and their family want. Later chapters in this book explore these issues statistically.

## Note

1    These children may present all three of the difficulties which another manager singled out as difficult for foster carers – sexualised behaviour which raises fears of allegations, attachment disorders, which make it difficult for carers to care for children who make only a superficial emotional response, and violent behaviour which is obviously hard to handle in the home.

Chapter 11

# Children and Outcomes

We actually do reasonably well overall. For the, if you like, the vast majority of our children, I think we do quite well and…stability is good, the number we've got in family placements is good…we perform quite well. The trouble is, I suppose I'm mainly involved in the problems…there is the group, it's probably quite a relatively small percentage, which are the young people, the kids with the greatest and most complex needs and they feel pretty unstable, and I guess that's the case in every Local Authority. (Manager)

## Introduction

Our case studies suggested that there were three primary determinants of outcome: the child's age and behaviour, their view of where they wish to be, and the quality of their carers. The next four chapters pick up these themes. They are concerned with outcomes and what determines them. One of their purposes is to test the hypotheses that the case studies provide.

Our primary concern is with what can be done to produce better outcomes, so we want to know whether these are affected by differences between councils, in the kinds or quality of placements or between social work teams. First, however, we need to explore the relationship between the children's characteristics and their outcomes. We can then examine whether the differences between children may explain any apparent effects of the councils, teams and placements that serve them.

## Method

We looked at three main groups of variables:

1.  Basic characteristics: age, sex, ethnic origin.

2. Care careers: age at first entry, repeat admissions, length of care career, whether latest admission within the last year.

3. Behaviour and experience: family difficulty score, challenging behaviour score, school performance score and care acceptance score.

We related these to four measures of outcome. Three of these measures (the A1 'three placements', D35 and the new PSA Indicator) have already been described in Chapter 9. However, we also used a measure of 'doing-well' that will be described later.

Typically we found that sex and ethnic origin were not related to these outcomes and they therefore appear rather little in the chapter. We then used a variety of statistical techniques to explore the apparent effects of combinations of the other variables on outcomes.

The design of the study means that our conclusions are less certain than we would like. Two difficulties are particularly important. First, we can never be sure that we have taken account of all the important differences between children. So it may be, for example, that we attribute to councils effects that actually arise from differences in the children they serve. Second, much of our information is collected at only one point in time, so we are unable to measure improvement directly by comparing our outcome measures at two points in time.[1] Instead we measure apparent improvement by seeing if the children appear to be doing better than expected given, for example, their need code on entry to the system.

These difficulties are to be expected. Our study is broad and exploratory. Many of the questions we are asking are new or, at the least, are being asked in new ways. We are, for example, not aware of any similar statistical investigation of the effects of local councils or departments on outcomes. This then is new territory. The journey is, we feel, an exciting if difficult one. The results are much more clear-cut and plausible than we had expected. We hope that the reader will equally feel that the effort is worthwhile.

## Stability: the A1 measure

Our individual reports for the 13 councils showed that those children who had three or more placements in a year differed from the others. Briefly, they showed more challenging behaviour, were less likely to accept that they needed to be looked after, and showed a greater variety of difficulties at school. They were also consistently less likely to have high ratings for emotional well-being, or attachments to at least one adult, or to be settled in their placements.

There was, however, one caveat to these findings. The differences were only apparent among those who were aged 11 or over. In some councils there was evidence that a few children under this age might be moving placements because of extremely difficult behaviour. The numbers, however, were not large enough to reach statistical significance. In general the conclusion was that some adolescents were having three or more placements for reasons connected with their behaviour and personality. Younger children seemed to be having three or more placements for other reasons.

These findings chimed with some of the opinions expressed by social workers and managers. The stereotype of a 'high mover' was definitely a teenager. By contrast they also talked of occasions when three placements in a year represented good practice. The most common example involved a baby moved from a hospital, to a short-term placement and then within a surprisingly short interval to an adoptive placement. One manager could speak for a number:

> An across the board indicator across ages probably isn't helpful. A high indicator of moves amongst teenagers, assuming it's the same teenagers, you know what I mean, doing this, bouncing around, is, well, it's logical...you can understand the reasons. With younger children I think it's more complex quite often and needs sometimes close examination. (Manager)

We checked our local findings against the data from all 13 councils. We found that those children with three or more placements were more likely:

- to be aged 11 or over
- to enter for the first time over the age of 11
- to have had repeat admissions
- to have higher challenging behaviour scores
- to have lower school performance scores
- to be slightly less likely to accept care.

We examined the pattern of findings for those over and under the age of 11.

When the young person was aged 11 or over, those with three or more placements were again more likely than others to have entered over the age of 11, to behave in a challenging way, to be doing badly at school and to reject care.

When the child was under 11, those with three or more placements were more likely to be performing badly at school and to be having repeat admissions (possibly because a repeat admission within a year already provides a minimum of two placements). They did not differ in other ways. So with the exception of their school performance (which could be explained by the effects of the moves themselves), they did not appear unduly difficult.

Table 11.1 illustrates these findings. As can be seen the difference between high and low levels of challenging behaviour seems to make no difference. Children with high levels of challenging behaviour move more but only if they

**Table 11.1** Level of challenging behaviour by three or more placements by age

| Aged 11 or over at census | | | | Three or more placements in year | | |
|---|---|---|---|---|---|---|
| | | | | No | Yes | Total |
| No | Level of challenging behaviour | Very low | Count | 368 | 60 | 428 |
| | | | % within Level of challenging behaviour | 86.0% | 14.0% | 100.0% |
| | | Low | Count | 446 | 82 | 528 |
| | | | % within Level of challenging behaviour | 84.5% | 15.5% | 100.0% |
| | | High | Count | 277 | 49 | 326 |
| | | | % within Level of challenging behaviour | 85.0% | 15.0% | 100.0% |
| | | Very high | Count | 300 | 78 | 378 |
| | | | % within Level of challenging behaviour | 79.4% | 20.6% | 100.0% |
| | | Total | Count | 1391 | 269 | 1660 |
| | | | % within Level of challenging behaviour | 83.8% | 16.2% | 100.0% |
| Yes | Level of challenging behaviour | Very low | Count | 304 | 55 | 359 |
| | | | % within Level of challenging behaviour | 84.7% | 15.3% | 100.0% |
| | | Low | Count | 510 | 90 | 600 |
| | | | % within Level of challenging behaviour | 85.0% | 15.0% | 100.0% |
| | | High | Count | 328 | 86 | 414 |
| | | | % within Level of challenging behaviour | 79.2% | 20.8% | 100.0% |
| | | Very high | Count | 485 | 258 | 743 |
| | | | % within Level of challenging behaviour | 65.3% | 34.7% | 100.0% |
| | | Total | Count | 1627 | 489 | 2116 |
| | | | % within Level of challenging behaviour | 76.9% | 23.1% | 100.0% |

Source: CIS and Social Worker data.

are aged over 11. Children with very high levels of challenging behaviour are more likely to have three or more placements in both age groups. Only those over the age of 11 with very high levels of challenging behaviour have a very high level of movement on this measure. Other groups must generally acquire three or more placements for reasons unconnected with their behaviour.

We next looked at the relationship between our variables taken as a set and whether or not the child had three or more placements at the end of the year. Our best 'model' suggested that three or more placements were more likely when:

- the child had experienced a repeat admission $(p < .001)^2$
- was aged 11 or over $(p < .001)$
- had a relatively low school performance score $(p = .007)$
- had a relatively high challenging behaviour score $(p = .142)$
- was aged 11 or over and had a relatively high challenging behaviour score $(p = .013)$
- had been looked after for less than a year $(p = .025)$.[3]

One striking feature of this model is that although it passes the relevant levels of significance with flying colours it is not a useful predictor. The model successfully predicts 99.7 per cent of those who did not have three or more placements. However, its success in predicting those who did have three or more placements is extremely poor. It fails to predict 97.2 per cent of them. It seems that our measures are largely irrelevant to the question of who has three or more placements. We return later to the question of why this should be so.

## Stability: the D35 measure

We carried out a similar analysis for the long-term stability (D35) measure. As will be remembered this is defined as the proportion of those who have been continuously looked after for four years who have been fostered with the same carer for at least the last two. Comparisons across the whole group showed that:

- those aged 11 or over, those who were first looked after above this age, males, and those with repeat admissions were less likely to score 'positive' on this measure (D35)
- those who had high challenging behaviour scores and low school performance were also less likely to score 'positive' on this measure (D35)

- the associations between challenging behaviour and low school performance were much stronger among those aged 11 or over than among younger children.[4]

We used the same variables to predict 'positive scores' on this measure.

**Table 11.2** Logistic regression predicting D35 stability measure

| Independent variables | B | SE | Wald | df | Sig. | Exp(b) |
|---|---|---|---|---|---|---|
| Experienced a repeat admission | −.606 | .127 | 22.709 | 1 | .000 | .546 |
| Challenging Behaviour Score | .339 | .323 | 1.100 | 1 | .294 | 1.403 |
| Eleven years or over at census date | −.119 | .154 | .603 | 1 | .437 | .888 |
| Interaction between behaviour score and aged 11+ at census | −.463 | .176 | 6.938 | 1 | .008 | .630 |
| Acceptance of care score | .246 | .072 | 11.542 | 1 | .001 | 1.279 |
| Constant | −1.073 | .461 | 5.407 | 1 | .020 | .342 |

Source: CIS and Social Worker data. Note: Table restricted to those looked after continuously for 4 years or more.

In this combined analysis children were less likely to be stably fostered if:

- they had had a repeat admission
- they were aged 11 or over *and* behaving in a challenging way[5]
- they did not accept their need for care.

This equation successfully predicted 65 per cent of those who were stably fostered and 61 per cent of those who were not. In this case, our measures, while clearly not the whole story, were obviously a very important part of it.

## Stability: the new measure

Finally, we carried out a similar analysis for the PSA 'new indicator' measure. As will be remembered this focuses on those who are under 16 and have been looked after continuously for at least two and a half years. The measure is the proportion of this group who have been placed for adoption in the past year or looked after in the same placement for the past two years. Comparisons across the whole group showed that:

- those aged 11 or over, and those with repeat admissions were less likely to score 'positive' on this measure

- those who had high challenging behaviour scores and/or low school performance scores were also less likely to score 'positive' on this measure

- the associations between this measure and challenging behaviour and low school performance were stronger among those aged 11 or over than among younger children.

We again tried to predict the measure on the basis of the same variables as the last. We found that:

- children with repeat admissions were less likely to be successful on this measure

- children over the age of 11 and displaying difficult behaviour were less likely to be successful on this measure.

Once we had taken these variables into account, neither being a teenager nor showing challenging behaviour were significantly associated with the outcome.[6]

This model predicts 89 per cent of those who were successful and 26 per cent of those that were not.


## The 'doing-well' score

We calculated a 'doing-well' score in addition to our other three measures of outcome. We asked the social workers to rate six measures of outcome. All were on a four-point scale from 'very poor/many problems' to 'very well/few problems'. These related to:

- emotional well-being

- behaviour

- positive adult ties

- settled in current placement or where currently living

- getting on in education/occupation

- safe and doing well.

The correlations between these variables varied from .55 to .74. We added them together to form a 'doing-well' score with the high scores being the more favourable ones. As can be seen this measure might be expected to be high among those who, in the language of our case studies, had a 'strong base' in the care system.

The variables we used to predict this measure were necessarily rather different from those that appear earlier in this chapter. It is, after all, rather obvious that a measure that covers schooling and behaviour will relate to measures of behaviour and school performance. For these reasons we concentrated on measures of family difficulty and care career and included the number of placements the child had had. Table 11.3 gives the details of our 'best' model. (Those unfamiliar with tables of this kind may like to refer to the note at the end of the chapter for suggestions on how to read them.)[7]

**Table 11.3** Regression equation for 'doing-well' measure

| Model | | Unstandardised coefficients[a] | | Standardised coefficients[a] | | |
|---|---|---|---|---|---|---|
| | | B | Std. Error | Beta | t | Sig. |
| 1 | (Constant) | 1.189 | .015 | | 79.380 | .000 |
| | More than one admission | −1.631E-02 | .003 | −.088 | −5.378 | .000 |
| | Log of days since last admission | 1.458E-02 | .001 | .222 | 13.724 | .000 |
| | Age at census | −5.170E-03 | .000 | −.230 | −13.871 | .000 |
| | Family Difficulty Score | −3.321E-02 | .006 | −.097 | −5.929 | .000 |
| | Child accepts need to be looked after | 2.100E-02 | .002 | .202 | 13.037 | .000 |
| | Number of placements | −2.976E-03 | .000 | −.155 | −9.238 | .000 |
| | Sex | 1.567E-02 | .003 | .084 | 5.489 | .000 |

[a] Dependent variable: 'Doing-well' measure.
Source: CIS and Social Worker data.

The equation we produced explained relatively little of our measure.[8] The associations were, however, highly significant. The children and young people who scored 'worst' on the 'doing-well' measure tended to be male, older, to have spent relatively little time looked after since their last admission, to have had had more than one admission and to have had a relatively large number of placements. In addition they were more likely not to accept that they needed to be looked after and to have families that had either abused them or were marked by domestic violence or substance abuse. In short, it was not easy for them to be looked after and not easy for them to be at home. This dilemma was equally signalled by the failures of the attempts to return home and the number of placements they had had.

## Conclusion

This analysis suggests a number of interesting conclusions:

- Difficult behaviour and poor performance at school were much more strongly linked with instability among those who were aged over 11 than among the younger age group.

- Even in this older group these problems accounted for very little of the movement measured by the 'three placements' in a year variable.

- The problems were more successful in predicting failure on the new PSA indicator.

- They were much more successful in predicting failure on the long-term D35 indicator.

At first sight these findings are rather disparate. At the same time they do seem to connect with those in Chapter 9. The difficulty of predicting the A1 three placements measure on the basis of the difficulties of particular children may arise because much movement, particularly in the early stages of a care career, is intentional. It therefore does not reflect the characteristics likely to predict placement breakdown. Children move because adults want them to move and this may be particularly true of children under the age of 11.

The longer a child remains looked after the more likely it is that he or she will have a placement that is meant to last. Breakdowns are therefore likely to be much more important sources of movement. It is therefore not surprising that the children's difficulties are important predictors of 'failure' on the new PSA and D35 measures.

## Notes

1  There is also the possibility that our outcome measures are affected by differences in perception between councils rather than by differences in performance. For example, social workers in councils that serve many 'emotionally troubled' children may raise their threshold for a rating of 'emotional disturbance' simply because they are so used to it. We do not think this is a serious problem. If it were we would expect, for example, that councils that had higher proportions of children who entered at a late age (who tend to be more disturbed) would do better with these children than other councils. This does not seem to be the case.

2  Contrary to our general rule we quote significance levels since a number of them are low.

3  These findings are based on children of school age. We can include a wider range of children by leaving out the school performance score. This leaves the results essentially unchanged with the exception that 'the combined effect' of displaying challenging behaviour and being over the age of 11 becomes highly significant.

4  The interactions were significant.

5    In this book we report significant interactions when (a) we have also included the individual terms in the interaction (i.e. in this case, age and the challenging behaviour score) and (b) the addition of the interaction terms significantly increases the power of the model.

6    Models that include interaction terms always include the terms that make these up as independent variables (e.g. if we include the interaction of behaviour and age we always include both behaviour and age). It can occur that these variables do not have significant coefficients. In such cases we only accept the model if it accounts for a significantly higher proportion of the variation than was the case for the model without the interaction term.

7    A regression uses some 'facts' about children (e.g. their age and family difficulty scores) to estimate another 'fact' (e.g. a score to measure how well they are doing). It does this through an equation that looks roughly like this 'Estimated score for child = (a number × age) + (another number × family difficulty score)'. The important columns in Table 11.3 are those that give the 'standardised coefficients'. These say how large the effect of a given variable is, after taking account of the others. A standardised coefficient of -1 (the lowest possible) would mean that the effect was very large and tended to reduce the score. A standardised coefficient of 1 (the highest possible) would again mean that the effect was very large but that it increased the score. The column under 'Sig.' says how likely it is that a coefficient of this size would be found if it was zero in the underlying population.

8    The adjusted R square was less than .18. In part this may be because of the crude nature of the measures. The more 'noise' there is in a variable the less it is likely to explain. In our case the same variable can have different meanings and consequences in different circumstances. For example, a child who returns to the care system to be fostered again with her grandmother when her mother goes temporarily into hospital may be counted as a repeat admission but may well not experience it as such. In addition we have not yet taken account of the quality of placement.

Chapter 12

# Placements and Outcomes

Quantitative statistics don't mean very much unless outcomes are effectively evaluated. Measuring the reasons for quality of provision is essential to obtaining a true picture. (Team Leader for Supervising Social Workers)

## Introduction

Our case studies, like other research (for summaries see Sinclair 2005 and Sinclair 2006), suggested that outcomes depended on the quality of the placement as well as on the characteristics of the child. In many respects what may matter is not whether a child is in foster care or residential care but how good or bad is the unit or placement in which they happen to find themselves.[1] How far does our statistical evidence reinforce or counteract this evidence? This issue is the focus for this and the next chapter.

In this chapter we ask three questions:

1. Were the children doing better in some kinds of placement than they were in others?

2. Were some kinds of placements seen as being of higher quality than others?

3. Were children in higher quality placements (as rated by the social workers) doing better than those in average or below average placements?

## Does the type of placement help predict outcomes?

Did our ability to predict outcomes improve with the addition of information on the kinds of placement the children had experienced? To explore this question we looked at the placements the children had at the beginning of the year and their outcomes at the end of it. Any child who was in residential care at the beginning of the year had, by definition, a 'bad' effect on the D35 indicator. In other respects:

- Children who had been placed in residential care or in agency foster placements at the beginning of the year did 'worse' than expected on both our 'doing-well' measure and the new PSA indicator.

- There were no differences between these groups on our three placements measure.

- Children fostered at the beginning of the year, particularly those fostered with family and friends, did better than expected on both our 'doing-well' measure and the new indicator.

In part these findings explained each other. For example, a fostered child could not be in residential care at the same time. So if foster children were doing better, children in residential care were likely to be doing worse.

A further caveat was that some at least of the findings might reflect selection and cost. The poor 'doing-well' scores of those who had been in residential care are not surprising: these young people had to be very troubled to get there. As already explained we could not take the children's backgrounds fully into account. Councils may also be unwilling to keep children for long periods in residential care because of the cost. This kind of care is therefore likely to be less stable. The comparatively poor performance of agency foster care on both the new stability indicator and the doing well measure may similarly reflect intake and cost.

As a check on these findings we analysed the kinds of placement by whether they were in the social workers' eyes 'fully successful'. By this we meant that they had lasted as long as needed and had met their aims. This measure is based on a professional judgement of how well a placement is doing and should take into account the child or young person's background.

As explained in the last chapter the social workers were very unlikely to say that a current placement had not lasted as long as needed. For this reason we concentrated in Table 12.1 on the previous placement rather than the current one. This in turn restricted our analysis to those who had had a previous placement in the last six months.

Obviously a placement may 'fail', not because it is inappropriate but simply because it is more likely to be used in difficult situations. We tested this idea with children's homes placements and placements with parents. We found that if one takes account of behaviour, age and age at entry, children's homes are not significantly less 'successful' than other placements while placements with parents are not significantly more 'successful'.

**Table 12.1** Last completed placement by full success

| Last placement | | Last placement fully successful | | |
| --- | --- | --- | --- | --- |
| | | No | Yes | Total |
| Foster with relatives | Count | 57 | 137 | 194 |
| | % within Last placement | 29.4% | 70.6% | 100.0% |
| Foster other | Count | 389 | 422 | 811 |
| | % within Last placement | 48.0% | 52.0% | 100.0% |
| Children's home | Count | 106 | 34 | 140 |
| | % within Last placement | 75.7% | 24.3% | 100.0% |
| Secure unit | Count | 9 | 9 | 18 |
| | % within Last placement | 50.0% | 50.0% | 100.0% |
| Hostel | Count | 43 | 25 | 68 |
| | % within Last placement | 63.2% | 36.8% | 100.0% |
| Placed for adoption | Count | 9 | 9 | 18 |
| | % within Last placement | 50.0% | 50.0% | 100.0% |
| Placed with parents | Count | 54 | 78 | 132 |
| | % within Last placement | 40.9% | 59.1% | 100.0% |
| Lodgings etc. | Count | 42 | 42 | 84 |
| | % within Last placement | 50.0% | 50.0% | 100.0% |
| Residential school | Count | 14 | 10 | 24 |
| | % within Last placement | 58.3% | 41.7% | 100.0% |
| Other residential | Count | 19 | 10 | 29 |
| | % within Last placement | 65.5% | 34.5% | 100.0% |
| Other form of placement | Count | 42 | 19 | 61 |
| | % within Last placement | 68.9% | 31.1% | 100.0% |
| Total | Count | 784 | 795 | 1579 |
| | % within Last placement | 49.7% | 50.3% | 100.0% |

Source: Social Worker data.
Note: Table is restricted to those with a placement completed in last six months.

By contrast a similar test for relative placements tends to confirm their 'competitive advantage'. Such placements increased the odds of full success by 80 per cent.

**Table 12.2** Logistic regression predicting whether last placement a success

| Independent variables | B | SE | Wald | df | Sig. | Exp(b) |
|---|---|---|---|---|---|---|
| Challenging Behaviour Score | −.691 | .061 | 126.447 | 1 | .000 | .501 |
| Entry when aged 11 or over | −.380 | .140 | 7.393 | 1 | .007 | .684 |
| Aged 11 or over | −.633 | .138 | 21.011 | 1 | .000 | .531 |
| Kin placement | .587 | .184 | 10.155 | 1 | .001 | 1.799 |
| Constant | .657 | .088 | 55.376 | 1 | .000 | 1.930 |

Source: Social Worker data.
Note: Table is restricted to those with a previous placement.

What happens if the analysis is restricted to children whose first previous place-ment was in foster care? Relative foster care is still more likely to be seen as suc-cessful – indeed it increases the odds of success by 140 per cent.

There was a fourfold variation between councils in the proportion of com-pleted placements that were with kin (5–22%). We wondered whether kin care would be less successful among those councils that made more use of it. Our rea-soning was that in these councils there would be more pressure on relatives to 'volunteer' and that the placements would be less successful as a result. There was no evidence for this. So as far as this piece of evidence went, the local councils with low usage of this type of placement would be safe in seeking to expand their use of relative foster care.[2]

There was, however, one related finding. Relative placements made up nearly a quarter (24%) of the placements intended for care and upbringing, but only six per cent of the much larger number of placements with other purposes. It was striking that the 'competitive advantage' of relative placements was restricted to the 55 per cent of them intended to provide care and upbringing. In these place-ments a kin placement increased the odds of 'success' by 320 per cent after we had taken account of relevant background variables. The comparable increase among the other group was six per cent and a long way from being significant.[3]

## Were some kinds of placement seen as being of higher quality than others?

We asked the social workers to rate the quality of the children's placements. They used a three-point scale: above average, average and below average. Understand-ably they were reluctant to label current placements below average. As a result the average rating of the last or latest placement was definitely 'above average'. Fifty-eight per cent were rated as 'above', and only five per cent as below.

This score differed significantly between placements. Table 12.3 compares the ratings for these different kinds of provision. The lowest was placement with parents. The 'best' was placement with adoptive parents, followed by placements in ordinary foster care and in residential schools.

**Table 12.3** Average placement quality scores by type of placement

| Last/latest placement | Quality of placement score (Mean) | N | Std. Deviation |
|---|---|---|---|
| Foster with relatives | 2.51 | 588 | .59 |
| Foster other | 2.63 | 2360 | .52 |
| Children's home | 2.36 | 313 | .57 |
| Secure unit | 2.33 | 18 | .48 |
| Hostel | 2.29 | 161 | .54 |
| Placed for adoption | 2.83 | 355 | .38 |
| Placed with parents | 2.04 | 343 | .65 |
| Lodgings etc. | 2.16 | 110 | .69 |
| Residential school | 2.56 | 74 | .49 |
| Other residential | 2.53 | 73 | .60 |
| Other form of placement | 2.26 | 71 | .67 |
| Total | 2.53 | 4466 | .58 |

Source: Social Worker data.

Among the commonly used placements 'ordinary' foster placements scored 'best', foster placements with relatives 'next best' and 'children's homes' worst. Table 12.4 gives more detail on this comparison.

Placements in children's homes in the independent sector were more likely to be seen as of high quality than those in the public one (see Table 12.5).

Previous work (Gibbs and Sinclair 1998; Hicks *et al.* 2007) has also suggested that placements in the independent sector have in certain respects better outcomes than those in the statutory sector.[4] Gibbs and Sinclair put forward two possible explanations. First, they provided evidence that the greater distance between the young people's homes and units in the independent sector provided some protection against the 'delinquent cultures' in which some young people were involved. Second, they suggested that distance also meant that the independent homes drew on a wider catchment area and so could provide a more

**Table 12.4** Three types of placement by quality of placement score

| Last/latest placement | | Quality of placement score | | | |
| --- | --- | --- | --- | --- | --- |
| | | Below average | Average | Above average | Total |
| Foster with relatives | Count | 29 | 225 | 334 | 588 |
| | % within Last/latest placement | 4.9% | 38.3% | 56.8% | 100.0% |
| Foster other | Count | 49 | 758 | 1553 | 2360 |
| | % within Last/latest placement | 2.1% | 32.1% | 65.8% | 100.0% |
| Children's home | Count | 16 | 167 | 130 | 313 |
| | % within Last/latest placement | 5.1% | 53.4% | 41.5% | 100.0% |
| Total | Count | 94 | 1150 | 2017 | 3261 |
| | % within Last/latest placement | 2.9% | 35.3% | 61.9% | 100.0% |

Source: Social Worker data.

**Table 12.5** Quality of placement score by type of agency

| Quality of placement score | | Type of agency | | |
| --- | --- | --- | --- | --- |
| | | Local authority | Independent | Total |
| Below average | Count | 9 | 7 | 16 |
| | % within Type of agency | 4.8% | 5.7% | 5.2% |
| Average | Count | 113 | 5 | 164 |
| | % within Type of agency | 60.4% | 41.8%1 | 53.1% |
| Above average | Count | 65 | 64 | 129 |
| | % within Type of agency | 34.8% | 52.5% | 41.7% |
| Total | Count | 187 | 122 | 309 |
| | % within Type of agency | 100.0% | 100.0% | 100.0% |

Source: Social Worker data. Note: Table is restricted to children whose last or latest placement was in a children's home.

specialist service. This in turn made it easier for them to be clear about their methods and objectives.

These explanations suggest that 'out of county' placements may in some instances work better than local ones. Table 12.6 is restricted to children in council provision and compares the quality of local and 'out of county' placements in three types of placement. In the case of relative foster care and children's homes, placements 'outside the county' attracted significantly higher ratings for quality.

**Table 12.6** Within and 'out of county' placements by quality in three types of placement

| Last/latest placement | | | | Quality of placement score | | | |
|---|---|---|---|---|---|---|---|
| | | | | Below average | Average | Above average | Total |
| Foster with relatives | Sector | LA within boundary | Count | 27 | 172 | 217 | 416 |
| | | | % within Sector | 6.5% | 41.3% | 52.2% | 100.0% |
| | | LA outside boundary | Count | 0 | 21 | 62 | 83 |
| | | | % within Sector | 0% | 25.3% | 74.7% | 100.0% |
| | | Total | Count | 27 | 193 | 279 | 499 |
| | | | % within Sector | 5.4% | 38.7% | 55.9% | 100.0% |
| Foster other | Sector | LA within boundary | Count | 27 | 492 | 1042 | 1561 |
| | | | % within Sector | 1.7% | 31.5% | 66.8% | 100.0% |
| | | LA outside boundary | Count | 11 | 129 | 272 | 412 |
| | | | % within Sector | 2.7% | 31.3% | 66.0% | 100.0% |
| | | Total | Count | 38 | 621 | 1314 | 1973 |
| | | | % within Sector | 1.9% | 31.5% | 66.6% | 100.0% |
| Children's home | Sector | LA within boundary | Count | 9 | 105 | 55 | 169 |
| | | | % within Sector | 5.3% | 62.1% | 32.5% | 100.0% |
| | | LA outside boundary | Count | 0 | 8 | 10 | 18 |
| | | | % within Sector | 0% | 44.4% | 55.6% | 100.0% |
| | | Total | Count | 9 | 113 | 65 | 187 |
| | | | % within Sector | 4.8% | 60.4% | 34.8% | 100.0% |

Source: Social Worker data.

Placements in the independent sector were more likely to be outside the county boundaries. The apparent advantage of independent over local council homes disappears if account is taken of this fact. Independent homes within the councils boundaries were not seen as 'better' than similar local council ones. Nor were those outside the council boundaries seen as 'better' than council ones that were also outside these boundaries.[5]

As we have seen earlier, completed placements with relatives are more likely to be seen as 'successful' by social workers. On the other hand such placements are less likely to be seen as high quality. Presumably their other advantages, the commitment of the carers, the maintenance of family ties and so on, compensate for this disadvantage.

Why should out of county placements with family and friends be seen as of higher quality than similar local placements? It could be a matter of chance.[6] If this is not so, it may reflect the extra commitment of kin who apply from outside the county, the extra quality needed to persuade social workers that an out of county placement is acceptable (although this does not seem to apply to ordinary placements) or the fact that such placements are more protected by distance from the conflicts with birth parents that seem to characterise placements of this kind (see Sinclair 2005).

## Quality of care score and the stability outcome measures

Does quality of care influence outcome? The answer is likely to depend on the kind of outcome we have in mind.

We begin our analysis by looking at stability. Tables 12.7 and 12.8 show how far those who are 'stable' on our three placements and long-term (D35) stability measures also have high quality placement scores.

Tables 12.7 and 12.8 both show a significant association. However, the trend for those doing well on the three placements measure to be in better quality placements is very slight. The association between quality and the D35 measure was stronger. It was also stronger than the association with the new PSA indicator.[7]

The explanation for this contrast may well have to do with the purposes of placement. We have argued that children often acquire three or more placements in a year because of movements that were intended. If so, their early moves may well be from or to 'good' placements. By contrast those who have been continuously looked after for four years or more are much less likely to make intended moves. Those who are in high quality placements may therefore be unlikely to move at all.

**Table 12.7** Quality of placement and three or more placements in a year

| | | Quality of placement score | | | |
|---|---|---|---|---|---|
| Three or more placements in year | | Below average | Average | Above average | Total |
| No | Count | 121 | 1074 | 1816 | 3011 |
| | % within Three or more placements in year | 4.0% | 35.7% | 60.3% | 100.0% |
| Yes | Count | 52 | 286 | 414 | 752 |
| | % within Three or more placements in year | 6.9% | 38.0% | 55.1% | 100.0% |
| Total | Count | 173 | 1360 | 2230 | 3763 |
| | % within Three or more placements in year | 4.6% | 36.1% | 59.3% | 100.0% |

Source: CIS and Social Worker data.
Note: Table restricted to those present at the end of year.

**Table 12.8** Quality of placement and D35 stability measure

| | | Quality of placement score | | | |
|---|---|---|---|---|---|
| D35 stability measure | | Below average | Average | Above average | Total |
| Not positive | Count | 42 | 251 | 312 | 605 |
| | % within D35 stability measure | 6.9% | 41.5% | 51.6% | 100.0% |
| Positive | Count | 16 | 195 | 415 | 626 |
| | % within D35 stability measure | 2.6% | 31.2% | 66.3% | 100.0% |
| Total | Count | 58 | 446 | 727 | 1231 |
| | % within D35 stability measure | 4.7% | 36.2% | 59.1% | 100.0% |

Source: CIS and Social Worker data.

There was a similar contrast between those under and over 11. Under the age of 11 those with three or more placements were less likely than others of similar age to be in average or below average placements (see Table 12.9). Among those aged 11 or over we found the opposite: those with three or more placements were more likely to be in above average placements. This difference between the two groups is very unlikely to occur 'by chance'.[8]

**Table 12.9** Quality of placement by three placements by age

| Aged 11 or over at census | | | Three or more placements in year | | |
| --- | --- | --- | --- | --- | --- |
| | | | No | Yes | Total |
| No<br>Group quality of care rating | Below average | Count | 486 | 74 | 560 |
| | | % within Group quality of care rating | 86.8% | 13.2% | 100.0% |
| | Above average | Count | 906 | 194 | 1100 |
| | | % within Group quality of care rating | 82.4% | 17.6% | 100.0% |
| | Total | Count | 1392 | 268 | 1660 |
| | | % within Group quality of care rating | 83.9% | 16.1% | 100.0% |
| Yes<br>Group quality of care rating | Below average | Count | 709 | 264 | 973 |
| | | % within Group quality of care rating | 72.9% | 27.1% | 100.0% |
| | Above average | Count | 910 | 220 | 1130 |
| | | % within Group quality of care rating | 80.5% | 19.5% | 100.0% |
| | Total | Count | 1619 | 484 | 2103 |
| | | % within Group quality of care rating | 77.0% | 23.0% | 100.0% |

Source: CIS and Social Worker data. Note: The table is restricted to those present on census date.

A similar analysis with the other two measures of stability did not produce this significant contrast. In each case, however, the association between quality and the indicator was much stronger among those aged over 11.

We have already demonstrated that the reasons for movement seem to be different in the cases of younger and older children. These data suggest that the association between movement and quality of placement may also be different. So quality of placement may affect movement but only in certain conditions. We suggest that these are:

- That the placement is intended to last.
- That the child has the age and the temperament to influence the decision to end unsuitable or unsatisfactory placements.

We pursue this idea in the next chapter.

## Quality of care score and the 'doing-well' outcome measures

Were children doing better in high quality placements? Table 12.10 uses a 'well-being score' which divides our 'doing-well' measure into high and low scorers. Those with high scores are assumed to have a relatively high level of 'well-being'. As can be seen those in the 'better' placements also did better on this measure and this proved to be so among those of all ages.

**Table 12.10** 'Doing-well' and quality of placement score

| | | Quality of placement score | | | |
|---|---|---|---|---|---|
| Well-being score | | Below average | Average | Above average | Total |
| Low | Count | 161 | 869 | 691 | 1721 |
| | % within Well-being score | 9.4% | 50.5% | 40.2% | 100.0% |
| High | Count | 40 | 787 | 1907 | 2734 |
| | % within Well-being score | 1.5% | 28.8% | 69.8% | 100.0% |
| Total | Count | 201 | 1656 | 2598 | 4455 |
| | % within Well-being score | 4.5% | 37.2% | 58.3% | 100.0% |

Source: Social Worker data.

Table 12.11 gives our 'best' combination of predictors for the 'doing-well' measure.[9]

The analysis suggests that other things being equal children had higher 'doing-well' scores when:

- the quality of placement was relatively high
- the child had not had more than one admission
- the social worker did not consider the child disabled
- the child had spent a relatively long time being looked after since the last admission
- the child was relatively young
- the child's family was not very problematic
- the child accepted the need to be looked after
- the child had had a relatively low number of previous placements
- the child was female.

The quality of care score had a much more significant relationship with 'doing-well' than any other variable. In this it contrasted with the influence of the

**Table 12.11** Quality of placement and other predictors of 'doing-well'

| Model | Unstandardised coefficients[a] | | Standardised coefficients[a] | | |
| | B | Std. Error | Beta | t | Sig. |
|---|---|---|---|---|---|
| 1 (Constant) | 1.031 | .016 | | 63.138 | .000 |
| Quality of placement score | 5.181E-02 | .002 | .330 | 22.322 | .000 |
| More than one admission | −1.832E-02 | .003 | −.099 | −6.454 | .000 |
| Social worker considers child disabled | 2.936E-02 | .004 | .116 | 7.992 | .000 |
| Log of days since last admission | 1.286E-02 | .001 | .195 | 12.735 | .000 |
| Age at census | −3.652E-03 | .000 | −.163 | −10.321 | .000 |
| Family Difficulty Score | −3.428E-02 | .005 | −.100 | −6.540 | .000 |
| Child accepts need to be looked after | 1.648E-02 | .002 | .159 | 10.848 | .000 |
| Number of placements | −2.622E-03 | .000 | −.137 | −8.723 | .000 |
| Sex | 1.219E-02 | .003 | .066 | 4.549 | .000 |

[a] Dependent Variable: 'Doing-well' measure.
Source: CIS and Social Worker data.

council. Information on which council was looking after a child did not add to our ability to predict how well they were doing.

## Conclusion

These analyses suggest some differences between placement types:

- Residential care appears to be more successful if it is 'out of county' and this characteristic accounts for the apparent greater success of the independent sector.

- Care by kin appears to be seen as of lower quality than 'ordinary foster care' but in long-term placements its results, as judged by the social workers, appear more satisfactory.

These analyses also suggest that good quality placements go with better outcomes and may well, as our case studies suggest, be crucial in bringing them about. The only caveat on this conclusion is one made in the last chapter. When the child is under the age of 11, movement between placements may have different origins and significance. Therefore, it is not surprising that in this group movement was not related to placement quality in the same way as it was among older children.

As we will see, these are the conclusions that we reach at the end of this book. At this point we need to note a number of problems with all the analyses we have presented so far.

First, the judgements are not made independently of each other. For example, a social worker who felt that a child was doing well might find it difficult to judge that a placement was below average.

Second, it may have been difficult for social workers to separate their judgements of the quality of the placement from their judgements of its appropriateness. So social workers who were reluctant to use residential care may have judged the placement only average, even though in its own terms it was excellent.

Third, for many purposes, the judgements are made at the wrong time. We asked about the last/latest placement that was made. Clearly the last placement cannot directly affect earlier ones so that its association with measures of movement is problematic.

Fourth, the judgements are likely to be made at a point where the placement will, as it were, have settled down so that it is difficult to separate the effect of the child on the placement from the effect of the placement on the child. 'Easy children' may well appear to have high quality placements simply because they have done nothing to upset them.

It would, in many ways, have made our task easier if we had been able to ask about the quality of a placement before a child was ever in it. This would have made it easier to judge whether outcomes varied with placement quality after allowing for differences between the children they took. It would also have been easier if we had had judgements of the placements made by people who were not judging the outcomes for the child. These considerations led us to look separately at the effects of foster care and residential care and to carry out the rather more complicated analyses we report in the next chapter.

## Notes

1   See, for example, Berridge and Brodie 1998; Hicks *et al.* 2007; Sinclair and Gibbs 1998 for residential care and Farmer *et al.* 2005 and Sinclair *et al.* 2005 a and b for foster care. Much of this work is summarised in three overviews by Archer *et al.* 1998, Sinclair 2005 and Sinclair 2006.

2   They may, of course, be using other ways of supporting relative placements. We have no evidence on this.

3   The addition of the interaction term between the aim of care and upbringing and placement with kin adds significantly to the predictive power of our equation (chi square = 8.62, df = 1, $p < .01$). In this model neither placement with kin nor placement for care and upbringing were significant suggesting that the advantage of relative placements lies in their ability to provide care and upbringing.

4   In these studies the independent agencies volunteered. Arguably only those who were proud of their service did so. This could account for the differences. Independent placements in this study were not volunteered in the same way.

5   If anything the reverse was the case but the small number of local council homes involved would make this an unsafe generalisation.

6   One reason may simply be chance. A much higher proportion (54%) of those placed with relatives were placed with siblings than found among those fostered with strangers (31%). The existence of such joint placements means that tests based on the assumption that observations are independent are not safe guides. In general we have dealt with this situation by relying on the fact that both the differences between placements and the numbers themselves have been very large (as in the 54% as against 31% difference reported above which relates to roughly 3000 children) or alternatively using multi-level models to test the effects of different kinds of placement. Unfortunately we had no way of telling which siblings were fostered with each other and the numbers placed with relatives out of county were small so we could not use either of these approaches.

7   Tau b was .16 for the D35 stability measure, -.06 for the three placements measure and .09 for the new indicator. All these were significant at .001 or beyond but the correlation for the D35 stability measure is clearly larger.

8   Statistics for under 11 in Table 12.7 are chi square = 5.36, df = 1, $p = .021$ and for the over 11 Table chi square = 17.33, df = 1, $p < .001$. Tarone's test for homogeneity gives statistics of chi square = 18.45, df = 1, $p < .001$.

9   These come from our standard list of variables with the addition of a measure of disability but exclude variables such as measures of challenging behaviour that have an association with the score almost by definition.

Chapter 13

# Carers, Homes and Outcomes

## Introduction

Our last chapter dealt with quality of placements 'across the board'. In the present one we look at quality within placement type. We want to know whether a high quality foster placement produces better outcomes than a low quality one. We ask similar questions about residential care. In doing so we are able to overcome some of the methodological problems we outlined in the last chapter.

## The fostering quality score

The provision of a good quality placement has been vital. (Social Worker)

Love children, get on well with professionals. (Supervising Social Worker)

This carer provides a resource for teenage girls. I feel the facts that she has fairly clear expectations and does not expect a great deal back emotionally are key to her success in achieving stable placements. (Supervising Social Worker)

Warm caring and committed, understands issues for children who have had to leave their country, as has been an asylum seeker herself. (Supervising Social Worker)

Comments in the social workers' questionnaires left no doubt that they considered the quality of the foster placements vital. They also highlighted the particular qualities they valued. They wanted carers who were warm, loving and committed, flexible, able to deal with the children's families, realistic and clear in their expectations, and able to work with professionals. They also emphasised the need to match children on the grounds that different foster families suited different children.

In all of this their comments match the research. Essentially this suggests that carers do best if they combine warmth with clarity of expectation, an approach commonly known as authoritative parenting. The research also suggests that carers vary in their ability to deal with different children (see Sinclair 2005 for summary of evidence).

In the light of this previous evidence we asked the supervising social workers a series of questions about the council foster carer households used in the sample. A number of the questions focused on the approach of the main carer and their family. We therefore asked whether the carer was accepting, clear about what they wanted, easily upset by the child's behaviour, able to see things from the child's point of view, part of a family which wanted them and so on. These questions went very closely together so that carers who were rated highly on one were also likely to be rated highly on others. We therefore added them together to form a composite 'fostering quality score'.

The maximum possible score was 32. A quarter of the carers scored at this level and nearly four out of ten scored 30 or over. A quarter scored 25 or under and were thus seen as less caring and committed.

We looked at the ratings of placement quality made by the social workers for children who were fostered on the census date. Where we had a fostering quality score for their carer we could compare this with the quality rating. Statistically the association was very highly significant but it was not very strong (tau b = .22, $n = 821$, $p < .001$). In part this may be because the measures related to different things. For example, a social worker may have felt that the quality of placement was not particularly high because it was a long way from the child's school. This, however, would have nothing to do with the quality of fostering provided by the carer. That said, the relationship was, as can be seen from Figure 13.1, a reassuringly consistent one.

Three categories of carers scored significantly lower than others: those who were subject to an accusation, those who were deregistered and those who had left of their own accord. These characteristics may have disenchanted those making the ratings. Alternatively it may be that foster care is subject to a 'Darwinian' process so that those who are less suited to fostering are more likely to leave.[1]

We divided this score into roughly equal thirds. Councils varied very significantly in the proportion of their carers whose ratings fell into these divisions. At one extreme staff in one council rated nearly half its carers (49%) in the lowest third and just over a fifth (21%) in the top third. Comparable figures for another council were a quarter (24%) of their carers in the lowest third and a half (53%) in the highest one.[2] We turn now to the question of whether quality of foster care makes a difference to outcomes.

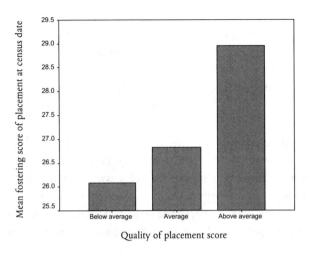

Source: Social Worker data.

**Figure 13.1** Relationship between fostering quality and placement quality

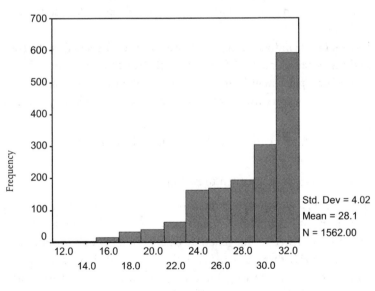

Source: Social Worker data.

**Figure 13.2** Distribution of fostering quality score

## Multi-level model: foster care

Anyone reading our case studies in Chapter 10 would find it hard to doubt that foster carers have a key influence on the length of a placement. Social workers, team leaders, and the managers we interviewed on the telephone concurred. Their replies repeatedly emphasised the importance of foster carers in reducing undesired moves. They were equally emphatic about the need to support and train the carers they had.

As we have seen the statistical data from the social workers suggested that the effect was only marked where the child was relatively old. This too fitted with the case studies. There were a small number of examples where young children remained for years in foster families where they were acutely unhappy or were even badly treated. As we have seen, however, the statistical data on the effects of good placements were not conclusive. We wanted to explore this issue in other ways.

We chose to do this by linking our data on foster carers to our data on placements. In many cases this was not possible. Some councils could not make this link in their client information systems.[3] In other cases the foster carers involved in past placements had left fostering and we had no information on them. There were, however, more than 4000 placements ($n = 4054$) where we had a quality score for the carers and could link them to the placements. We used these to test our hypothesis.

Our work on the individual reports to each of the 13 councils suggested that we should test a rather more elaborate model than the simple one that 'good carers ensure long placements'. Instead we tested the hypothesis put forward in the last chapter that carers with high fostering scores ensure long placements in two conditions:

1.  The child is old enough to 'break' the placement if he or she is unhappy there.

2.  The placement is intended to be long-term.

In order to test this hypothesis we defined 'old enough' as at least 11 years old when the placement began. We excluded placements made from the community on the grounds that these would generally be expected to be short-term. We then tested the hypothesis that placements with carers with high fostering scores would last longer after allowing for the age of the child and the length of placement for which the carer was registered.[4]

To do this we used a multi-level model provided by the computer programme MlWin. This technique is often used in educational research. It allows the researcher to distinguish between the effects of different levels (for example, school, class and child) on certain outcomes such as examination performance.

$\text{lnpleng}_{ij} \sim N(XB, \Omega)$

$\text{lnpleng}_{ij} = \beta_{0ij}\text{cons} + 0.357(0.144)\text{goodfos}_{ij} + 0.000(0.000)\text{sel11} + \\ \quad {}_{ij} + 0.000(0.000)\text{sel2plus}_{ij} + 0.491(0.083)\text{minapp}_{ij}$

$\beta_{0ij} = 2354(0.528) + u_{0j} + e_{0ij}$

$[u_{0j}] \sim N(0, \Omega_u) : \Omega_u = [0.989(0.201)]$

$[e_{0ij}] \sim N(0, \Omega_e) : \Omega_e = [2478(0.185)]$

$-2 * loglikelihood(IGLS) = 3246.468(805 \text{ of } 4054 \text{ cases in use})$

Sources: CIS data and Social Worker data.

**Figure 13.3** Multi-level model for length of placement and fostering score

We used it initially to explore the effects of foster placements on the length of time for which foster children stayed in the placement.

Figure 13.3 will mean little to most people. Even those who are used to multi-level models will find the variables unintelligible. It is, however, useful to have the figure as an aid to explanation. Essentially it concerns the relationship between placement length (*lnpleng*)[5] and two characteristics of the placement: the carers' fostering score (*goodfos*) and minimum length for which the carer was approved (*minapp*). The two other terms in the equation are there to restrict the calculations to those over 11 at the start of placement and to placements that were not made from the community. The result of these restrictions, combined with the need to focus on placements where we could relate the fostering score to placements, was that our sample was reduced from 4054 to 805.

The equation suggests that carers with high fostering scores do tend to have longer placements.[6] The influence of the fostering score is, however, much less than that of the length of time for which the carer is approved.[7] Clearly there are a large number of factors that we did not take into account – for example the potential length of the placement before the child reached 18, the difficulty of the child and so on. We did in fact create models that took these factors into account. Those we tried mildly strengthened the relationship between the length of placement and the fostering score without, however, ever making it very strong.

A difficulty about this analysis is that it only deals with placements. Well-being and the measures of stability have to do with the individual children. So we needed an analysis that dealt with them. In order to do this we looked at those children who were fostered at the start of the census year. The aim was to relate the fostering quality score of their carer at that point to the measures of how well they were doing (the 'doing-well' score) on their last or latest placement at

least six months later. As a number of carers had more than one child in the placement we continued to use a multi-level model.

This analysis established the following:

- According to this analysis half the variation in our 'doing-well' measure
  was 'down to' the foster placement.

- In keeping with the above the fostering score was very strongly related to
  the 'doing-well' measures after allowing for the other variables in the
  equation ($t = 6.4$, $p < .001$).

- Those fostered with relatives were also doing better although the
  significance level was low ($p = .05$).

- The combination of the fostering score and whether or not the carer was
  a relative appeared to account for most of the variation associated with
  the foster placement.

Other things being equal children were also doing better in these analyses if:

- they had been looked after for a relatively long time

- they were under 11

- they had not had a repeat admission

- they had not had a lot of problems at home (i.e. they did not have a high
  family difficulties score).

Therefore, we are led to the same conclusion that we tentatively reached in
Chapter 12. As far as we can see, the quality of placement is key to how well the
child is doing.

In the sample as a whole the fostering score at the turn of the year was not
related to any of the three main stability measures.[8] This is not surprising. All
these variables relate to changes of placement. In the case of two of the indicators
the relevant changes may have taken place before the start of the census year. In
the case of the 'three placements' indicator the child or young person may well
move from their 'turn of the year' placement to a perfectly satisfactory one.

All this, however, did not mean that the quality of placement was irrelevant to
whether or not the child moved in the coming year. There was a relationship but it
was not the same among children who were under and over 11. Our analyses
showed that:

- In the sample as a whole, children with high quality placements were no
  more or less likely than others to stay in the same placement for the next
  year.

- If the child was aged 11 or over at the census date, he or she was more
  likely to stay in the same placement for the year if the placement was of

high quality. (This finding held if we took account of the minimum length of time for which the carer was approved and/or the challenging behaviour score.)

- If the child was aged less than 11, he or she was less likely to stay in the placement for the year if the placement was of high quality. (This finding also held when we took account of the minimum length of time for which the carer was approved and/or the challenging behaviour score.)

We also looked at whether children with high quality placements at the turn of the year were more or less likely to have a set of placements described by the social workers as 'fully successful' or as a 'failure' (i.e. one at least of the last three placements that did not fully meet its purposes and one at least that did not fully meet the child's needs). This analysis showed that:

- 'Failure' was more likely when the fostering quality score was low and particularly so if we took account of the challenging behaviour score.

- 'Full success' was also more likely when the fostering quality score was high and remained so when we took account of the challenging behaviour score.

The upshot of these analyses is that they support the different strands of qualitative data and of those using social workers' ratings of placement quality. The quality of the carers can have an impact on placement length. On average, however, this is only the case where the child is older and where the intention is that the placement lasts. In most cases, these two conditions do not hold. For this reason the quality of carers is probably not a powerful weapon in the armoury of managers seeking to reduce the quantity of movement in the care system. Conversely measures of this movement are probably only a very weak and highly indirect measure of the quality of carers.

It does not follow that the quality of carers is unimportant among those who are under the age of 11. On the contrary it is strongly related to our measures of success and to our measure of 'doing well'. This is true for those aged 11 or over and for those under the age of 11. One of the most disturbing features of this study was the number of young children in our case studies who had remained for prolonged periods with carers with whom, according to their later account, they were acutely unhappy.

## Quality of care: variations between residential units

This young person has done excellently due to being able to have specialist residential education. He's been very lucky. (Social Worker)

High levels of staff and use of agency staff can make it difficult to provide good levels of support and consistency for young people. *Ad hoc* decision-making can lead to confusion and misunderstanding. (Manager)

Very efficiently run unit and well-resourced with committed and well-trained staff. (Manager)

Comments by social workers and others again emphasised the importance of and, perhaps more often, the lack of high quality residential care. The qualities they wanted varied to some extent with the kind of placement required. In general they emphasised consistency, the quality of education and the quality and quantity of staff.

With the exception of the apparent emphasis on staff ratios[9] all this was in keeping with the research. This again suggests that children's homes work best if they are able to combine warmth and clarity. In addition they generally have to have good strategies for dealing with difficult behaviour and education. In achieving this, much depends on the head of home and on the degree to which he or she can work with their staff in an agreed approach (see, for example, Hicks *et al.* 2007; Sinclair and Gibbs 1998).

The information available was not sufficiently standard to allow us to develop a reliable way of coding the different types of residential unit.[10] It was clear, however, that they served a variety of purposes. There were schools, secure units, assessment units for mothers and babies, medium-term units of uncertain purpose, short-term homes for disabled children, and long-term units variously offering therapy, preparation for independent living, preparation for living with a family, or places where children could put down roots. Some had a number of sub-units whose character may have varied, some kept a mix of children for short and long periods and a handful appeared to have a staff team looking after one child. Some units had education on the premises, but were clearly not schools in the ordinary sense of the word.

As in the case of foster care we computed a measure of quality for residential care. This was based on aspects of residential care known to be related to the functioning of units. It included ratings for managing behaviour and education, the relationship between staff and residents, the effectiveness of any key worker system, and the overall quality of care. We were able to collect this information on 184 residential units. It correlated, although not very strongly, with the social workers' measure of quality of placement.[11]

This further measure of residential care showed considerable variation (see Figure 13.4).

In many councils we found it very difficult to get ratings made of the 'independent' residential units. Although the councils must, in a sense, have had very

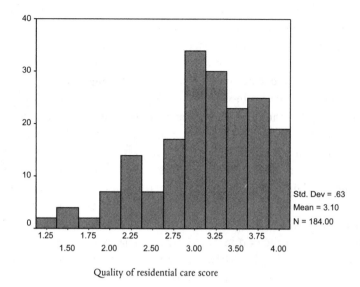

Quality of residential care score

Source: Social Worker data.

**Figure 13.4** Rating of residential units

considerable experience of them through the young people placed there, there did not seem to be an easily accessible 'institutional memory' of what the units were like. This appeared to us odd. Residential units are known to range widely in quality and cost, while costing on average around £64,000 a year per place. We had therefore expected that councils would make as much effort as they could to check the quality of care or even develop a common database on these units with other councils. When we raised these issues with the councils, they either said that they were developing practice in this respect (e.g. through placement exit interviews and independent reviewers) or that we had failed to tap into the experience that they had. Other councils may wish to develop their practice in a similar way.

## Was quality of care score related to length of placement?

Residential units that kept their residents for a relatively short time tended to score low on our quality of care score. The correlation between this score and the average length of stay was quite low ($r = .23$, $p = .002$). Moreover it could occur for different reasons.

On the one hand 'short-stay' residential homes may find it harder to provide high-quality care. For example, those that deliberately set out to offer short-stay care may pay less attention to education than, say, residential schools that keep their young people for a relatively long time. In addition it may be difficult to create a strong benign culture in a situation where there is a high turnover and a wide variety of young people are brought together.

While it is probable that short lengths of stay make it more difficult to provide quality care, it is also possible that causation can work the other way. It is known that residential units vary widely in their impacts on young people. In some the residents are very likely to be bullied, sexually harassed, and led into crime (Gibbs and Sinclair 2000). Others by contrast are benign places where there are good relationships between staff and residents and between the residents themselves (Hicks *et al.* 2007). It seems likely that young people will stay longer in such places than they do in others. Their social workers will be less likely to remove them and they themselves will be less likely to run away. What evidence did we find that this might be the case?

In tackling this problem we used a similar approach to that employed for foster care. We faced, however, the difficulty that we did not have the same standard data for residential homes that we had for foster carers. So we knew that some homes kept their residents for a much shorter time than others. However we did not always know whether a home was intentionally 'short-stay' or not. It was therefore difficult to determine the effect of quality of care, after allowing for whether a home was short-stay or not. In order to overcome this problem we excluded a quarter of the homes that seemed to keep their residents for a particularly short time.[12]

Our analysis of the remaining residential units showed that other things being equal:

- Children with high difficult behaviour scores tended to have shorter stays.
- Children with a need code of disability tended to have longer stays.
- Children seeking asylum tended to have shorter stays.
- Children in a local council unit tended to have shorter stays.
- Children in homes with a high standard of care score tended to have longer stays.

Much of this may have to do with the role of the units. Those with a need code of disability were primarily in residential schools, where lengths of stay are longer. Asylum seekers may be in relatively short-stay hostels. Local council units may have to accommodate a wide variety of young people, some of whom, for example those on remand, may have intentionally short stays. As already suggested, it is probably harder to provide a high quality of care in homes where some or all stays are short.

All this could explain the association between standard of care and length of stay. However, it is also possible that the associations between difficult behaviour and a low standard of care score on the one hand and short lengths of stay on the other also reflect the effect of unintentional breakdowns, decisions by social workers to remove young people from homes where they are unhappy and so on.

Our lack of detailed knowledge of the units also made it difficult for us to explore their effects on the 'doing-well' score. We knew that some units were likely to be dealing with 'more difficult' young people and thus have on average lower 'doing-well' scores. We did not know which these were. There was, however, one set of findings in which we had some confidence and which we discuss below.

The quality of care score for residential units was significantly associated with our school performance score. This remained the case if we took account of the degree to which the young person displayed challenging behaviour and of whether or not they were seeking asylum (asylum seekers did much better on this score and those with challenging behaviour much worse). The association was much stronger when we looked at those who were still in the same residential unit on the census date – the point to which our scores referred. It was positive but not significant among the remainder.

In theory this positive association between school performance and residential unit could arise from selection. It is also possible that 'good units' tended to select on the grounds of educational performance in the first place. If this were the case we would expect to find that good units had young people with less difficult behaviour. This was not so. The challenging behaviour scores differed little by unit after we had taken account of whether or not the young person was seeking asylum. It was also possible that 'good' units tended to exclude those whose performance at school was poor after their arrival. If this were the case we would expect to find that school performance among those who had left was worse in the case of the good units. This was not so.

So if selection does not explain these differences in the school performance of residents what does? The alternative explanation is that they reflect the differing impact of the homes. This is in keeping with the association with the quality of care score. It is also in keeping with a large swathe of research in this area. This research also suggests that the impact of residential homes, while powerful, tends to be short-lived. Too often it does not survive the residents' departure. Where it does survive it is often the 'bad habits', for example, the tendency to abscond or to criminal behaviour that persist (see Sinclair 2006 for a summary of the evidence).

Therefore habits of school attendance or effort may not always outlast the setting in which they were acquired. Hence, perhaps, stems the lack of significant association between school performance and the quality of residential care in their former unit.[13]

We tested one final hypothesis which was that placement in residential care might serve to control rapid movement. In order to do this we looked at those who were in placement at the beginning of the year and explored whether, after allowing for behaviour and other variables, they were more or less likely to have had three or more placements at the end of the next year. The association was sometimes positive and sometimes negative depending on the variables in the equation but was never significant. Our conclusion was that in most cases placement in residential care did not restrain rapid movement, leastways among those in it at a particular point in time.

## Conclusion

These findings strongly suggest the following conclusions:

- Quality of placement can affect stability but only when the child is over the age of 11 and the placement is meant to last.

- The quality of a placement can affect its success and the well being of the child irrespective of the child's age.

- Foster care by relatives is seen as being of lower quality than other foster care, but this deficiency is more than made up by other factors, arguably the greater commitment of the carers, so that it is relatively more successful than other forms of foster care.

An observational study of this kind cannot prove these conclusions. They are, however, likely. In particular the conclusion that the quality of placement is important fits with all the research in this area of which we are aware. The safest approach for the moment is to act as if it is true.

It follows that:

- Care needs to be taken that the requirements of performance indicators do not lead to young children staying on in placements where they are deeply unhappy, a situation that did occur in our case studies.

- The quality of the placements is of paramount importance. Everything possible should be done to ensure that placements are of the highest quality.

In general, improvements in placement quality are likely to depend on selection, support, training and the refusal to use placements that are of low quality. So far research has largely ignored selection. It has failed to find evidence that support or training improves outcomes. Further research on what might work in this area is vital.

That said, social workers do distinguish between good and less good placements. Children do the same. Why cannot local councils make more use of this information? By doing so they should be able to weed out bad placements and identify others that need more support.

## Notes

1   Other work in the Social Work Research and Development Unit (SWRDU) has suggested that carers who scored low on a similar score were more likely to experience placement breakdown (Sinclair *et al.* 2005a) and that breakdowns commonly precipitate a decision to cease caring (Sinclair *et al.* 2004).

2   In some councils carers who had been there for longer scored better and in others the reverse was the case. In a two-way analysis of variance with the fostering quality score as the dependent variable the interaction between high (above the median) length of registration and local council was just significant ($p = .043$). There was no obvious explanation for this finding. It may well be the result of chance. Another curious finding concerned the relationship between quality score and the 'minimum period of approval'. Again there was no overall effect but an interaction by local council ($p = .003$). We have no explanation for this either. Examination of the data suggested that if there was an effect it was confined to a very small number of councils where recent changes had meant increases or drops in the average quality of short-term carers – a group where such rapid changes would be more likely as turnover among them is not inhibited by obligations to long-term foster children.

3   This might be seen as a limitation. In practice there was no evidence that those councils that could make the link made any use of it. Our own view is that there would be some value in routinely monitoring placement length and breakdown by foster carer. This information could alert managers to carers associated with an unexpectedly high degree of movement. This does not mean that this information should be used without further enquiry. Breakdowns are an occupational hazard of fostering. However, a system that refuses to re-employ carers experiencing breakdowns without further enquiry is said to have dramatically reduced fostering breakdowns in at least one area in Illinois, USA.

4   The councils told us whether the carers were approved for short-term, intermediate or long-term fostering (we left the definition of these terms to them). Our rough and ready coding was: 1 = short-term, 2 = medium-term, 3 = long-term.

5   Strictly speaking this is the natural log of (placement length plus one). Placement length itself varies from 0 to 6465 days and is strongly skewed. The transformation was chosen to produce a more normal distribution. It was necessary to add one in order to avoid taking the natural log of nought. For ease of exposition we talk in the text of 'placement length'.

6   The figures in brackets are the standard deviations of the coefficients. A coefficient divided by this standard deviation is distributed as t and is significantly different from zero if it is greater than 1.96.

7   After applying the two restrictions the addition of the term 'minapp' reduces the overall chi square by 128 with one degree of freedom. The corresponding figure for the fostering score was 4.8.

8   These analyses, like all those in this section of the book, were only carried out on those fostered at the beginning of the census year. There is, of course, a trivial relationship between being fostered at the beginning of the census year and being positive on the D35 indicator.

9   Neither Sinclair and Gibbs (1998) nor Hicks *et al.* (2007) could find any relationship between staffing level and their measures of the quality of home environment. It was, however, apparent in both studies that staff believed there was.

10  It seems likely that further analysis and coding of the actual paper forms would enable us to do better in this respect. Unfortunately this was not within the capacity of this study due to time and funding constraints.

11  There was a correlation of .305 (tau b) between the score for placements at the census dates and the social workers' ratings of the quality of the last/latest placement. This was significant at a level of significance way beyond .001 but is clearly not as high as it might have been.

12  Our criterion was that the standard deviation should be greater than 130 days. This excluded 25 per cent of the homes all of which also had low average lengths of stay.

13  This interpretation is largely based on previous research. We did find a positive association between the quality of care score and school performance of former residents. The fact that this was not significant may simply reflect the relatively low numbers involved in this analysis.

Chapter 14

# Teams and Outcomes

There used to be 12 or 13 what we called district child care teams and I grouped them together because I said 12 was far too many and we were going to have seven. But I think that, I think those cultures of difference and boundaries, boundaries go up and, and they stay up for a very long time and they do help make people safe, I think, and they allow people to compete as well. (Manager)

## Introduction

The myriad decisions that together make up the care system almost always involve social workers. By and large, these work in teams. Their decisions are supervised, monitored and signed off by their team leaders. In what follows we first describe the teams, the views of the team leaders and the resources available to them. We then try to assess the impact of the different teams on choice of placements, care careers, and outcomes.

The information we will use comes partly from the client information system, and partly from team leaders. The information system gave us the names of the current social work teams of children in the sample. The leaders of these teams responded to questionnaires we sent them. Two-thirds (65%) of them sent us completed questionnaires and their teams covered two-thirds (67%) of the children in the research.

## Kinds of team

Our 13 councils organised their teams in different ways.

Some councils had broad 'Children and Families' teams. These dealt with all the children referred from the community, supported families with children in need and supervised children who were looked after.

Other councils divided the work of Children and Families teams. Part of the work was given to 'long-term teams' and part to 'Referral and Assessment' teams. This group would normally serve an area of a council. It could be further broken down into a Referral team, Children in Need teams which gave long-term support to families with children in the community, and 'Looked after Children teams' which supervised children in the care system. Two councils divided their teams by age and made further distinctions in terms of whether the children were looked after or in the community.[1]

So far we have been describing different ways of dealing with the needs met by Children and Families teams. There were also specialist teams. The most common of these were leaving care teams (hardly ever more than one per council), and teams for disabled children. Others were known by a variety of names and included teams with special responsibility for children needing permanent placements, a team for the children of homeless families and a team providing solution-focused therapy for families (see Table 14.1).

**Table 14.1** Types of social work team

| Type of social work team | Frequency | Per cent | Valid per cent | Cumulative per cent |
|---|---|---|---|---|
| Children and families | 29 | 16.7 | 16.7 | 16.7 |
| Referral and Assessment | 33 | 19.0 | 19.0 | 35.6 |
| Long-term | 44 | 25.3 | 25.3 | 60.9 |
| Children in need | 17 | 9.8 | 9.8 | 70.7 |
| Looked after children | 19 | 10.9 | 10.9 | 81.6 |
| Permanency | 3 | 1.7 | 1.7 | 83.3 |
| Leaving care | 8 | 4.6 | 4.6 | 87.9 |
| Disabled children | 13 | 7.5 | 7.5 | 95.4 |
| Homelessness | 1 | .6 | .6 | 96.0 |
| Asylum seekers | 3 | 1.7 | 1.7 | 97.7 |
| Health | 1 | .6 | .6 | 98.3 |
| Teenagers' families | 1 | .6 | .6 | 98.9 |
| Other | 2 | 1.1 | 1.1 | 100.0 |
| Total | 174 | 100.0 | 100.0 | |

Source: Team Leader data.

## How many social workers did the teams have?

We asked the team leaders to tell us how many social workers they were meant to have (their 'Full Time Equivalent (FTE)' establishment). We included in this the team leaders themselves, as well as anyone called a senior social worker, senior practitioner or social worker. Overall 60 per cent of the teams had establishments of five to eight social workers. Roughly a fifth fell below this range and a fifth above it (see Figure 14.1).

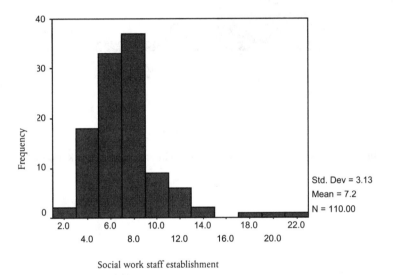

Source: Team Leader data.

**Figure 14.1** Social work staff establishment per team

We also asked about the number of staff in post. The teams responding to our questionnaires had a total of 735 full time equivalent social workers including agency workers or an average of 6.7 per team.

We compared the number of social workers actually in post with the establishment and calculated a vacancy rate (see Figure 14.3). Fifty-six per cent of the teams had no vacancies. A fifth had vacancies of 20 per cent or more (equivalent to one full-time post in a team with an establishment of five staff).

The vacancy rate was 22 per cent on average in the London councils and eight per cent on average in teams in other councils, a significant difference.[2] Policy makers may need to take account of such geographical differences. There is little point in increasing the numbers of social workers nationally if the problem is that social workers cannot afford to live and work in London.

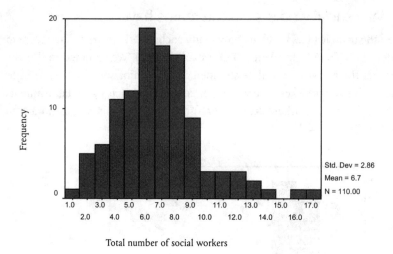

Source: Team Leader data.

**Figure 14.2** Number of FTE social work staff (including agency workers) per team

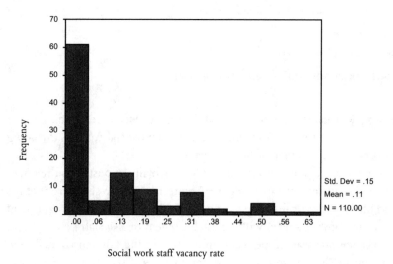

Source: Team Leader data.

**Figure 14.3** Vacancy rates in teams

## Caseloads

We also asked about the number of cases handled by the teams. Overall they were dealing with 12,765 cases with an average of 113 cases per team and 17.4 cases per social worker.

Some of these cases took more time than others. We wanted to take these differences into account. To do this we asked how many cases of different kinds were currently on the teams' books and how much of the overall time each group of cases was estimated to take. In this way we could see if a group of cases was taking more or less time than its numbers would suggest.

We used this comparison to calculate a 'weighting' for different kinds of case. If a group of cases made up 30 per cent of the teams' clients and took up 30 per cent of its time the weighting for this kind of case was 30/30 or 1. If a group of cases made up 30 per cent of the teams' clients but took up 15 per cent of its time the weighting was 15/30 or .5.

On average across 110 teams the weightings were:

- Children in need        0.57
- 'Other' cases           0.68
- Care leavers            0.75
- Duty cases              0.89
- Looked after            1.11
- At risk                 1.33

This in turn allowed us to calculate an 'adjusted caseload size' that we defined as the ratio of the adjusted number of cases (sum of weighted cases) to the number of social workers (including agency workers).

As can be seen from Figure 14.4, the average adjusted caseload was around 20. There were, however, four teams with very high adjusted caseloads per social worker of 67 or over. These teams had a major effect on analyses that used the adjusted caseload measure. We have therefore left them out of these analyses.

## Resources available to teams

We gave team leaders a list of 17 problems that might lead to 'undesirable moves'. The list covered lack of appropriate placements, and problems connected with schools, courts, contacts, matching and carers. The team leaders were asked to rate their importance in leading to undesirable movement on a four-point scale ranging from 'no significance' to 'very significant':

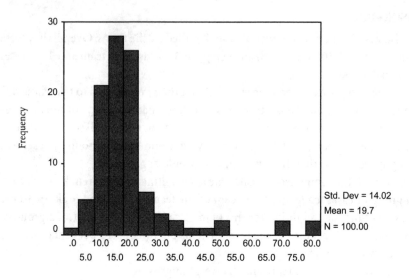

Adjusted cases to social workers' ratio

Source: Team Leader data.

**Figure 14.4** Adjusted cases to social workers' ratio

- The highest average rating was given to 'lack of long-term placements'. More than half (52%) of the team leaders thought that this was a 'very significant' source of undesirable movement. A further 38 per cent thought it significant.

- The next highest rating was given to 'need for a special fostering scheme' with 34 per cent rating this as 'very significant' and 50 per cent rating it as 'significant'.

- Other high ratings were given to the need for residential placements, school exclusion, lack of resources to support contact, problems connected with matching and the lack of training for carers.

We also asked the team leaders about how easy it was for them to get access to a list of 14 resources. Table 14.2 shows how many said that these resources were at best available only after a long delay and how this varied with the age of the child.

Table 14.2 has three main messages:

1. Team leaders thought that resources were short for all groups.

2. Resources became shorter as the child became older: they were in more plentiful supply for those under five than they were for those

aged five to 11, who in turn were seen to be better served than those aged 12 or over.

3. Children with specialised needs were in certain respects (e.g. availability of adoptive placements) less well served than others.

**Table 14.2** Resources and expected delays by age of child

| | % Unavailable or available only after long delay | | |
|---|---|---|---|
| Child: | Under 5 yrs (%) | 5–11 yrs (%) | 12+ yrs (%) |
| Choice of emergency placements | 66 | 70 | 86 |
| Choice of short-term placements | 43 | 64 | 84 |
| Choice of long-term placements | 85 | 95 | 94 |
| Well matched LT placements | 79 | 92 | 95 |
| Well matched placements in residential care** | – | – | 88 |
| Specialised foster care for children with challenging behaviour** | – | – | 98 |
| Therapeutic residential placements** | – | – | 96 |
| Appropriate arrangements for supervised contacts | 34 | 41 | 49 |
| Adoptive placements for disabled children*** | 88 | 97 | – |
| Adoptive placements for minority ethnic children*** | 74 | 89 | – |
| Adoptive placements for two or more children*** | 40 | –* | – |
| Other adoptive placements*** | 32 | 70 | – |
| Intensive packages for children returning from care | 28 | 31 | 60 |
| Other key resources | 46 | 56 | –* |

Source: Team Leader data.

* Not enough team leaders answered these questions to allow percentages.

** These questions were not asked about children under 12.

*** Questions about adoption were not asked about young people aged 12 or over.

The most important sources of support outside of social services were schools and, to a lesser extent, the Child and Adolescent Mental Health Service (CAMHS). We asked the team leaders about these possible sources of support. Understandably they were keener to talk about problems with these services than about what was going well. In practice, as we will see below, they varied in their views about the quality of these services and the degree of collaboration they received from them.

## Variations between councils in resources

The team leaders' replies suggested that some councils provided more resources than others. There were significant differences between team leaders in different councils in how far they pointed to problems over long-term contacts ($p = .047$), the availability of adoptive parents ($p = .002$), inappropriate insistence on contact by the courts ($p = .012$), and carer support ($p = .052$).

There also seemed to be differences in the views that team leaders in different councils took of schools and the CAMHS service. These differences were small but significant ($p = .043$) in the case of schools but much more pronounced ($p < .001$) in the case of CAMHS. There was no obvious reason for these differences.[3] For example the various scores did not differ by whether or not the council was in London.

## Can external resources reduce pressure on teams?

We wanted to see whether high caseloads or lack of resources might create a sense of 'work pressure' in teams that in turn might lead to worse outcomes among the children. We based our measure of 'work pressure' on the team leaders' answers to three statements:

1. We have the resources to deal with our work to a reasonable standard (scoring reversed).

2. We have to cut corners and leave non-urgent work.

3. We are operating at a dangerously low level of resources.

In replying to these statements the team leaders used a four-point scale (from 'strongly agree' to 'strongly disagree'). Team leaders who agreed with one statement were very likely to agree to the others. Those who disagreed with one were likely to disagree with others.[4] We made our 'work pressure score' by adding the responses together.

We related this score to our measures of resources. These included:

- adjusted caseload size (see earlier)

- a 'placement availability score' which summarised the availability of all forms of placement including (for adolescents) residential care and specialised foster care[5]

- a 'field resources score' which summarised the availability of supervised contacts and packages for children returning home (we did not use the need for 'other key resources' because many team leaders did not routinely complete this item)[6]

- an 'adoption resources score' which summarised the information on adoptive placements with the exception that the item on placements for siblings aged 5 or over was omitted for lack of responses[7]

- a school support score[8]

- a CAMHS support score.[9]

We looked first at whether teams with high 'work pressure' scores were more likely to have unallocated cases, low staff ratios and children who did not get full assessments when they should have done so (see Table 14.3). This proved to be so.

**Table 14.3** Correlations between different measures of 'pressure'

| | | Work Pressure Score | Adjusted cases to social workers ratio | Team has unallocated cases | Looked after children receive full assessments |
|---|---|---|---|---|---|
| Work Pressure Score | Pearson correlation | 1 | .449 | .315 | .492 |
| | Sig. (2-tailed) | . | .000 | .002 | .000 |
| | N | 94 | 94 | 94 | 89 |
| Adjusted cases to social workers ratio | Pearson correlation | .449 | 1 | .306 | .242 |
| | Sig. (2-tailed) | .000 | . | .002 | .021 |
| | N | 94 | 96 | 96 | 91 |
| Team has unallocated cases | Pearson correlation | .315 | .306 | 1 | .137 |
| | Sig. (2-tailed) | .002 | .002 | . | .196 |
| | N | 94 | 96 | 96 | 91 |
| Looked after children receive full assessments | Pearson correlation | .492 | .242 | .137 | 1 |
| | Sig. (2-tailed) | .000 | .021 | .196 | . |
| | N | 89 | 91 | 91 | 91 |

Source: Team Leader data.

Table 14.3 suggested that perceived work pressure does go with other measures in ways that 'make sense'. This encouraged us to test some more hypotheses. These were that our work pressure score would reflect:

- the adjusted caseload size of the social workers
- the social worker vacancy rate
- the quality of administrative support as perceived by the team leader
- the ratio of computers to social workers
- the field resources score
- the placement availability score
- the CAMHS and school scores
- the council in which the team was.

We found that our measure of work pressure differed significantly by council. It was also higher where caseloads were relatively high. It was lower (i.e. 'better') where vacancies were few or non-existent, the team leader said there was good collaboration with CAMHS, and field resources were, on our measure, relatively generous.[10]

We looked at the effect of these variables when 'taken together'. This suggested a simpler picture. In this a feeling of work pressure reflected:

- adjusted caseload size (the higher the caseload the higher the pressure)
- field resources score (the greater the resources the lower the pressure).

The effect of the council is through these variables rather than independently of them. In other words councils appeared to affect the pressure on social workers because they had more or less generous staffing ratios and resources for family support rather than through other means. Table 14.4 set outs the relevant analysis.

## Do teams influence the choice of placement?

The standard placement in all councils is foster care. Nevertheless some councils use foster care more than others. Similarly councils differ in their use of adoption, fostering with relatives, placement with parents and residential care. We wished to know whether these differences reflected the views and resources of teams within the councils.

Before doing this we wanted to measure one other variable. Social work is partly a matter of balancing risks and rights. If children are left at home they may be harmed. At the same time an over-zealous policy of removing them from their

**Table 14.4** Factors associated with work pressure in teams

| Work pressure score | | Unique method (ANOVA[a,b]) | | | | |
|---|---|---|---|---|---|---|
| | | Sum of squares | df | Mean square | F | Sig. |
| Covariates | (Combined) | 36.532 | 2 | 18.266 | 7.221 | .001 |
| | Adjusted cases to social workers ratio | 21.691 | 1 | 21.691 | 8.575 | .005 |
| | Field resources score | 15.966 | 1 | 15.966 | 6.312 | .014 |
| Main effects | LA | 49.139 | 12 | 4.095 | 1.619 | .104 |
| Model | | 92.767 | 14 | 6.626 | 2.619 | .004 |
| Residual | | 189.721 | 75 | 2.530 | | |
| Total | | 282.489 | 89 | 3.174 | | |

[a] Work pressure score by LA with Adjusted cases to social workers ration, Field resources score.
[b] All effects entered simultaneously.
Source: Team Leader data.

families could infringe the rights of parents and children, overwhelm the resources of the care system and risk harming the children in other ways. We expected that teams would balance these risks in different ways and that this might affect their policies on returning children to their own homes, their use of adoption and their readiness to use care by relatives. We therefore asked the team leaders two questions designed to measure 'family-mindedness'.[11] Teams serving disabled children were less 'family minded' than others. This, however, may be a matter of chance. Overall there were no significant differences on this score by type of team or by council.[12]

We assumed that the likelihood of placement would depend on the council, the particular characteristics of that team and the characteristics of the children served by it. This 'multi-level' model suggested that:

- After allowing for age at entry, ethnicity, and repeat admissions children aged less than eight were more likely to be placed for adoption at the end of the year if their teams had a relatively high ratio of staff ($p < .001$).

- Teams 'under pressure' were similarly less likely to make adoptive placements.

- The association between placement for adoption and the adoption resources score was in the predicted direction but not significant.

- None of our team variables were associated with placement with parents.

- After allowing for age at entry, a behavioural reason for admission and repeat admissions, those aged 11 or over were more likely to be in residential care at the end of the year if the team leader was not 'family minded', although the association was not strong ($p < .05$).

- None of our team variables was associated with placements with relatives, although the differences between teams in the proportion of these placements seemed to be very large.

The one strong association in this set of findings was that between caseload size and placement for adoption. Arguably adoption requires social workers to have enough time to give this aspect of their work priority.[13] It is therefore not surprising that staff teams with a relatively low proportion of social workers were not particularly successful in making adoptive placements.

As can be seen we were not particularly successful in predicting type of placement from team characteristics. This did not mean that teams made no difference. According to our model the likelihood of placement with relatives had much more to do with the team than it did with the council. The same was true of residential care. This suggests that the likelihood of these placements does depend on the team but that our measures did not pick out the teams most likely to make these placements.

## Do teams influence care careers?

Some teams were defined by their particular roles in the children's care careers. So, some dealt with assessment, others with children in need and yet others with children looked after on a long-term basis. In such teams there was an obvious connection between the type of team and the career movements the children made. In looking for any effect of teams on placement movement we therefore looked within 'team type'.

We looked at repeat admissions, turnover among those who were admitted during the year and turnover among those who were present at the beginning of the year. We found few associations:

- After allowing for relevant variables, teams with 'family minded' team leaders were less likely to have repeat admissions among those admitted in the year (a barely significant association).

- Again after allowing for relevant variables, teams with apparently abundant 'field resources' were significantly more likely to attempt rehabilitation with those who entered in the year (a significant association).

There was significant variation between the social work teams in the proportions of those looked after for a year or more who ceased to be looked after during the year. These proportions were not, however, significantly correlated with any of our team measures.

## Do teams influence measures of stability?

We analysed our data on placement stability in the same way. In each analysis we took account of age, age at admission and the experience of repeat admissions.

Teams with unallocated cases and/or with high work pressure scores did not differ on the new (PSA) indicator or the stable fostering (D35) indicator. They were, however, more likely to have children who had had three or more placements at the end of the year. It is not clear why this should be. Possibly, the lack of resources leads to rushed ways of working and emergency placements.[14] These in turn lead to more work and more pressure.

Young people aged 11 or over and served by teams that had relatively high placement availability were less likely to have three or more placements in a year. This was not true among young people under 11. Once again it is not clear why this should be. Possibly a lack of suitable placements leads to placement break-down among older children whereas among younger children it leads to problems in moving them on from placements.

Teams with high school support scores tended to do well on all three stability measures. It seems unlikely that movement among children who have been fostered for four years or more is sufficiently frequent for it to lead to a deterioration of relationships with local schools. It seems more likely that good relationships with local schools have a positive effect on this indicator. If this is so they may also have a positive effect on the other indicators.

## Did the teams influence our measure of 'doing-well'?

We examined whether teams varied in their apparent effects on the well-being of their clients. Our conclusion was that any influence was likely to be very small.

None of the attributes of teams were significantly associated with our 'doing-well' score after we had taken account of the characteristics of the users. This does not, of course, mean that teams had no influence. It may be simply that our measures were too imprecise or that we were trying to measure the wrong things. That said, any influence is unlikely to be large. We return to this issue in our next chapter.

## Conclusion

The teams in this study differed in a lot of ways. They had differing purposes and served differing kinds of children. According to the team leaders, some teams were under more pressure than others and some were better served by outside agencies. Pressure tended to be high when adjusted caseloads were high and field resources low. These associations may or may not reflect cause and effect. It is probably safest to assume that they do until proved otherwise.

The team leaders themselves described the kinds of resources they wanted. Generally they felt there was a need for more long-term carers, and more special fostering. They also wanted more support for contact, less school exclusion and more or better training for carers. Their views varied between councils and responses to their views would need to vary accordingly.

The children were more likely to use particular kinds of placement in some teams than they were in others. There were also differences between teams in the chances that a child would go home or have a repeat admission. We were not able to say for sure why teams differed in these ways. The team leaders' views seemed to be influential. For example, children were more likely to go home if they had team leaders who felt that they had more by way of field resources. Team resources may also be important with teams under pressure making them less likely to make placements for adoption.

Some measures of outcome also varied between teams. Those that were under pressure were more likely to have children who had moved three or more times in a year. The better the apparent support from schools the better the team was likely to do on all the measures of stability. This association may or may not arise from cause and effect. There is, however, no harm in assuming that it does. Better collaboration between schools and social services can surely only do good.

Overall these findings show that councils need to keep their social work teams 'on side'. Without their help they may find it hard to increase care by family and friends, increase adoption, or do well on some measures of stability. At the same time there seem to be limits to the effects of teams. There are not large differences between teams in the well-being of the children they serve.

## Notes

1   These two councils made age a key principle in organising their teams. In addition all the leaving care teams dealt with older young people (16 or over or, in one case, 14 or over), teams serving asylum seekers were more or less confined to older children and one team offered a specialist service to families and carers with teenage young people.

2   Mann–Whitney U test, $Z = 3.06$, $p < .001$.

3  The school support score was significantly lower among teams that only served looked after children ($p < .01$ in a Kruskall Wallis analysis that only considered the five main types of team). This may well be a chance finding. If it is confirmed in other research, the reason may be that these 'looked after' teams often deal with children who are placed outside their councils and that it is more difficult to create good relationships with schools in these circumstances. Alternatively it may be that schools are more prone to exclude looked after children in the knowledge that there is someone to take responsibility for them in the day – an approach that social workers are unlikely to approve of.

4  The inter-correlations varied from .47 to .56.

5  We standardised the figures for each response so that they had a mean of 0 and a standard deviation of 1. A measure based on these standardised scores would have had a Cronbach's alpha of .87. However we had complete information for only 63 teams. In order to cope with the problem of missing variables our score was based on the average value of responses to all variables.

6  We used a similar procedure for the field resources score where the initial Cronbach alpha was again .87.

7  We followed the same procedure and the reliability score was .77.

8  The school score was based on two questions 'Schools are too keen to exclude looked after children' and 'Schools are generally keen to work with us over looked after children'. Both questions were answered on a four-point scale.

9  The CAMHS questions were 'Confidentiality is a problem in our work with CAMHS', 'CAMHS give a high priority to work with looked after children', 'Our work with CAMHS raises problems over the way cases are understood'. These questions were answered on a four-point scale.

10  Our measures of quality of administration, rate of computers per social worker and placement availability were not significantly associated with work pressure. The computer rate was associated with lower pressure after allowing for its association with social worker caseloads. This, however, reflected the effect of two rather extreme outliers and it seemed safer to exclude them from the analysis.

11  'Family contact should hardly ever be restricted even in cases of abuse' and 'Contact with families should be actively managed and supervised where there is any risk'.

12  This statement may seem to be different from the preceding one. In practice, however, it is unsafe to pick out one category of team as being significantly different from the others when the significance is not very large and the difference among the categories taken as a set is not significant.

13  Alternatively teams specialising in adoption may be well-staffed. This is unlikely as the two 'permanency' teams did not have a particularly 'good' staffing ratio.

14  Emergency placements influence the three placements measure since they are likely to be followed by another in the near future. They do not have so much influence on the PSA or D35 measures since these are affected by any move irrespective of whether or not it is to an emergency placement.

Chapter 15

# Councils and Outcomes

## Introduction

Outcomes vary with the children, placements and teams involved. How far do they also depend on the councils by whom the children are served? This is a crucial question. Government policy on child care is delivered through these councils. The electorate holds them accountable for the effect of their actions. Naturally all parties assume that the council's writ can and should run in all parts of the child care system. Where there is a child protection scandal, it is not only the social workers who are named. Councils and chief officers are also held to account.

This book has shown that this assumption of council responsibility is in many ways right. We have found major differences between councils over whether they return children to their homes, the proportion of looked after children who have repeat admissions, the use of care orders and the kinds of placements provided. Councils also differ in the kinds of children they look after. These differences in the children, however, do not fully explain the differences in practice. In many respects there is no doubt that the council's writ does indeed run.

Despite this evidence, it is still not clear how much influence a council has. Appendix II gives some reasons for this uncertainty. In this appendix we look at national statistics on the official indicators of council performance in the field of children's services. It is natural to think that all these indicators are related to some underlying measure of 'organisational excellence'. If this were so we would expect that the indicators would show considerable consistency. Excellent councils who scored high on an indicator in one year should do so in the next. Those who scored 'well' on one indicator should also tend to score high on the others and to have a high overall 'star rating'. Appendix II shows that very little of this is true.[1]

All this points to a key problem. Councils are bureaucratic and political bodies. They depend on rules and filing systems and the willingness of individuals to follow guidance that can never fully cover the situations they meet. As argued in the introduction there is no adequate theory of how such bodies can influence the complex dealings of the front line workers on whom the care system depends. This chapter wrestles with the question of how councils might be able to ensure effective practice.

## Method

The chapter begins with a brief analysis of material from our telephone interviews with managers. We use this to explore the way in which they saw themselves as influencing events. Our main method is statistical. Different councils serve different kinds of children. We need to see whether, after allowing for these differences, children in some councils do better than expected.

## Introducing changes

The officers we spoke to were concerned with policy. The most common aim, for example, was to keep children out of the care system. The mere assertion of such a policy was obviously not in itself enough to bring about what they wanted. To achieve their aims the councils had a number of tools at their disposal.

The most obvious of these tools was the *provision of resources*. For example, if the council provides a large number of children's homes, these are obviously more likely to be used. In practice councils were generally trying to restrict the use of residential care. Similarly most were reluctant to authorise the use of the independent sector. Nevertheless there was a considerable variation in the attitudes of key officers to these different provisions. As we have already pointed out, there are major variations in the extent to which councils make use of them.

A second tool involved *staffing policies*. Commonly the officers spoke of their difficulties or success in recruiting and keeping social workers and foster carers. They detailed the methods that they used to do this: for example, the level of remuneration they offered or the training and support they gave to foster carers. Potentially these policies could also rely on the information available on quality of performance – for example, through Independent Reviewing Officers, exit interviews or annual appraisal. In practice, however, the need to retain and support staff seemed to take precedence over the need to monitor their performance – a point to which we return later.

A third tool involved *procedures*. There was at the time much interest in the introduction of placement panels of various kinds. The aim here was to ensure common policies were followed and to test and improve the quality of the decisions made. Some specialised panels were meant to allow 'bargains' to be struck between the different parties who were paying for the placements.

Fourth, councils could use *structural changes* or *pilot projects* to concentrate attention and expertise on particular issues – for example, through the development of dedicated multi-disciplinary teams to promote the education of looked after children or the provision of specialist teams for asylum seekers or long-term looked after children. Large authorities would commonly introduce a change in one or two areas as a means of testing out its effects, keeping down the initial expense or capitalising on some *ad hoc* funding that happened to be available.

The way in which councils were able to combine these different sources of influence could be seen in the changes they had introduced. In analysing these we concentrated on those that councils told us had clearly 'worked'. One had increased the number of children looked after by 19 per cent over the course of the year. This reflected a judgement that the council had been keeping children in the community when it was far too risky to do so. Another council had reduced its use of agency foster placements by 18 per cent over the year, judging them expensive and inappropriate. A third council seemed to have avoided the association, found in some councils, between repeat admissions and loss of a chance for adoption. Again this seemed to reflect conscious policy.

These changes seemed to have been produced by attention to the 'levers' we have described above. So they involved:

- *Policies* – all the councils had clearly formulated views on the changes they wanted to achieve.

- *Procedures and organisation* – the council seeking to increase its adoption rate was a small one and relied on the assistant director to sign off all care plans. This officer insisted that any plan to rehabilitate a child should be accompanied by a plan for permanence if that failed. The council reducing its use of agency foster care also relied on review and placement panels to implement its policies.

- *Staffing* – the procedures were implemented by staff signed up to the policies and were a way of getting the message across to social workers who needed to take account of them if, for example, they were to get the placements they wanted or their plans approved. In the council with the increase in the number of children in the looked after system this had partly been achieved by changing the personnel in the assessment team.

- *Resources* – in the council with the change in adoption policy this had been accompanied by an increase in the number of social workers involved in finding adopters. The council seeking to reduce its use of agency foster care had mounted a sustained recruitment campaign and increased its use of in-house carers by 24 per cent over the year.

In these ways changes were brought about not by the use of 'one policy lever' but rather by a coherent combination of the methods we have discussed.

## Variations by councils

Was our ability to predict our outcome measures improved by adding information on the local councils? The answer varied by the outcome measure considered.[2] After allowing for the background variables there were still very highly significant variations by local council on the 'three placements' and new PSA stability indicators. There was also a slight variation in 'doing-well' by council but no variation in the D35 measure. These are interesting results. We consider them below in more detail.

## Variations between councils on the A1 (three placements) measure

The councils varied very significantly on the 'three placements' measure. This effect ceased to be significant if the two 'worst' performing councils were omitted. Both these councils (and the next 'worst' performing council) had special looked after teams. We tested the idea that councils with these teams would not do well on the measure.

Figure 15.1 describes the differences between these councils and others. As can be seen councils with the teams did indeed have higher adjusted rates of children with three or more placements.[3]

There are three reasons for being wary about this result. First, it was only one of a number of hypotheses we tested – this one may have proved correct by chance. Second, the reasoning behind our hypothesis turned out to be wrong.[4] Third, one possible reason for the effect, if it is a true one, is that some of the looked after teams were quite new. At the time of our study they may have still been reviewing their children and making some placement changes as a result.

We wondered whether councils would have high proportions with three or more placements if many of the moves were planned rather than forced. There was some evidence that this was so. We calculated the proportion of those with fully successful placement histories among those with three or more placements. This measure correlated positively with the councils' adjusted 'three placements' indicator,[5] although the correlation fell just short of significance. So more of the completed placements in councils who score high on this measure are seen as successful and thus as having done their job.

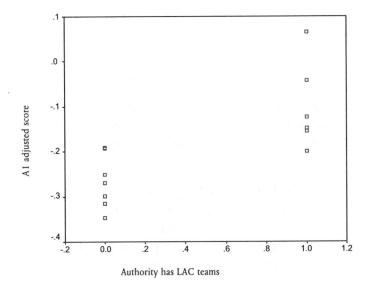

Source: CIS data. Note: .0 = Councils without LAC teams ($n = 7$); 1.0 = Councils with LAC teams ($n = 6$). The analysis was based on the 13 councils. Two of the councils without LAC teams had exactly the same score and are represented by one square.

**Figure 15.1** Adjusted three placements score and type of council

Therefore, it seems that differences between councils on the 'three placements' measure are not fully explained by differences in the children they look after. It is less clear what it is that councils do that brings these differences about. The use of looked after children's teams may have an effect but we need further research to be sure. The differences may also reflect variations in conscious policy (for example, over the speed with which adopted children are processed and placed).

## Variation between councils on the 'new PSA indicator'

Our conclusions on the 'new indicator' were very similar to those that we reached on the three placements (A1) measure. Councils undoubtedly affect it. It is much harder to know why.

The reasons for this difficulty may be that the explanations for doing well or badly are relatively specific to the council. One council was doing outstandingly well on this measure after allowing for differences in intake. Despite this, its overall official rating for serving children was very low. In this council a new management team was striving to improve the authority at the centre and were concerned about drift. So the indicator may simply have reflected reluctance on the part of social workers to move children whom the management would rather have placed elsewhere. Another council was also doing very well on the measure but was marked by much tighter central control. Here the good performance may have reflected rapid moves into final placements.

Our conclusion therefore is that the new PSA indicator does provide interesting information about a council's performance. Of itself, however, it does not, without further analysis, show whether that performance is good or bad.

## Lack of variation by council in the D35 measure

Our knowledge of the councils did not improve our ability to predict which children would do well on the D35 measure. This was surprising.[6] Why was it so? The most likely explanation for the lack of variation is that once a child has been looked after for four years all councils are agreed that the best place for him or her is likely to be a stable foster placement. They do not, however, differ sufficiently in their ability to affect the variables that produce such placements.

Again this result foreshadows our central conclusion: councils can affect decisions (for example, over the speed at which children return home). Where there is widespread agreement on what the decisions should be outcomes depend on day-to-day practice. The quality of this varies a great deal but not in a way that councils find it easy to control.

## Differences in 'doing-well'

There was a highly significant difference between councils in the 'doing-well' score. There are two important caveats. First, the result is more a tribute to the numbers in the analysis than to the additional explanatory power gained by including the councils in the analysis.[7] The effect of the councils was very small.

How did the councils make their influence felt? In part, it seemed, this was through the social work teams. Our 'multi-level' model took account of certain characteristics of the children. After we had done this, the teams accounted for only 2.7 per cent of the variation in our measure of 'doing-well'. The councils accounted for none of it.

Therefore, it seems likely that if councils are to make life better for their looked after children they will have to rely on their carers. It was interesting that the average authority measure of quality of carer (judged by the supervising social worker) was positively associated with the average measure of client well-being (based on ratings by the social worker) (tau b = .46, $p$ = .028).

We looked further at this result using a 'multi-level' model. This suggested that children were more likely to do well 'in care' if:

- they were first looked after when they were quite young

- they did not have particularly serious problems at home

- they were not considered disabled by the social workers

- their council had a 'retention' policy as measured by the average length of time the children had been in care since their last admission

- the average quality of the foster carers as measured by the supervising social workers was high.

So councils may do better if they take the children in young, keep them a long time and ensure that those who look after them are 'good parents'.

We need to be careful with these results. Statistically we are only dealing with 13 councils. 'Doing-well' is measured at only one point in time. The findings that relate specifically to councils are barely significant. Even if we accept them, we need to be cautious about acting on them. Taken to extremes they would suggest that councils should aim to take in children as young as possible, and then avoid having them adopted or returned home. This would be morally unacceptable.

In the end we need to look at the results along with our other findings and our case studies. Taken together these suggest that children do better in care if:

- they know what is planned for the long-term and are happy with this

- they have good foster carers.

It must surely make sense for councils to try and bring this about.

## Conclusion

This chapter has been concerned with two questions:

1. What aspects of the care system are associated with differences between councils?

2. How far can councils use the power they seem to have to influence outcomes?

Both our qualitative and our quantitative evidence suggest that the power of the councils is considerable. They formulate policy. They also implement it through their use of resources, their staffing policies, their procedures and the way they structure themselves and pilot new provisions and resources.

At the same time there may be limits to what they can do. The 'three placements' indicator did vary by council as did the new indicator. The D35 indicator did not. In addition there was only a very slight variation in terms of our measure of 'doing-well'. Even this slight effect disappears if we take account of the influence of social work teams.

These findings are in keeping with those of our earlier chapters. As we have seen many of the moves recorded in the 'three placements' and new PSA indicators are planned from the beginning of the placement. In this sense they reflect decisions and plans that can be written down. It is in the area of conscious decision that the councils' influence lies. So it is no surprise that councils differ on these measures.

These considerations may also explain why there was so little variation between councils in either the children 'doing-well' or the stability of long-term placements. There are not differences of policy on the proper treatment of those who have been looked after for four years. All are agreed that long-term foster care is likely to be the best place for them if this can be ensured. This makes it less surprising that lack of success on this measure is so strongly related to the children's characteristics. It also makes it less surprising that differences between councils in organisational arrangements were not associated with differences on this measure.

In the end our results suggest that councils are most likely to promote the well-being of their children if:

- they are able to provide them with long-term security
- they give them good foster carers.

Their ability to do this depends ultimately on the skill and commitment of the social workers and foster carers themselves.

## Notes

1 The lack of correlation between the performance indicators need not mean that councils do not influence them. If, however, they do, this must be through means that are highly specific to the indicator concerned. It is also possible that indicators vary for reasons that have nothing to do with what the council does. For example, Appendix II provides evidence that indicators relating to education are influenced by the social characteristics of the geographical area.

2 We first carried out the logistic and OLS regressions described earlier, then added information on 12 councils as dummy variables and then compared the omnibus model chi square or analysis of variance tables as appropriate allowing for the additional degrees of freedom.

3 Mann–Whitney U test $Z = 2.714$, $p = .007$. The adjusted rate was the average standardised residual, i.e. a measure of how far each child in the council was doing better or worse than predicted on this score.

4    We thought that the division of responsibility might lead community teams that had made emergency placements to defer the decision to seek a permanent placement so that when one was found after six months the effect on the new indicator would be negative. If this was so, it would be expected that the effect would be apparent on relatively recent entrants but not on others. This did not turn out to be so. In practice the effect was only significant for the A1 'three placements measure' and was equally apparent irrespective of how long the child had been looked after.

5    Spearman's Rho = .5, $p$ = .08, two-tailed.

6    Its correlation with the new indicator was .72, that between the new indicator and the A1 measure was -.53 and that between the D35 measure and A1 was negative and not significant (-.3).

7    The adjusted R square rose from .174 to .182.

Chapter 16

# An Overview

## Introduction

This book has been about the movement of children in care. Most people believe that children who are looked after move too much. At the same time most agree that not all their moves are bad – some moves, for example to adoption, are seen as good. The assumption behind the research was that moves take their meaning from a wider context: their effect on the children's chances of achieving a permanent base in which they can grow up happily, attached to those looking after them and without further disruption.

This assumption led us to ask three questions:

1. What kinds of children are looked after?

2. How do they move into, out of and within the system?

3. How far do their chances of stability and well-being depend on: (a) their own characteristics; or (b) the particular placements, social work teams or councils they happen to have?

In broad outline we found that the care system was dealing with a number of distinct groups with different needs and prospects. Whatever their differences most of the children looked after at any one point in time were not going home in the near future, not going to be adopted and not going to achieve a long-term placement in care. Prior to a long-term placement, they often moved a good deal. Some of those who were placed long-term were happy and wished, despite the statistical probabilities against, to stay 'forever'. Others were weakly attached to placements or moved from placement to placement, unable either to go home or find a place to be in care. The challenge is to increase the number of children who are with their families, adopted or in long-term care and who can stay happily and safely where they are.

Our case studies left us in no doubt that success in meeting this challenge depends on the relationships the children make. The key ones are clearly likely to be in long-term placements with their families, with adoptive parents or with a foster family. Not all children, however, can achieve such long-term relationships immediately. There may also be a need for adults who are a safe refuge, while, for example, a child tries out a return to their family or goes to a residential school. Some children may also need to change if they are to have a chance of a permanent placement. Others who have a family of their own may not want a new one but need a place from which to launch themselves into the adult world. We argue that in such cases relationships with carers again have a key role to play.[1]

These ideas are hardly new. Our recommendations are meant to give them more depth. We provide evidence that councils can bring about much of what we suggest – for example, increases in the use of adoption and care by family and friends. However councils seemed less able to influence a key determinant of the children's relationships and well-being: the quality of their placements. Here too we have suggestions to make.

## The study

The study took place in 13 councils in England: four county councils, two unitary councils and four London and three metropolitan boroughs. The councils were not randomly selected but, as far as we could check, our key samples almost exactly represented the national picture.

The research focused on all children who had been looked after at any point in a year whose last day (census date), as agreed with individual councils, varied between 31 May 2003 and 30 June 2004. It drew on administrative data on all children looked after in the agreed years ($n = 7399$), questionnaires from social workers on those looked after in the last six months of the years ($n = 4647$, response rate 71%), and from team leaders ($n = 114$, response rate 66%). We had additional data on foster households ($n = 1585$) and residential units ($n = 315$). Telephone interviews with 54 managers provided a managerial context and case studies of 95 children illustrated, deepened and tested the conclusions. Each council received an individual report on its own data of approximately 25,000 words.

## What kinds of children are looked after?

Our sample contained a number of relatively[2] distinct groups of children:

- Young entrants (43%)[3] – these children were under the age of 11. They were looked after primarily for reasons connected with abuse and neglect and had many difficulties at home.

- Adolescent graduates (26%) – these young people had first been admitted under the age of 11 but were now older than this and still in care. They had generally entered the system for reasons of abuse and neglect, had difficulties at home, at school and with behaviour.

- Abused adolescents (9%) – these young people were first admitted over the age of 11 for reasons of abuse or neglect. On average their behaviour was significantly more challenging than that of the adolescent graduates and they were also doing much worse at school.

- Adolescent entrants (14%) – these young people were first admitted when aged 11 or over and were looked after primarily because relationships at home had broken down. Their families had fewer problems in their own right than those of the previous groups but they themselves showed more challenging behaviour and were doing worse at school.

- Children seeking asylum (5%) – these were almost invariably over the age of 11. They were looked after because they had no families and not because their families had problems. They were doing comparatively well at school and displayed less challenging behaviour than any other group.

- Disabled children (3%) – these children were said to be looked after because they were disabled. They had comparatively high levels of challenging behaviour but their families were not said to have many problems in their own right.[4]

## The key challenges

The groups differed from each other in many ways. For the purposes of the study the key difference lay in the aims, lengths and nature of the placements. Around six out of ten of the young entrants, adolescent graduates and disabled children had last or latest placements that were meant to lead to adoption or to give care and upbringing. The comparable figures for adolescent entrants, asylum seekers and even abused adolescents were all much lower.[5] In keeping with this, sizeable proportions of adolescent entrants (60%), abused adolescents (49%) and asylum seekers (40%) had last or latest placements that had lasted less than six months.

In practice only the adolescent graduates had had the time to achieve a really long placement. Among those in this group who were over 16 nearly four in ten were in a foster placement that had lasted for two years or more. In none of the other groups were as many as a quarter of the young people of this age in foster placements that had lasted this long. At the census date just over a quarter of the adolescent graduates who were over 17 had placements that had lasted for five years or more. Even in this group, however, a long placement was not assured. Just under a third had placements that had lasted for less than a year.

Children may, of course, achieve permanence through adoption or return home. These options were not available for many of our sample. Adoption was possible for young entrants who had started to be looked after under the age of five. Nine per cent of those in our sample were adopted in our census year. More may have been adopted later. Only a handful (23 out of more than 4500) of children first looked after over the age of five were adopted in the census year.

The chance of return home varied with time since arrival. We estimated that just under half (46%) of those who started to be looked after would leave within a year. Two-thirds (63%) of those doing so went home. Among those who had been looked after for a year or more the chance of leaving within the next year was very low (around 5% for children aged between 11 and 15). Only about a fifth of those who did leave after a year were known to go home. At any particular point in time around three-quarters of our sample had been continuously looked after for more than a year. Their chance of going home was low.

Many of those going back home did not stay there. Around four in ten of our sample and half of those over 11 had had more than one admission.[6] Councils who returned high proportions of children had, on average, higher numbers of children with repeat admissions. Those who had gone home and come back had more placements and were, on our measures, doing worse than others of similar age and age at first admission.

These features of the care system resulted in a build up of children who were not going to leave in the near future but who were not, in the end, going to have a long-term stable placement. This is a key challenge. The aim of policy must be to reduce the number of these children, while seeking to ensure that those who are in long-term placements are doing well and those who are not are nevertheless as secure as possible.

## Could more go home safely?

There were very large differences between councils in the proportions of children returning home within the first year. These differences were not explained by differences in the children. So it seems likely that on average more could go home. The question is whether they could do so safely.

In general the children who were least likely to go home were those who were 'vulnerable' in the sense of being younger, disabled, abused or neglected. Children who came from families where there was domestic violence or drug or alcohol abuse were as likely as others to go home but more likely than others to have had a repeat admission. The same was true of children with challenging behaviour. Safe returns would require plans to deal with all these 'risk factors'. They would also need resources. Social work teams were statistically more likely to try return home when the team leader believed that community resources were good.

Our case studies also emphasised aspects of practice around return. There was the need to consider a wide range of placements and not just return to mothers – placements with fathers, kin, and friends could all 'work out'. There also needed to be clarity about what was planned and the conditions for its success. Social workers had to work purposefully, if possible with the agreement of all concerned, in order to achieve the plan at measured but urgent pace. There had to be a realistic assessment of whether the conditions for return were met and a fall-back plan if they were not.

Other things also helped. These included continuity. The more the child was able to share the placement with their siblings, avoid a change of school, begin a longer term placement with known carers, and maintain contact with the relatives to whom they were to return the better. 'Good' carers who were able to sympathise with the parent(s), support the child and work with the social workers were highly valuable. Overall, there was a need for adequate staffing to enable purposeful social work, avoid drift and allow thorough assessment.

IMPLICATIONS:

High priority should continue to be given to ensuring return home where appropriate, but this requires careful assessment of the relevant risks, good practice and appropriate resources (cf. Biehal 2006; Farmer, Sturgess and O'Neill 2008).

## Should there be more shared care?

Shared care might reduce the need for full admission to the care system. Some councils were enthusiastic about its possibilities. As some made much more use of this than others, its use could be increased.

In general we tried to exclude 'planned series of short breaks' from the study. There were, however, case studies of children who had received them in the past or were currently receiving them despite being looked after. Some children had received shared care over a prolonged period with different carers. This practice appeared to lead to insecurity. By contrast regular breaks with the same carer could appear very successful.

There were two specific reasons for considering more 'shared care'. First, children who had repeat admissions rarely returned to their former carers. A few had done so in our case studies and were very glad about it. An increase in this practice might limit the damage associated with failed returns home. Second, some disabled children appeared to have no placement other than a residential one. One of our case studies of a disabled young person provided a very successful example of a combination between residential care, care with known foster carers and care at home. This could be a promising model for other disabled children or even children who are not disabled.

**IMPLICATIONS:**

(a) The effects of failed returns home should be reduced and the benefits of shared or rotating care increased by ensuring that wherever possible children go to carers they know and trust; (b) There should be more use of foster placements in conjunction with residential care, particularly residential care for disabled children; (c) Brief breaks should, if possible, be with the same carer(s).

## Is there a role for 'treatment'?

In a previous study in the 1980s around one in nine of the placements were 'for treatment'.[7] We found only one in a hundred of the last or latest placements had this aim. Team leaders felt that this was a gap and wanted more special fostering schemes and specialist residential care. Children or young people who probably needed to 'change' and therefore some form of 'therapy' included:

- those who had great difficulty in trusting adults and therefore in committing themselves either to foster carers or their own families

- those (often teenage entrants) whose behaviour threatened any placement whether with their family or in care.

Carers are likely to have a key role in dealing with these difficulties. Children are unlikely to learn to trust adults if those with whom they live are untrustworthy. They are unlikely to learn to behave well at home if the adults where they are living ignore good behaviour and they themselves get what they want by behaving badly.

Fortunately there is some evidence from other research that foster care, at least, may provide an answer to some of these problems.[8] In the long run, however, change that relies on a benign environment is only likely to last if it is followed by another equally benign one. Return home is unlikely to succeed unless the original problems have been addressed.

Those who are not going home also require coherence between placement and subsequent environment. For them too a continuing relationship with some stable adult is likely to be crucial.[9] We consider below those with a stable placement history. Those without one are known to do badly on leaving care. There is evidence that leaving care teams can play a useful role with these young people, not least by dealing with their recurrent crises over accommodation for which appropriate provision has to be made (for this and much more evidence on leaving care, see Biehal *et al.* 1995; Broad 1998; Sinclair *et al.* 2005b; Stein 2004; Wade and Dixon 2006).

We described those seeking asylum and others entering over 16 as using the care system as a 'launch pad'. The case studies suggested that the young people required a room of their own, respect for their individuality, encouragement with their education or employment, practical help with these if necessary, space within which to work and a trusted adult who was prepared to listen and encourage. Some needed space within which to work out relationships with their own families. Those seeking asylum might also need help with finding their own relatives, getting in contact with members of their own communities and with dealing with their own legal position (cf. Wade, Mitchell and Baylis 2005).

IMPLICATIONS:

Councils should return to the view that placements can provide treatment, but ensure that these placements are part of a coherent plan.

## Should there be more adoptions?

An increase in the number of adoptions would lower the number of young entrants and, over time, the number of adolescent graduates. There were wide differences in the likelihood that children of similar characteristics would be adopted in different councils. So an increase in the number should be possible.

In part these differences between councils arose because attempted rehabilitation virtually prevented adoption in some councils but not in others. Resources may also play a part. Adoption was more likely if the social work team serving the child was relatively well-staffed. It was less likely if the child was no longer a baby, had siblings, was said by the social worker to be disabled and came from a minority ethnic group. Teams or workers dedicated to placing such hard to place children might increase their chances of adoption, although we ourselves have no evidence of this.

Our qualitative data (mainly from our interviews with managers) emphasised the likely importance of:

- clear policies on adoption
- investment in advertising and local recruitment of adopters
- adequate staffing of 'adoption and fostering' teams
- procedures that ensure adoption is considered in all care plans for children under five and that these are 'signed off' at a suitable level

- 'parallel planning' for young children returned home (a possible explanation for differences between councils in the effects of failed returns home)

- being prepared to consider adoptions by carers and to deal with their likely concerns over loss of income and support – a practice that was endorsed by some of our 13 councils and also by other research (Sinclair 2005).

IMPLICATIONS:

An increase in the number of adoptions is possible and desirable. It is likely to depend on decisiveness,[10] good practice, a high level of appropriate resources and appropriate council policies and procedures.

## Could there be less movement within the system?

Most placements were meant to end. Nearly half of those in the social work sample who had arrived within the last year had placements with short-term aims such as assessment, while half of those in their second or third year had placements with medium-term aims (for example, preparation for a long-term placement or adoption). Only among those who had been looked after for more than three years did most placements have the long-term aim of care and upbringing. Overall only four in ten of the last or latest placements were meant to provide such long-term care.

In keeping with this social workers thought in terms of sequences of placements. These sequences were dominated by a 'family ideal'. They tended to be seen as successful when they ended in homely placements (adoption, foster care or the child's own home) and unsuccessful in other cases. Difficulties in achieving successful sequences included use of residential care for disabled children, the lack of foster placements for children with challenging behaviour, and, in some areas, the lack of 'matches' for black and minority ethnic minority children. Such children might be placed out of county and then moved in order to bring them closer to their families, bring about a better match or (as the social workers sometimes saw it) save money.

IMPLICATIONS:

The number of intended moves could be reduced by: (a) broadening the scope of some initial placements so they were able to take children of varying kinds and for varying lengths of time thus avoiding the need for interim placements before a final placement is found; (b) increasing the availability of local placements able to take challenging children and black and minority ethnic children; (c) accepting that local placements are not always best (see below); (d) Increasing the councils' commitment to certain groups so that the plan is to keep them until they are ready to move rather than to move them on.

## Can care itself offer more permanence?

Care can offer long-term placements in a family setting. As we have seen it is only likely to do this where the child is an adolescent graduate. Even for these the chances of a really long placement vary. Some councils have very few 'adolescent graduates' over the age of 16. Possibly they have reduced their numbers through the use of residence orders. Others have large numbers. We cannot comment on these differences in policy.

We used our case studies to distinguish between children who had different levels of commitment to care. Some children had a base in care. They were happy where they were, wished ideally to 'stay for ever' and had the amount of contact that they wanted with their families. Others were weakly based in care. They were not going home and had reasonably stable care careers but were not committed to their current placement. Others had no place to be. They were not going home, were not committed to their current placement and had very unstable care careers.

Some of these differences arose from the nature of the placements. Temporary or residential placements did not seem to attract the same commitment as long-stay ones in foster care. Most, however, depended on where the children's allegiance lay and the quality of the carers. Other things helped: a clear plan so that all knew what they stood; the presence of siblings; a school where the child was happy. Counselling could help a child to come to terms with leaving their family. The key threats were the way the child behaved and a reluctance to accept a need to be looked after.

Statistically long placements are threatened by difficult behaviour among those over 11. Some young people mourned the loss of placements that had disrupted. Others were about to leave long-term placements because they were 18 and before they were ready to do so.

IMPLICATIONS:

(a) Long-term placements should be treated on the same assumptions as adoption and placements at home, carefully made and reviewed, recognised as permanent, supported at times of threat, on occasion allowed to persist despite disruption, and not arbitrarily ended at 18 (cf. Schofield 2002, 2003); (b) Young people in a settled placement should leave as children leave their parents: at their own pace, with the chance of return, and with back-up from those who have been looking after them (cf. Biehal 2005; Stein and Wade 2000).

## How should success be measured?

In order to test these conclusions we needed measures of both stability and well-being. Children do not want to stay with carers with whom they are unhappy. They do not want to leave placements where they are doing well. We measured four main outcomes. These related to:

1.  whether the child had had three placements in the year (a measure related to the official A1 indicator but differing from it in using information from the social workers as well as the client information system)

2.  the official D35 indicator (the proportion of children who had been looked after continuously for four years or more who had been fostered with the same carer for the past two)

3.  the new PSA movement indicator (the proportion of children under the age of 16 who had been looked after continuously for two and a half years or more and who were in the same placement for the past two or placed for adoption in the past year)

4.  a measure of 'doing-well' calculated from social work ratings of 'emotional well-being', 'behaviour', 'positive adult ties', 'being settled in current placement', 'getting on in education/occupation' and 'being safe and doing well'.

We examined how far movement or 'doing-well' reflected the characteristics of the child. Children who were over 11 and doing poorly on the indicators of movement differed from others of the same age. They showed more challenging behaviour and were less likely to be doing well at school, were also more likely not to want to be in care. Such characteristics were not important predictors of movement among those who were under 11.

IMPLICATIONS:

It is not enough simply to measure stability. We also need to take account of well-being. Insofar as we do use stability as a measure of success we need to be aware that: (a) the reasons for greater or lesser stability are not the same among children under or over 11 and; (b) that some children are more likely to do well and achieve stability than others.

## Does the kind of placement influence outcome?

Some kinds of placements seemed to have better outcomes than others. Comparisons, however, need to take account of differences in the children or rely on judgements that take these differences into account. It was interesting that once we had done this some of the differences between residential care and foster care disappeared. The findings still suggested that young people had higher well-being in foster care, but we thought it unsafe to assume that we had fully taken account of their backgrounds. It was also interesting that:

- Residential placements and placements with family and kin were seen by the social workers as being of higher quality when they were not within the local authority.

- This explained the perceived superior quality of residential placements in the independent sector.

- Social workers commonly saw placements with parents on a care order as achieving their purpose. Children were relatively more likely to flourish in these placements if (a) they did not accept the need to be looked after and (b) they did not have a need code of abuse.[11]

A number of findings related to placements with family and friends. These placements lasted longer than others and were seen as more successful by social workers. Children in them had higher well-being scores and this remained true when we allowed for other key characteristics. There were strong arguments for making more use of these placements.

Increased use of placements with family and friends should be possible. In different councils the proportion of foster placements that were of this kind varied from one in a hundred to more than a quarter. Moreover, councils that placed a relatively high proportion of their children with family and friends were doing as well with children in these placements as other councils that made less use of this provision.

The apparently good effects of placements with family and friends came with a 'warning'. The placements were only seen as more successful by social workers when they were also intended to be long-term. They were also seen as lower in quality. The case studies certainly illustrated their virtues ('naturalness', continuity, the commitment of family members, the maintenance of family ties). They also illustrated their problems – the ill-health of grandparents, the poverty of many carers, their lack of experience with very challenging children, quarrels between carers and birth parents (see also Farmer and Moyers (forthcoming); Hunt, Waterhouse and Lutman 2007; Sinclair 2005).

IMPLICATIONS:

Councils need to widen choice of placements through: (a) accepting that placements 'out of county' can play an important role; (b) considering placements with parents particularly when the child is not at risk of abuse and does not want to be looked after; (c) making more use of care with family and friends, while remaining aware of its potential drawbacks and particular needs for support. Councils need to be aware of the lack of evidence for differences in outcome between foster and residential care, after allowing for differences in intake, as the costs of the two forms of provision may differ.

## Does quality of placement affect outcomes?

We measured the quality of placements through ratings by social workers and also used separate ratings by supervising social workers and others of the quality of foster carers and of residential units.

Our general conclusion was that quality of placements and quality of foster carer were both very strongly related to our measure of 'doing-well'. The higher the quality the better the child did. This conclusion held when we took account, as far as we could, of the children's characteristics.

Quality of foster care and quality of placement were also related to the length of placement but only if the placement was intended to last and the child was over 11. When this was so children lasted longer in the 'better' placements. Again, this conclusion also held when we took account, as far as we could, of the children's characteristics.

The quality of the residential unit was also related to turnover and to how well the child was doing in terms of education.

IMPLICATIONS:

High quality placements are central to children's well-being and the stability of long-term placements for children over 11. The central aim of management must be to enable, acquire and promote such placements.[12]

## How far can councils influence outcomes?

Much policy assumes that councils are in a position to bring about what the government wants. Our recommendations also assume that councils can, for example, ensure that more children are adopted or fostered with relatives.

If councils do have this kind of impact there are likely to be differences between them in the outcomes they achieve. In certain respects this was true. As we have seen councils varied significantly in their willingness to return children to their homes, the proportion of entrants who had previously been admitted, and the kinds of placements they made. The likelihood of a positive result on the three placements and PSA measures similarly varied with council after taking account of the children's characteristics.

These variations in practice and provision were not explained by differences in clientele although these were also very large. There were qualifications. In some respects the social work teams appeared more potent influences on placement decisions than the council. This was particularly so in relation to placements with friends and family. Nevertheless our findings left no doubt that councils and teams could influence those aspects of movement about which they could take decisions (for example, whether a child should go home).

Our interviews with managers suggested that they did this through a combination of:

- policies (e.g. guidelines on the 'threshold' for looking after children)
- central procedures and bodies (placement panels, procedures for signing off care plans and the like) through which the policies were implemented and whose key members were 'signed up' to the policies
- resource provision (e.g. recruitment of additional foster carers in order to reduce reliance on the independent sector)
- cultural change (e.g. replacing a team that had a particular approach to risk assessment with another).

Councils seemed less able to affect those variables such as 'happiness' or the achievement of a long-stay foster placement (the D35 measure) that depended heavily on the quality of placements and practice. All our evidence suggested that the quality of a child's current placement had a far stronger impact on how well he or she was doing than either the council or the child's social work team.

IMPLICATIONS:

Councils can and should influence the choice of provision available for children in care along with the choices that are made. They have much greater difficulty in influencing the outcomes for children in these placements and this must be a key focus for their efforts.

## Improving the quality of placements

This study has shown that social workers can identify 'good placements'. This ability is potentially a powerful tool for improving quality. Children, their social workers and independent reviewers and supervising social workers all know a lot about placements. This knowledge could be used to guide the choice of place-ments, influence the market, improve the quality of the workforce and end place-ments that are not working out. In practice we did not find evidence that this was happening in any systematic way.

This lack of attention to quality may reflect government targets. These do not focus on the quality of the children's placements. With the exception of education where outcomes depend quite heavily on the social characteristics of the area (see Appendix II), they have little to say about how the children are doing. Instead they rely on 'proxies' that are easier to measure than well-being, and may or may not relate closely to it. Managers and practitioners in our study felt that the spirit behind the targets was good but that the measures themselves should not guide individual practice or be taken as an accurate indicator of a council's performance.

Our own analysis of three years' national data supported this view. It sug-gested that the measures were not stable over time, weakly correlated with each other at best, and weakly correlated if at all with inspectors' judgements on how well the council was doing (see Appendix II). Evidence from the study itself showed that the data used for the indicators was, in some councils, very poor. Adjustments for the quality of data and for the children's characteristics produced league tables for our 13 councils that were very different from the 'official' ones. Overall this part of our analysis led us to conclude that the measures could provide useful feedback to managers and did help to focus minds on general issues. They were not, however, the heart of the matter and should not deflect attention from those things that were.

**IMPLICATIONS:**

It is possible to pick out good residential units, good carers and placements that are working. Councils must use this knowledge in a systematic way to guide practice, commissioning and quality assurance. Inspections should focus on the degree to which they make these judgements accurately and act on them appro-priately.[13]

## Support from central government

The research was commissioned as part of the government initiative *Quality Protects*. This was very popular in our councils. It also highlighted some of the ways central government can support practice. Government can provide leader-ship on values. It can deliver resources. It can oversee the system for seeing whether these resources are well spent. Clearly it also has other 'levers', for example, legislation and high level re-organisation. None of our suggestions, however, require levers other than leadership, resources[14] and quality assurance.

IMPLICATIONS:

Our qualitative evidence suggests that *Quality Protects* was an effective approach to promoting change. The government would be able to promote the lessons of this study using similar strategies. More specifically it can use its leadership to promote a view of care as based on relationships, and consider the implications in terms of funding and quality assurance.

## Conclusion

This final chapter has argued that care should be built around the children's relationships both those they make with their real or adoptive parents and families, and those they make while in care. This way of looking at care suggests some changes – better supported and assessed rehabilitation, more use of adoption, a form of foster care that is more genuinely 'permanent', and the use of carers and residential units both to promote change and to support children outside the placement itself.

Our emphasis on relationships poses a problem. Of their nature they are individual, partial, and unpredictable. Councils themselves do not have relationships – or at least not in the same sense. They are corporate parents, not real ones. They work through paper, committees and bureaucratic rules. We believe, however, that with skill they can nurture and enable the relationships that children in care can make. In this way they will make the best use of the greatest wealth that the care system has: the commitment and human qualities of those who make it up.

## Notes

1   These ideas are clearly related to Bowlby's (1979) ideas, particularly those which relate to the concept of a safe base.

2   The groups were partly defined in terms of government 'need codes' (abuse or neglect, disability etc). By definition a child cannot have more than one need code. So a child who was, for example, disabled and abused would have only the one label. For these reasons, the differences between the groups are less sharp than they appear. That said, we have shown that the differences are real and have real consequences, for example, for the children's careers in care.

3   There is a slight overlap between these groups. For example, some disabled children had entered under the age of 11. Where a child could have been put in more than one group, we put him or her in the last group in the list to which he or she belongs.

4   The percentage of disabled children depended very much on the definition of disability. Those defined as disabled by the social workers constituted a much higher percentage of the six month sample (16%). As explained in the body of the book the correlates of disability defined in these different ways were sometimes the same but not always.

5   20% (adolescent entrants), 27% (asylum seekers), 40% abused adolescents.

6   This figure is based on information from social workers and the client information system.

7   Rowe, Hundleby and Garnett 1989. Their figures are not strictly comparable with ours as they focused on placements that started and/or finished whereas we focused on individuals including those who did not move at all.

8   Chamberlain (1998) discusses relevant evidence on a form of treatment foster care involving the use of a social learning approach with challenging children. Children who 'bottle up emotions' and generally display the 'stoical' behaviour characteristic of 'inhibited attachment' are more likely to change this behaviour if they live with carers who are 'child oriented'. This was not true of behaviour that resembled 'disinhibited attachment' the other main branch of reactive attachment disorder (Sinclair *et al.* 2005b). As far as we know, there is no strong evidence that any therapeutic approach is successful with this form of the disorder.

9   For evidence of the continuing importance of relationships on leaving care see Sinclair *et al.* 2005b.

10  For evidence on the importance of early decision and much else see Howe 1997 and Selwyn, Frazer and Quinton 2006.

11  This reflects an analysis not reported in the main text. Briefly an analysis of variance using our measure of 'doing-well' as the dependent variable showed a highly significant main effect ($p < .001$) for 'not accepting need to be looked after' and an even more significant interaction between this acceptance and being placed with parents. There was a similar effect for abuse considered on its own. The combination of need code of abuse and acceptance of the need for care left both interactions significant, albeit in the case of the need code at a low level of significance ($p = .036$).

12  There is abundant other evidence that placements can affect outcome. For relevant evidence on residential care see Sinclair (2006) and on foster care Sinclair (2005).

13  Suggestions for improving the quality of placements usually focus on training. In principle this must be right. In practice there is a lack of evidence that any current form of training can improve outcomes (see Sinclair 2005 for foster care and Sinclair 2006 for residential care).

14  It would cost money to enable young people to stay with their carers beyond the age of 18 or to keep places free so that a young person can return to them if return home fails to work out. Evidence that residential care is not apparently more effective than foster care does suggest that those who use much of it might save resources by reducing its use. Specialist foster care, however, is unlikely to be cheap. So the suggestions we put forward will probably depend on resources and the force of the argument that can be put for getting them.

# Representativeness of the Study Samples

## Introduction

In this Appendix we examine three aspects of the representativeness of the study. First, we look at the characteristics of the 13 councils that took part in the study, particularly their relationship to comparator councils that are closest in terms of deprivation levels and demography. Second, we demonstrate that the study included a sample of looked after children ($n = 7399$) similar in their basic characteristics to those found at national level. Third, we compare the characteristics of the sub-sample of children (for whom we had received a detailed questionnaire from their social workers – $n = 4647$) who were looked after, or ceased to be looked after, by the 13 councils during a specified six month period with those of the main sample for the same six month period.

## The 13 participating councils

Before considering comparators, Table AI.1 sets out some of the key demographic characteristics of the 13 councils that participated in the study. As can be seen, the 13 councils included three outer London and one inner London, three 'unitaries', four shire counties and two metropolitans. In terms of location the 13 councils were spread throughout the standard regions of England – the two regions not represented in the study were the South West and the East of England.

The councils ranged from the large, with two containing a population of about three-quarters of a million, to the moderately sized with populations of less than a quarter of a million. More precisely, the study contained two councils in the lowest population quartile, three in the second quartile, four in the third and four in fourth, or highest, population quartile. Not surprisingly, the shire counties had the lowest number of people per hectare of land whereas the outer and inner

**Table AI.1** Demographic characteristics of 13 participating councils

| Council | Type of council | Location | Population | Density pop per hectare | LAC per 10,000 < 18 |
|---|---|---|---|---|---|
| 01 | Outer London | London | 219,100 | 34.2 | 40.2 |
| 02 | Outer London | London | 298,300 | 19.9 | 46.8 |
| 03 | Shire County | North West | 678,700 | 3.3 | 33.3 |
| 04 | Shire County | E. Midlands | 743,000 | 2.9 | 32.9 |
| 05 | Metropolitan | North East | 191,000 | 13.3 | 63.3 |
| 06 | Unitary | Yorks & H. | 247,900 | 34.8 | 98.2 |
| 07 | Inner London | London | 174,400 | 140.8 | 88.2 |
| 08 | Outer London | London | 250,600 | 65.1 | 101.2 |
| 09 | Unitary | Yorks. & H. | 155,000 | 1.8 | 53.0 |
| 10 | Shire County | West Midlands | 286,700 | .9 | 28.4 |
| 11 | Shire County | South East | 758,600 | 3.8 | 43.3 |
| 12 | Unitary | Yorks. & H. | 183,100 | 6.7 | 45.5 |
| 13 | Metropolitan | Yorks. & H. | 477,800 | 13.1 | 68.5 |

London councils had the highest density of population – the contrast between the West Midlands' shire county with less than one person per hectare and the inner London council with 140 could not be sharper. Finally, the last column of the table sets out the rate of looked after children per 10,000 of the population aged under 18. Again, reflecting the national picture, the range is considerable from a low of 28 to a high of 101.

These then are some of the basic characteristics of the 13 councils in the study. We turn now to a consideration of their 'comparators', that is, the other councils they resembled.

Annex G of the report on performance indicators (Commission for Social Care Inspection 2004) contains a list of comparator groups for each of the 148 councils in England (City of London and the Isles of Scilly are not included). Each council is listed in alphabetical order along with the 15 comparator councils, presented in order, that are closest to that council in terms of deprivation levels and demography. For example, the first five comparator councils closest to Bolton on these criteria are, first, Tameside, followed by Oldham, Walsall, Rochdale and Derby.

From this list it is possible to ascertain that the 13 councils in the study featured as comparators for 104 of the 148 councils (70.3%) in England. This overall figure can then be broken down to provide a more detailed picture to show the number of occasions the 13 councils appeared as one of the first five comparators, as one of the first ten comparators and as one of the 15:

- as one of the first 5: 55 of 148 (37.2%)

- as one of the first 10: 88 of 148 (59.5%)

- as one of the 15: 104 of 148 (70.2%).

Viewed another way, of the 135 councils that were not in the study (148 – 13 = 135), only 26 had lists that did not contain comparators from among the 13 participating councils. In addition, on eight occasions within the study one or more of the 13 appeared in the list of comparators for each other.

On this basis alone, the results from the study are highly relevant to a large proportion of the councils that share similar characteristics to the 13 in the study.

## The study sample compared to national statistics

Table AI.2 sets out details for the basic characteristics of the looked after children in the York study, set alongside comparable national information.

As can be seen, the characteristics of the study sample, based on information contained in the management information systems of the 13 councils, are very similar to the national picture based largely on the SSDA 903 returns made by councils each year at the end of March.

Three important variables in the SSDA 903 returns are 'category of need', 'placement' and 'legal status'. Table AI.2 indicates that for the first two the project and national sets of statistics are very close.

This is less so when it comes to legal status where national figures suggest that a larger proportion of children looked after at the end of March 2004 were on 'other orders' than was the case for the study sample. However, the proportions that were voluntarily accommodated were very similar in the two samples. The main contrast used in the book is between those who were voluntarily accommodated and the others.

The following PAF indicators are particularly relevant to the present study:

- A1 PAF indicator – the proportion of children looked after at 31 March with three or more placements in the last 12 months.

- D35 PAF indicator – the proportion of children looked after continuously for at least four years, and of those the number and

**Table AI.2** Comparison of study sample with national statistics

|  |  | Study (%) | National (%) |
|---|---|---|---|
| Age | Under 1 | 4.1 | 4.2 |
|  | 1–4 | 13.8 | 14.7 |
|  | 5–9 | 21.2 | 20.8 |
|  | 10–15 | 43.4 | 43.3 |
|  | 16 & over | 17.5 | 17.0 |
| Sex | Male | 56.3 | 55.5 |
|  | Female | 43.7 | 44.5 |
| Ethnic group | White | 78.2 | 80.0 |
|  | Other | 21.8 | 20.0 |
| Category of need | Abuse/neglect | 64.3 | 62.5 |
|  | Disability | 3.6 | 3.9 |
|  | Parental illness | 5.5 | 5.7 |
|  | Family acute stress | 6.8 | 6.9 |
|  | Family dysfunction | 8.3 | 10.0 |
|  | Unacceptable behaviour | 2.1 | 2.8 |
|  | Low income | .2 | .2 |
|  | Absent parenting | 9.1 | 8.0 |
| Placement | Foster placements | 70.1 | 68.0 |
|  | Children's homes/hostels | 11.3 | 11.4 |
|  | Adoption | 5.0 | 5.4 |
|  | Placed with parents | 8.1 | 9.6 |
|  | Other | 5.5 | 5.6 |
| Legal status | Accommodated under S.20 | 28.6 | 31.4 |
|  | Care orders | 59.2 | 64.4 |
|  | Others | 12.2 | 4.2 |
| A1/D35/New PI | PAF A1 | 13.4 | 12.9 |
|  | PAF D35 | 50.1 | 49.3 |
|  | New PI | 65.6 | 64.9 |

Sources: National statistics based on the 2004 annual SSDA 903 returns.

proportion of them who have been in their foster placement for at least two years.

- New PSA indicator – the proportion of children aged 16 and under who have been looked after for at least two and half years, and of those the number and proportion who have been in the same placement for two years, or placed for adoption.

Table AI.2 again indicates a very close match on these three measures between project and national statistics.

## The questionnaire to social workers

Our sample in the 13 councils consisted of 7399 looked after children, 5413 of whom were still looked after at the census date (the date at which we collected the information in each council). A further 988 children had been looked after at some time during the previous six months and the remaining 998 had been looked after during the six month period prior to that.

Our six month sample ($n = 6401$) comprised the 5413 children who were still looked after at the census date and the 988 who had been looked after at some time during the previous six months. In addition, we were able to identify the relevant social worker and send them a questionnaire about a child's recent placements. The question we address here is whether the sub-sample of children for whom we received a questionnaire from their social workers ($n = 4647$) represented a biased or unbiased sample of all the children in the study who had been looked after in a specified six-month period.

Not surprisingly, given the high response rate (72.6%) from social workers, the columns of figures in Table AI.3 show close correspondence. Therefore, there is strong evidence to conclude that the questionnaire returns from social workers represent an unbiased sample of children looked after in the six-month period. We have already provided evidence that the main sample is highly representative of the situation in England as a whole. We can therefore be reasonably confident that this is true of the six-month sample as well.

**Table AI.3** Comparison of the 6-month sub-sample with the sample based on the social worker questionnaire returns

| | | 6 month sub-sample (%) | Social worker Q. returns (%) |
|---|---|---|---|
| Age | Under 1 | 4.0 | 3.8 |
| | 1–4 | 15.3 | 14.6 |
| | 5–9 | 20.6 | 20.1 |
| | 10–15 | 40.8 | 41.3 |
| | 16 & over | 19.4 | 20.2 |
| Sex | Male | 56.3 | 56.4 |
| | Female | 43.7 | 43.6 |
| Ethnic group | White | 78.3 | 77.6 |
| | Other | 21.7 | 22.4 |
| Category of need | Abuse/neglect | 61.8 | 60.6 |
| | Disability | 3.3 | 3.5 |
| | Parental illness | 5.9 | 5.5 |
| | Family acute stress | 7.9 | 7.7 |
| | Family dysfunction | 8.6 | 8.5 |
| | Unacceptable behaviour | 2.9 | 2.9 |
| | Low income | .3 | .3 |
| | Absent parenting | 9.3 | 10.8 |
| Placement | Foster placements | 70.1 | 69.7 |
| | Children's homes/hostels | 11.3 | 11.2 |
| | Adoption | 5.0 | 5.4 |
| | Placed with parents | 8.1 | 7.5 |
| | Other | 5.5 | 6.2 |
| Legal status | Accommodated under S.20 | 31.5 | 31.4 |
| | Care orders | 54.4 | 54.6 |
| | Others | 14.1 | 14.0 |
| A1/D35/New PI | PAF A1 | 13.2 | 12.6 |
| | PAF D35 | 50.1 | 50.5 |
| | New PI | 65.6 | 65.5 |

Sources: Client Information Systems in 13 councils and Social Worker data.

# Analysis of National Data

## Introduction

Two performance indicators (A1 and D35)[1] have provided a key focus for the book. This appendix uses national data to explore these and other indicators.

There are four key questions:

1. Are the indicators consistent across time, so that a council that appears to score highly in one year also scores highly in the next?

2. Do the performance indicator scores relate to each other and to the ratings of council performance for the area 'serves children' and the overall 'star' rating?

3. How do the stability measures relate to social conditions and the way the councils' care systems operate?

4. Is it possible to derive an economical description of the operation of the council's systems and then explain variations in this by reference to social and other factors?

These questions all bear on the central concern of the book of how far and in what way can managers influence the operation of the care system.

If there is no relationship between scores over time this would imply that it was very difficult for councils to score consistently on the indicators. Organisational structure, long-serving managers and other factors that tend to be stable over time are therefore unlikely to have much effect. Some consistency across time is therefore almost a necessary condition for a useful organisational indicator. The converse, of course, does not apply. It is perfectly possible to have a consistent indicator that is essentially not under an organisation's control. However, it is reasonable to suggest that the test of consistency is one that all indicators should pass.

The issue of how indicators relate to each other and to overall judgements of performance is equally important. If there is some general factor of 'organisational excellence' one would expect a high degree of association between different measures. If there is no such consistency both managers and inspectors face a more difficult task. In such cases the strategy that, for example, produces a 'good score' on, say, the A1 indicator might not produce a high score on indicators concerned with care leavers' subsequent employment (Indicator A4). Managers have, as it were, to solve a number of different problems and not just one. Inspectors are likely to find councils who score well on one indicator yet poorly on another. In reaching an overall judgement on the council they have to give a weighting to one indicator as against another, a more difficult task than simply, as it were, aggregating them.

The question of how scores relate to social and other conditions is relevant both to whether they can be influenced and how this may be so. If it was found that a score was very strongly related to social conditions there might be little that a council in unfavourable conditions could do about it. By contrast if it could be shown that an indicator related to factors within the council's control this could be helpful.

The search for simpler patterns of operation is relevant to all the questions raised above. The reduction of a complex but potentially confusing set of scores to a smaller number may help managers and inspectors. Managers may find they have fewer problems to solve. Inspectors may have to make judgements on a smaller set of scores. If it is possible to 'explain' these scores this again may help both groups.

## Method

We used data from the following sources:

- National data submitted by the 150 local councils in England as part of their SSDA 903 statistical return. This requires each council to complete a form for every child who is looked after during the course of a year ending 31 March. The summary data for each council (but not individual child) is available electronically via the internet. The latest data set available for our analyses covered the year 1 April 2003 to 31 March 2004.

- Other national data sets that contain information at the level of the same 150 local councils. The different sources yielded a range of information, including data on population and population density, income support rates, unemployment, ethnicity and school absence. Perhaps the most useful source was the 'Income Deprivation Affecting Children' (IDAC) index developed by Michael Noble and his colleagues at Oxford University (Office of the Deputy Prime Minister 2005).

• The ratings for councils' performance for 'serves children' and overall 'star' rating.

We analysed the data using SPSS 11 for correlations, regression, and factor analysis.

## Are the performance indicators consistent over time?

Tables AII.1 to AII.8 give the correlations between successive scores on various indicators over the three years 2002, 2003, and 2004.

As can be seen in Table AII.1 there is a reasonably high correlation between 2002 and 2003 ($r = .626$) and also between 2003 and 2004 ($r = .537$) for the A1 Indicator.[2]

**Table AII.1** Correlations between successive A1 indicators (2002–2004)

|  |  | % with 3 or more placements 2002 | % with 3 or more placements 2003 | % with 3 or more placements 2004 – CF/A1 |
|---|---|---|---|---|
| % with 3 or more placements 2002 | Pearson correlation | 1 | .626 | .025 |
|  | Sig. (2-tailed) | . | .000 | .764 |
|  | N | 148 | 146 | 148 |
| % with 3 or more placements 2003 | Pearson correlation | .626 | 1 | .537 |
|  | Sig. (2-tailed) | .000 | . | .000 |
|  | N | 146 | 147 | 147 |
| % with 3 or more placements 2004 – CF/A1 | Pearson correlation | .025 | .537 | 1 |
|  | Sig. (2-tailed) | .764 | .000 | . |
|  | N | 148 | 147 | 150 |

Some of this continuity will be a continuity of children. Children who have been stable in one year are likely to be stable in the next. Relatively long-staying children in stable placements at the end of 2003 are quite likely to be in those same placements at the end of 2004. So some continuity is to be expected and is to be found between 2002 and 2003 and also between 2003 and 2004.

What is surprising is the degree of discontinuity between 2002 and 2004 ($r = .025$). This would suggest one of three things: there has been a major change in the way figures are collected; there have been major changes in the operation of various social services departments between those dates; or organisation has very little consistent effect on the figures at all.

Table AII.2 gives the correlations between successive years for adoption and fostering (Indicator B7). Unsurprisingly there is a high degree of consistency. This figure is no doubt influenced by the overall supply of foster carers and by policy on the use of residential care for teenagers.

**Table AII.2** Correlations between successive proportions of children fostered or adopted (Indicator B7)

|  |  | % fostered or adopted 2002 | % fostered or adopted 2003 | % fostered or adopted 2004 – CF/B7 |
|---|---|---|---|---|
| % fostered or adopted 2002 | Pearson correlation | 1 | .878 | .727 |
|  | Sig. (2-tailed) | . | .000 | .000 |
|  | N | 147 | 147 | 147 |
| % fostered or adopted 2003 | Pearson correlation | .878 | 1 | .788 |
|  | Sig. (2-tailed) | .000 | . | .000 |
|  | N | 147 | 148 | 147 |
| % fostered or adopted 2004 – CF/B7 | Pearson correlation | .727 | .788 | 1 |
|  | Sig. (2-tailed) | .000 | .000 | . |
|  | N | 147 | 147 | 147 |

There is no such consistency on the next indicator (C22) that relates to the fostering and adoption of children under the age of ten. The correlations in Table AII.3 are indeed significant. However a correlation of .2 accounts for only four per cent of the usual measure of variation. For practical purposes this is not very important. The probable explanation is that all authorities foster almost all children under the age of ten. They all have enough foster carers to do this, at the expense, if necessary of adolescents. So variations around this number probably reflect variations in the numbers placed with parents or adopted and so are not sufficiently large or systematic to yield high consistent variations.

**Table AII.3** Correlations between successive proportions of children fostered or adopted under the age of 10 (Indicator C22)

| | | % under 10 fostered/ adopted 2002 | % under 10 fostered/ adopted 2003 | % under 10 fostered/ adopted 2004 – CF/C22 |
|---|---|---|---|---|
| % under 10 fostered/adopted 2002 | Pearson correlation | 1 | .191 | .210 |
| | Sig. (2-tailed) | · | .020 | .011 |
| | *N* | 148 | 148 | 147 |
| % under 10 fostered/adopted 2003 | Pearson correlation | .191 | 1 | .114 |
| | Sig. (2-tailed) | .020 | · | .170 |
| | *N* | 148 | 148 | 147 |
| % under 10 fostered/adopted 2004 – CF/C22 | Pearson correlation | .210 | .114 | 1 |
| | Sig. (2-tailed) | .011 | .170 | · |
| | *N* | 147 | 147 | 147 |

The correlations between successive D35 measures, as set out in Table AII.4, are again 'reasonable'. They account for between 21 and 45 per cent of the variation depending on the correlation chosen.

**Table AII.4** Correlations between successive D35 indicators

| | | D35 % 2002 | D35 % 2003 | CF/D35 % 2004 |
|---|---|---|---|---|
| D35 % 2002 | Pearson correlation | 1 | .673 | .459 |
| | Sig. (2-tailed) | · | .000 | .000 |
| | *N* | 144 | 144 | 143 |
| D35 % 2003 | Pearson correlation | .673 | 1 | .518 |
| | Sig. (2-tailed) | .000 | · | .000 |
| | *N* | 144 | 146 | 145 |
| CF/D35 % 2004 | Pearson correlation | .459 | .518 | 1 |
| | Sig. (2-tailed) | .000 | .000 | · |
| | *N* | 143 | 145 | 148 |

Much of this may reflect consistency of individuals involved. For example, a long-stay child who moved in 2003 could not score well on this indicator in 2004. The fact that correlations are not higher could reflect the relatively low base of the indicator. In practice, however, there was not much evidence that this applied. The correlation was as high in the smaller unitary councils as among the others.

Table AII.5 gives the correlations between successive years of a new PSA indicator.[3] This concentrates on those under 16 and looked after continuously for 30 months. The relevant proportion is the number of these who have been in the same placement for the past two years or, alternatively, placed for adoption. As can be seen many of the correlations are rather low. The correlation between the measures for 2002 and 2004 accounts for about 4 per cent of the variation. This may, of course, reflect inaccuracies in the data on the new measure that will come to be ironed out. On the face of it, however, this measure does not appear to be a particularly stable measure of organisational performance.

**Table AII.5** Correlations between successive years on new PSA indicator

|  |  | % nupi 2002 | % nupi 2003 | % nupi 2004 |
|---|---|---|---|---|
| % nupi 2002 | Pearson correlation | 1 | .449 | .210 |
|  | Sig. (2-tailed) | . | .000 | .011 |
|  | N | 147 | 146 | 147 |
| % nupi 2003 | Pearson correlation | .449 | 1 | .318 |
|  | Sig. (2-tailed) | .000 | . | .000 |
|  | N | 146 | 147 | 146 |
| % nupi 2004 | Pearson correlation | .210 | .318 | 1 |
|  | Sig. (2-tailed) | .011 | .000 | . |
|  | N | 147 | 146 | 147 |

Table AII.6 presents the correlations between successive years on the adoption measure (Indicator C23). This shows some evidence of stability, although this is not marked. If one takes account of the proportion of children under the age of five in 2004 the correlation between 2003 and 2004 rises to .39, accounting for around 15 per cent of the variation.

Table AII.7 deals with the proportions of care leavers meeting certain criteria and getting one or more GCSEs at a level A–C (Indicator A2). The correlation between the two years of data available is relatively high and accounts for about 43 per cent of the variation.

**Table AII.6** Correlations between successive adoption performance measures (Indicator C23)

| | | Adopted as % of those LAC 6 months 2002 | Adopted as % of those LAC 6 months 2003 | Adopted as % of those LAC 6 months 2004 – CF/C23 |
|---|---|---|---|---|
| Adopted as % of those LAC 6 months 2002 | Pearson correlation | 1 | .457 | .390 |
| | Sig. (2-tailed) | . | .000 | .000 |
| | N | 141 | 131 | 133 |
| Adopted as % of those LAC 6 months 2003 | Pearson correlation | .457 | 1 | .421 |
| | Sig. (2-tailed) | .000 | . | .000 |
| | N | 131 | 140 | 133 |
| Adopted as % of those LAC 6 months 2004 – CF/C23 | Pearson correlation | .390 | .421 | 1 |
| | Sig. (2-tailed) | .000 | .000 | . |
| | N | 133 | 133 | 140 |

**Table AII.7** Correlations on education measure for 2003 and 2004 (Indicator A2)

| | | % ceased with 1 or more GCSE 2003 | % ceased with 1 or more GCSE 2004 – CF/A2 |
|---|---|---|---|
| % ceased with 1 or more GCSE 2003 | Pearson correlation | 1 | .654 |
| | Sig. (2-tailed) | . | .000 |
| | N | 136 | 133 |
| % ceased with 1 or more GCSE 2004 – CF/A2 | Pearson correlation | .654 | 1 |
| | Sig. (2-tailed) | .000 | . |
| | N | 133 | 141 |

Table AII.8 deals with the measure for further education, training, and employment (Indicator A4). The correlations are again reasonable, for example, that between the 2002 and 2003 measure accounts for nearly half the variation. As we will see later, there is evidence that the education indicators reflect social conditions in the authorities and these may account for some of the stability.

**Table AII.8** Education, employment and training: correlations between successive measures (Indicator A4)

|  |  | % in educ/train/ employ 2002 | % in educ/train/ employ 2003 | % in educ/train/ employ 2004 – CF/A4 |
|---|---|---|---|---|
| % in educ/train/employ 2002 | Pearson correlation | 1 | .701 | .462 |
|  | Sig. (2-tailed) | . | .000 | .000 |
|  | N | 128 | 120 | 119 |
| % in educ/train/employ 2003 | Pearson correlation | .701 | 1 | .589 |
|  | Sig. (2-tailed) | .000 | . | .000 |
|  | N | 120 | 135 | 126 |
| % in educ/train/employ 2004 – CF/A4 | Pearson correlation | .462 | .589 | 1 |
|  | Sig. (2-tailed) | .000 | .000 | . |
|  | N | 119 | 126 | 133 |

## Relationship of scores to each other and to the overall ratings of authority performance

We looked at the association between different measures of performance in 2004. For simplicity we begin with the relationships between those performance indicators that were specifically concerned with placement stability.

There are some predictable, albeit small, correlations between the proportion adopted or fostered in 2004 on the one hand and the proportion of children adopted or fostered under the age of ten and the D35 score on the other hand. These associations are to be expected simply from their definitions.

There are also significant correlations between the new PSA indicator and the two stability indicators (A1 and D35). Again this is almost certainly a matter of definition. The new PSA indicator can be seen in Table AII.9 as a cross between the other two.

It is striking that the new PSA indicator is essentially uncorrelated with any of the others and that the A1 and D35 indicators are not significantly correlated with each other.

This pattern of 'non-correlation' is essentially repeated in Table AII.10. There is one significant correlation ($r = .315$) between the education measure (A2) and the long-term stability one (D35). This may reflect an impact of

**Table AII.9** Correlations between selected stability performance measures in 2004

| | | % with 3 or more placements 2004 – CF/A1 | % fostered or adopted 2004 – CF/B7 | % under 10 fostered/adopted 2004 – CF/C22 | CF/D35 % 2004 | % nupi 2004 |
|---|---|---|---|---|---|---|
| % with 3 or more placements 2004 – CF/A1 | Pearson correlation | 1 | –.032 | .123 | .095 | –.388 |
| | Sig. (2-tailed) | . | .704 | .136 | .250 | .000 |
| | N | 150 | 147 | 147 | 148 | 147 |
| % fostered or adopted 2004 – CF/B7 | Pearson correlation | –.032 | 1 | .322 | .212 | .070 |
| | Sig. (2-tailed) | .704 | . | .000 | .010 | .397 |
| | N | 147 | 147 | 147 | 146 | 147 |
| % under 10 fostered/adopted 2004 – CF/C22 | Pearson correlation | .123 | .322 | 1 | .097 | –.006 |
| | Sig. (2-tailed) | .136 | .000 | . | .244 | .945 |
| | N | 147 | 147 | 147 | 146 | 147 |
| CF/D35 % 2004 | Pearson correlation | .095 | .212 | .097 | 1 | .446 |
| | Sig. (2-tailed) | .250 | .010 | .244 | . | .000 |
| | N | 148 | 146 | 146 | 148 | 146 |
| % nupi 2004 | Pearson correlation | –.388 | .070 | –.006 | .446 | 1 |
| | Sig. (2-tailed) | .000 | .397 | .945 | .000 | . |
| | N | 147 | 147 | 147 | 146 | 147 |

Note: We have used non-parametric correlations (Kendall's tau b) for this table.

long-term stability on education or the impact on both of challenging children. Both explanations may well apply. It is, however, striking that the correlation, though significant, is low ($r = .315$) and thus accounts for only about ten per cent of the variation.

**Table AII.10** Correlations between selected performance measures

| | | Adopted as % of those LAC 6 months 2004 – CF/C23 | % ceased with 1 or more GCSE 2004 – CF/A2 | % in educ/train/employ 2004 – CF/A4 |
|---|---|---|---|---|
| % with 3 or more placements 2004 – CF/A1 | Pearson correlation | .120 | .073 | .047 |
| | Sig. (2-tailed) | .157 | .391 | .591 |
| | N | 140 | 141 | 133 |
| % fostered or adopted 2004 – CF/B7 | Pearson correlation | .174 | .150 | −.028 |
| | Sig. (2-tailed) | .041 | .080 | .750 |
| | N | 138 | 138 | 132 |
| % under 10 fostered/adopted 2004 – CF/C22 | Pearson correlation | .077 | .040 | .039 |
| | Sig. (2-tailed) | .372 | .646 | .657 |
| | N | 138 | 138 | 132 |
| CF/D35 % 2004 | Pearson correlation | .008 | .315 | .156 |
| | Sig. (2-tailed) | .926 | .000 | .075 |
| | N | 139 | 140 | 132 |
| % nupi 2004 | Pearson correlation | −.096 | .078 | −.003 |
| | Sig. (2-tailed) | .261 | .360 | .977 |
| | N | 138 | 138 | 132 |

Table AII.11 presents the last set of inter-correlations. As can be seen these are all low but nevertheless positive and significant. This is encouraging. However, it is worth re-emphasising that the correlations are very low.

These findings demonstrate that inspectors have a difficult task. In judging councils they have to balance a large number of weakly correlated factors. How far do their overall judgements relate to these different performance indicators?

Table AII.12 shows the correlations between the ratings for whether the council serves its children well and its overall status on social services ('star

**Table AII.11** Correlations between selected performances indicators

| | | Adopted as % of those LAC 6 months 2004 – CF/C23 | % ceased with 1 or more GCSE 2004 – CF/A2 | % in educ/train/employ 2004 – CF/A4 |
|---|---|---|---|---|
| Adopted as % of those LAC 6 months 2004 – CF/C23 | Pearson correlation | 1 | .268 | .171 |
| | Sig. (2-tailed) | . | .002 | .054 |
| | N | 140 | 137 | 128 |
| % ceased with 1 or more GCSE 2004 – CF/A2 | Pearson correlation | .268 | 1 | .254 |
| | Sig. (2-tailed) | .002 | . | .004 |
| | N | 137 | 141 | 129 |
| % in educ/train/employ 2004 – CF/A4 | Pearson correlation | .171 | .254 | 1 |
| | Sig. (2-tailed) | .054 | .004 | . |
| | N | 128 | 129 | 133 |

rating') on the one hand and several of the individual performance measures on the other.

As can be seen for 'serves children' there are significant but low associations with the C23 adoption rating (tau b = .176) and the A4 measure of training (tau b = .229) and approaching significance on the A1 'three placements' in a year measure (tau b = -112). The other associations are not significant. It is particularly striking that there is no association whatsoever with the new PSA target.

We collapsed the four-part rating of how well the council served its children into two categories ('yes' and 'most' against 'some' and 'no'). We then tried to see how well the variables given in Table AII.12 predicted this. The answer was 'rather poorly'. Only two variables remained as significant in a backward conditional logistic regression. These were the further education, training and employment variable (A4) and the adoption variable (C23). Taken together they would have allowed a successful prediction in 64 per cent of cases. A 'guess' that the council would have been rated 'no' or 'some' would have been correct in 67 per cent of cases and correct for 62 per cent of cases for 'most' or 'yes' combined.

As a separate exercise we examined the relationship between the Performance Assessment Framework (PAF) indicators and the inspectors' rating for 'serves children' and their overall 'star' rating for that council. As a reminder, for

**Table AII.12** Correlations between performance measures and overall measures of performance

| Kendall's tau b | | Serves children | Overall star rating |
|---|---|---|---|
| CF/A1 – Stability of placements | Correlation coefficient | −.112 | −.152 |
| | Sig. (2-tailed) | .086 | .017 |
| | N | 148 | 148 |
| CF/B7 – LAC in foster care or placed for adoption | Correlation coefficient | .059 | .055 |
| | Sig. (2-tailed) | .373 | .388 |
| | N | 147 | 147 |
| CF/C22 – LAC in foster care or placed for adoption | Correlation coefficient | .092 | .180 |
| | Sig. (2-tailed) | .167 | .006 |
| | N | 146 | 146 |
| CF/D35 – Long-term stability of LAC | Correlation coefficient | .060 | .084 |
| | Sig. (2-tailed) | .361 | .194 |
| | N | 146 | 146 |
| % nupi 2004 | Correlation coefficient | .078 | .110 |
| | Sig. (2-tailed) | .240 | .089 |
| | N | 147 | 147 |
| CF/C23 – Adoptions of LAC | Correlation coefficient | .176 | .147 |
| | Sig. (2-tailed) | .010 | .027 |
| | N | 138 | 138 |
| CF/A2 – Educational qualifications of LAC | Correlation coefficient | .029 | .101 |
| | Sig. (2-tailed) | .674 | .128 |
| | N | 138 | 138 |
| CF/A4 – Employment, education and training | Correlation coefficient | .229 | .249 |
| | Sig. (2-tailed) | .001 | .000 |
| | N | 132 | 132 |

the year 2003/2004 there were 18 PAF indicators for Children and Family Services within the following five domains:

1. Domain 1 – National priorities and strategic objectives. Indicators A1 to A4.

2. Domain 2 – Cost and efficiency. Indicators B7 to B10.

3. Domain 3 – Effectiveness of service delivery and outcomes. Indicators C18 to C24.

4. Domain 4 – Quality of services for users and carers. Indicator D35.

5. Domain 5 – Fair access. Indicators E44 and E45.

The final indicator (E45 – Ethnicity of children in need) was included in the 2003/2004 report for information only and came with a warning that doubts remained over its interpretation. For this reason we excluded it and confined our analysis to 17 indicators.

The first task was to reduce the scores within each of the 17 indicators down to two categories – 'acceptable' (very good/good/acceptable) and 'not acceptable' (ask questions about performance/investigate urgently). Our initial attempts to create a global score based on the 17 indicators faced the problem of missing data – either because the value had been suppressed in the data set or the council had not submitted the data in the first place. This resulted in a correlation value of .29 between our global score and the inspectors' 'serves children' rating that, while significant in statistical terms, accounted for less than ten per cent of the variance.

Our next step was to remove some of the indicators that contained a great deal of missing data (for example, the indicators A4 and C18 both lacked data on 18 councils). Where councils had missing data on the remaining indicators we gave them the benefit of the doubt and treated their performance as 'acceptable'. This led to an improved correlation co-efficient of .39, again significant but still accounting for only 15 per cent of the variance. Though an improvement in method on our first attempt we were still not satisfied with this solution.

Given the possible bias in our previous method, and to maximise the amount of data that was available, we decided to look at the correlations between each of the five domains and both the inspectors' ratings for 'serves children' and their overall 'star' rating of the council. We were also able to do the same for a global score based on all 17 indicators. As a further refinement, as the data was not necessarily 'normally distributed', we calculated both the Pearson parametric '$r$' correlation and Kendall's 'tau b' non-parametric correlation.

Table AII.13 indicates that '$r$' and 'tau b' were reasonably close in each case and any slight difference did not substantially change the interpretation of the result. For example, the correlation between the Domain 1 score and the 'serves children' rating is .274 and .229 for '$r$' and 'tau b' respectively, in both cases the values are significant at $p = .002$. While many of the values throughout the table are significant they are low and account for a very small proportion of the variance.

**Table AII.13** Correlation between PAF domains and inspectors' ratings

|  |  | Serves children | | Overall 'star' rating | |
|---|---|---|---|---|---|
|  |  | r | tau b | r | tau b |
| **Domain 1** | r/tau | .274 | .229 | .318 | .256 |
| A1–A4 indicators | | | | | |
| (*n* = 126 councils) | *p* | .002 | .002 | .000 | .000 |
| **Domain 2** | r/tau | .240 | .207 | .253 | .215 |
| B7–B10 indicators | | | | | |
| (*n* = 145 councils) | *p* | .004 | .003 | .002 | .002 |
| **Domain 3** | r/tau | .433 | .396 | .349 | .278 |
| C18–C24 indicators | | | | | |
| (*n* = 95 councils) | *p* | .000 | .000 | .001 | .001 |
| **Domain 4** | r/tau | .152 | .172 | .146 | .139 |
| D35 Indicator | | | | | |
| (*n* = 146 councils) | *p* | .068 | .033 | .080 | .093 |
| **Domain 5** | r/tau | −.018 | .024 | −.122 | −.123 |
| E44 indicator | | | | | |
| (*n* = 148 councils) | *p* | .828 | .766 | .141 | .113 |
| **All domains** | r/tau | .480 | .428 | .417 | .376 |
| A1–E44 indicators | | | | | |
| (*n* = 87 councils) | *p* | .000 | .000 | .000 | .000 |

Source: Social Services Performance Assessment Framework Indicators 2003–2004.

## How do the stability measures relate to social conditions and the way the councils' care systems operate?

We set out to explain the key stability indicators of:

- measures of the social character of the areas (population density, proportion of ethnic minorities, rate of adults claiming social security, proportion of families headed by a lone parent, a measure of deprivation and average number of unauthorised absences per child of secondary school age)

- measures of the care system reflecting its population (age and sex of children)

- measures of practice in the care system (measures of speed of return to the outside world, proportion adopted, proportion fostered).

We chose the last measures on the grounds that these were all factors over which we thought a council could exercise some control.

Table AII.14 gives an equation predicting the measure of turnover for the A1 indicator. This accounts for a relatively low proportion (28%) of the proportion of children at the end of the year that had had three or more placements.

**Table AII.14** Regression equation predicting three placements measure

| | Coefficients | | Standardised coefficients | | |
|---|---|---|---|---|---|
| | B | SE | Beta | t | Sig. |
| (Constant) | .630 | 4.992 | | .126 | .900 |
| Measure of length of stay of discharges | −.199 | .065 | −.543 | −3.053 | .003 |
| Ratio of starts to children looked after | 8.104 | 3.682 | .264 | 2.201 | .030 |
| % aged under 1 | .409 | .184 | .181 | 2.215 | .029 |
| % aged 10–15 | .229 | .076 | .253 | 3.018 | .003 |
| Income deprivation affecting children index | 6.800 | 2.737 | .201 | 2.484 | .014 |
| Average stay on group data* | 5.011E–02 | .025 | .352 | 1.972 | .051 |

Note: * This is measured by allocating numbers to the grouped data provided in the national statistics. The latter do not provide specific data on lengths of stay.

The first two variables suggest that councils that have a high turnover (a high rate of children starting to be looked after and relatively low lengths of stay among those discharged) will tend to have high ('poor') scores on this A1 measure.

The other variables suggest that movement may be higher among children aged less than one and those aged 10–15. Data from the main project showed that movement was higher in this latter group than in the sample as a whole. This was not true for those children aged less than one. This group were, however, more likely to move often than those aged from two to nine and this probably explains the result. The association with measures of deprivation may reflect the influence of the latter on local schools and on teenagers. Difficulties at school and involvement in a delinquent sub-culture can both threaten placements.

There was little to explain variations on the new performance indicator. It is conceptually related to the D35 and A1 indicators. Unsurprisingly it is significantly associated with both of them. In other respects it was related to very little.

None of the social indicators were associated with it. It did not seem to matter whether the council fostered a high or low proportion of its children. It was not associated with measures of schooling or employment. Previously high rates of adoption in 2002 and 2003 seemed to somewhat depress the indicator ($r = -.17$, $p = .04$ and $r = -.16$, $p = .06$). Arguably a high rate of adoption removes young children who would otherwise remain stably placed. However, the effect, if any, is clearly very small. There was a slightly stronger correlation between the indicator and the ratio of new starts to existing children ($r = -.23$, $p = .005$). Arguably councils that take in a relatively high proportion of children have difficulty in getting all of them settled within 6 months (something the indicator encourages). Again, however, this effect is weak.

Performance on the D35 indicator is also difficult to explain. As can be seen from Table AII.15 this indicator is weakly and negatively related to the adoption rate in at least two years (2002, 2003). Presumably councils with relatively high adoption rates thereby reduced the number of long-staying foster children. This effect, which was in any case small, was not apparent in 2004.

**Table AII.15** Correlations between adoption rates (C23) and the D35 indicator

|  |  | D35 % 2002 | D35 % 2003 | CF/D35 % 2004 |
|---|---|---|---|---|
| Adopted as % of those LAC 6 months 2002 | Pearson correlation | −.277 | −.289 | .064 |
|  | Sig. (2-tailed) | .001 | .001 | .455 |
|  | N | 137 | 139 | 140 |
| Adopted as % of those LAC 6 months 2003 | Pearson correlation | −.232 | −.261 | −.037 |
|  | Sig. (2-tailed) | .007 | .002 | .663 |
|  | N | 135 | 137 | 139 |
| Adopted as % of those LAC 6 months 2004 – CF/C23 | Pearson correlation | −.260 | −.159 | .008 |
|  | Sig. (2-tailed) | .002 | .062 | .926 |
|  | N | 137 | 138 | 139 |
| D35 | Pearson correlation | −.765 | −.382 | .289 |
|  | Sig. (2-tailed) | .000 | .000 | .000 |
|  | N | 143 | 143 | 143 |

In 2004 there was an encouraging correlation between the long-term stability measure (D35) and GCSE performance (A2) (see Table AII.16). Obviously this could be interpreted in different ways. Those who do well on their GCSEs may be the kind of young people who do not disrupt placements. On the other hand good placements may last longer and produce good performance at GCSE. The correlation is certainly compatible with the last explanation. Unfortunately, and for no obvious reason, there are no similar correlations in the previous years.[4]

**Table AII.16** Correlations between the D35 measure and the measure of educational performance (A2)

|  |  | % ceased with 1 or more GCSE 2003 | % ceased with 1 or more GCSE 2004 – CF/A2 |
|---|---|---|---|
| D35 % 2002 | Pearson correlation | .129 | .001 |
|  | Sig. (2-tailed) | .139 | .989 |
|  | N | 133 | 137 |
| D35 % 2003 | Pearson correlation | .068 | .022 |
|  | Sig. (2-tailed) | .434 | .795 |
|  | N | 133 | 138 |
| CF/D35 % 2004 | Pearson correlation | .422 | .315 |
|  | Sig. (2-tailed) | .000 | .000 |
|  | N | 135 | 140 |

There were similarly small but encouraging correlations with the proportions of care leavers involved in employment or further education or training (see Table AII.17). The correlations would not be expected to be large – few, for example, of those involved in the 2003 D35 measure, and none of those in the 2004 one, would be in a measure applied to care leavers. So it is encouraging that in 2004 they are consistent.

**Table AII.17** Further education, training and employment measure (A4) with D35

|  |  | D35 % 2002 | D35 % 2003 | CF/D35 % 2004 |
|---|---|---|---|---|
| % in educ/train/employ 2002 | Pearson correlation | −.052 | .120 | .219 |
|  | Sig. (2-tailed) | .565 | .183 | .014 |
|  | N | 123 | 124 | 127 |
| % in educ/train/employ 2003 | Pearson correlation | −.068 | −.096 | .195 |
|  | Sig. (2-tailed) | .438 | .276 | .024 |
|  | N | 131 | 131 | 133 |
| % in educ/train/employ 2004 – CF/A4 | Pearson correlation | −.051 | −.062 | .156 |
|  | Sig. (2-tailed) | .565 | .484 | .075 |
|  | N | 131 | 131 | 132 |

## Explaining variations by reference to social and other factors

We used factor analysis to derive a more economical or 'parsimonious' description of the councils' operations and outcomes. Essentially this method seeks to account for a large number of different scores in terms of a much smaller number of different dimensions. Examples of other uses lie in the attempt to describe variations between individuals in answering intelligence tests in terms of variations on, say, a main 'factor' such as 'general intelligence' and perhaps one or more special abilities.

The factors or components derived by this method depend on the variables analysed and also on the particular technique used. In this case we used the default method in SPSS (principal components). We included all the performance measures discussed above for the number of years for which they were available, in this way giving them more weight than other variables.

We included some measures of the councils' operations in 2004. These were:

- percentage of those leaving who left within 6 months of arrival

- the ratio of those entering the system over the year to those present on 31 March 2004

- a measure of the average length of time those who were discharged over the year had spent since last starting to be looked after

- a measure of the length of time those looked after on 31 March 2004 had been looked after

- the proportion of children looked after on 31 March 2004 aged less than five

- the rate of children looked after per 10,000 of all children aged less than 18.

We also included measures of the social character of the area. These related to:

- rate of families headed by a lone parent

- a measure of economic deprivation ('IDAC index' – see description above)

- density of population

- proportion of the population aged under 18

- proportion of children who were white.

Finally, we included information on the type of council (Inner London,[5] Metropolitan, Shire, or Unitary) as binary variables.

There were 43 variables in the analysis and the first four components accounted for half (49%) of the variation.[6] These could be interpreted as:

- Component 1 – Social deprivation – This component was heavily loaded on high income deprivation (.85), high proportion of income support claimants (.82), high population density (.77), high proportion of lone parents (.73) and high proportion of ethnic minorities. Councils with high scores on this component would have a high rate of children looked after (.79), low proportions of children fostered or adopted and relatively poor scores on the 'proportion with one or more GCSEs' measure (-.52 (2003); -.45 (2004)).

- Component 2 – we interpreted this as an 'adoption' component. Councils that scored high on this component would look after relatively high proportions of children under five (.62), and have consistently high proportions adopted (.54 to .43 depending on the year). They would score consistently 'poorly' on the D35 indicator (-.59 to -.41 depending on the year), generally poorly on the A1 indicator (.56 (2002), .54 (2003), .22 (2004)) and somewhat poorly on the new PSA indicator (-.42 to -.37 depending on year). They would tend to be Metropolitan (.49) or Inner London (.49).

- Component 3 – this component is essentially a measure of turnover. Councils that scored high on this component would tend not to be Metropolitan (-.46) or Inner London (-.46) but would have high ratios of starts to children looked after (.74), low average duration of completed placements (-.69) and high proportions of those leaving would do so within 6 months of starting to be looked after (.63). They would tend to do 'badly' on the three placements measure (.45 to .60 depending on year) and to a lesser extent on the new performance indicator (-.47 to -.27 depending on year).

- Component 4 – from the factor loadings, we interpreted this component to be a measure of a commitment to fostering. Councils that scored high on this component would tend to have consistently high proportions of children fostered or adopted (.52 to .50) and consistently high scores on the D35 measure (.43 to .49) – a likely consequence of a commitment to fostering. For reasons that are less clear they would also tend to have high proportions leaving within 6 months (.54) and a low average duration of completed placements (-.45).

The first factor emphasises the importance of social factors in explaining some indicators. These are primarily concerned with adoption, fostering and performance at school. Clearly inspectors have to try to discount these social factors in judging performance. This again must make their task more difficult.

## Conclusion

The current performance regime seeks to identify high performers and distinguish from others who are less good or even require external intervention. It is widely assumed that performance indicators can help with this task. This may not be as easy as is sometimes thought.

One difficulty is that some indicators are not very stable. So it is doubtful that they are useful measures of a consistently high quality organisational strategy.

A second difficulty is that measures that are not connected 'by definition' are weakly correlated or not correlated at all with each other. It therefore seems that they are unlikely to reflect an all-encompassing dimension of 'organisational excellence'. It also follows that judgements of 'organisational excellence' are likely to require allocating 'weights' to different measures – a hard and potentially subjective task.

A third difficulty is that the measures are only weakly correlated with the relevant judgements of excellence ('serves children' and the overall 'star rating'). The strongest association is with a 'basket of measures' where we simply counted the number of times the authority was within the appropriate benchmark. Even this, however, accounts for less than a quarter of the variation.[7]

There could be various explanations for this. Inspectors may have been attending to different measures. They may differ between each other in the weights they give to the measures. The overall measure of performance may have low validity. Or the performance measures may actually have little bearing on performance. None of these explanations is particularly favourable to the idea that the measures provide a strong measure of performance.

A fourth difficulty is that some measures have to be interpreted in the light of social conditions in the area served by the council. Performance on the education measures is quite strongly linked to a component measuring the extent of the councils' social deprivation.

A fifth possible difficulty may be that there may be potential conflicts within the aims implied by the measures. For example, a good performance on the adoption measures may in the long run lead to difficulties in ensuring a good performance on the D35 measure.

These difficulties are clearly not fatal to the idea of performance measurement. Many of the 'difficulties' are based on correlations. These provide an appropriate method of analysis if the assumption is that there is a consistent gradation across a measure with low scores being consistently poor and high scores consistently 'good'. The introduction to the measures used to point out that essentially they needed further interpretation, so that both very high scores and very low ones might call for further investigation. This advice suggests that we need to be cautious in interpreting our figures. It does not, however, invalidate the analysis based on domains and on the basket of measures – there we did take account of the possibility that very high or very low scores might be equally problematic.

That said, the common assumption seems to be that the scores provide a kind of league table. On this assumption the analysis in this appendix would be appropriate. It is thus this assumption rather than the concept of scores *per se* that this appendix challenges. The new PSA target for those looked after for 30 months or more provides a particular example of this. On the evidence we have presented this is an unstable measure that is only related to others defined in a similar way. It appears to bear no relationship to how good the inspectors think the council is. The government may need to reflect on how much weight they should put on it.

## Notes

1   Indicator A1: The percentage of children looked after at 31 March with three or more placements during the year.

    Indicator D35: The percentage of children who had been looked after continuously for at least four years, and of those the number and percentage who were currently in a foster placement where they had spent at least two years.

    Fuller definitions of these indicators are provided by the Commission for Social Care Inspection (CSCI 2004).

2   As a guide a correlation of .5 'explains' about 25 per cent of the usual measure of variation.

3   New PSA target: Children under the age of 16 who have been looked after continuously for at least two and half years, and of those the number and percentage who had been in the same placement for at least two years, or placed for adoption, at 31 March.

4   This anomaly was not removed by analyses that took account of our social indices.

5   We omitted 'Outer London' as a kind of 'benchmark'.

6   We used the Varimax rotation in the belief that this would allow for easier interpretation.

7   There is an additional difficulty that we are correlating measures we assume to be roughly normally distributed with a 'serves children' measure that contains four values that may not be at equal intervals. A non-parametric measure such as tau b would be more appropriate. This, however, does not yield a measure of 'variance accounted for'. In practice wherever possible we have checked our Pearson correlations against a non-parametric one. There proved to be little difference in either size or significance.

# Monitoring and Quality Assurance

Councils participated in this study, at least partly, and probably in most cases primarily, because they were interested in placement stability. More specifically they wished to gain more control over the performance indicators that measured movement. Generally they wanted fewer moves.

Most managers and team leaders, however, had rather more complex attitudes. They approved of the spirit behind the indicators. They were overwhelmingly positive towards *Quality Protects*, the initiative within which the indicators are embedded. On the other hand they commonly pointed out that the indicators were poor guides to individual practice (for example, a rapid adoption might easily involve three placements and would usually be seen as good practice). Commonly they felt that the indicators were of interest and needed to be understood. They were not, however, unambiguous measures of how well a council was doing.

The project's findings supported this rather complex attitude. Most placements were not meant to be permanent. Most moves occurred because they were intended. Others have suggested that this implies that moves are mainly 'for administrative reasons'. This, however, raises the question of what 'administrative reasons' means. A child may return home because it is thought that that is the best step or because it is necessary that this should be tried before a judge will agree to adoption. Is this an 'administrative' decision? Similar questions are raised about the use of short-term and emergency placements, 'bridging placements', placements for assessment and so on. It could indeed be argued that short-term placements are 'administrative'. They occur for primarily logistical reasons. Yet if they did not exist, it would be necessary to ensure that children were placed immediately in placements that fitted their needs in the longer term. This would have major implications for the number of carers needed and for their qualities.[1]

So what did our study have to say about the performance indicators that were of such concern to the councils? That depends on what these indicators are intended to do. Briefly the study did not support the use of the indicators as part of a league table. The reasons are:

- the quality of the data – the major discrepancies between the information from social workers and from the client information system would make us very dubious about the reliability of the A1 indicator[2]

- the difficulty of interpreting indicators whose significance differs for different groups in the care system (children's behaviour is a much more powerful correlate of three placements in a year among older children than among younger ones)

- the lack of attention to failed attempts at rehabilitation

- the difficulty of adjusting the indicators for measures of input

- the influence on indicators of practices, which are not obviously good or bad in themselves[3]

- the possible perverse effects of the indicators on individual practice[4]

- the danger that the indicators will inhibit innovation (the suggestions we have made for brief overnight stays for adolescents or time limited treatment foster care could well lower performance on them)

- the lack of strong consistent correlations between the indicators themselves or between the indicators as a group and the overall judgements that are made of the quality of service provided by the authority.[5]

Appendix II contains some further analysis of the performance indicators that tends to strengthen these points. Briefly, it seems that the performance indicators are only weakly correlated with the overall measure of performance for children's services. They are also weakly correlated with each other and often with the same performance indicator in previous years. All this tends to suggest that either there is no stable overall dimension of 'organisational excellence' or that if there is performance indicators are not a particularly robust way of tapping it.

These considerations do not suggest that the indicators are useless. At the least they have two major virtues. First, they direct managers' attention towards actions that might be taken to influence matters at the level of groups rather than individuals. Second they raise questions. It would, for example, be odd to find that a council had almost no children in foster placements that had lasted for two years or more. There might be explanations – for example, the creative use of adoption, residence orders and special guardianship. It is, however, important that an authority asks itself such questions and satisfies itself as to the reply.

This in turn means that councils should value their information systems, and use them not only to raise questions but also to sample key groups. They may, for example, sample children who are apparently 'failures' on the D35 indicators and seek to understand in detail why they are not in stable foster placements. The result may support what they are doing or suggest that it may need to be modified (e.g. by the ability to combine fostering with residential education).

Overall therefore we would suggest that group performance indicators are in most cases ambiguous in their interpretation, poor guides to action at an individual level and a dubious basis for league tables at an aggregated one. Used with understanding they may nevertheless raise useful questions, assisting an authority towards becoming a 'learning organisation' and thus enhancing its contribution to the welfare of looked after children.

More fundamentally, however, we suggest that attention is primarily focused not on movement but on two related issues:

1. How well the children are doing.
2. The quality of their placements.

These are the variables that in our view matter. Good care rests on good carers and should yield good outcomes. Unfortunately these variables are difficult to measure and even more difficult to inspect.

A further difficulty is that it is very hard to separate out the influence of the child from the influence of the council. A council that only took in 'easy' children should, in principle, find it easy to have high scores on any 'doing-well' measure. Clearly this is a problem for researchers as well. Researchers, however, use elaborate methods to try and sort out the influence of 'input'. These are unlikely to be possible in the rough and tumble world of indicators.

We believe that despite these difficulties such a system should be possible.

First, social workers are able to pick placements that are going well or badly. They are also able to rate the quality of these placements. They do this for research studies and their ratings predict the future. In principle therefore it is possible to construct a rating system that does tap these essentially 'soft' variables.

Second, judgements of the quality of placements do not appear to be heavily 'contaminated' by judgements of how well the child is doing. If this were so we would expect that residential placements would attract low quality ratings when they do not. It should therefore be possible to make a judgement on whether children are not doing well because of poor quality placements.

Third, a crucial difficulty in inspection is that inspectors do not have time to inspect anything more than a tiny fraction of the children who are, say, fostered by a particular council. This sampling cannot be a reliable guide to the quality of foster placements as a whole.

Our suggestion is that those inspecting councils should focus on the quality and reliability of the council's own system of quality assurance rather than on the quality of the workforce. So they should be concerned with the principles behind the system, the accuracy and completeness of the judgements that are made, and the use that is made of these judgements (for example, on whether the council continues to use placements that it has found to be poor). This method of inspection should focus the council's attention on what is important, while avoiding some of the difficulties arising from lack of time.

It is not suggested that it would be easy for councils to put such a system in place or for others to inspect. This is, however, something which should be possible and on which development work could be done.

## Notes

1    This is for the reason given before. A child may need to be placed with their siblings with a Bangladeshi family capable of dealing with their particular needs and within reasonable distance of their own family and their school. It is unreasonable to expect that such carers can be available 'on tap'. Some holding arrangement is therefore necessary. It is probably also true that some carers want children 'long-term' whereas others are well able to cope with the comings and goings of children but do not want a long-term emotional commitment. An insistence that all placements are expected to last long-term if necessary is therefore likely to result either in inappropriate placements or in the loss of some carers with much to give.

2    We adjusted the measure to allow for information from the social workers. If the analysis is restricted to the cases on which we had information from the social workers the correlation between the official A1 measure and our measure would be .68, thus accounting for less than 50 per cent of the variation.

3    For example, a practice of keeping children for long periods on care orders at home is not obviously good or bad in itself but will have a negative impact on the D35 indicator and a positive one on the new '30-month' indicator.

4    For example, we have noted that some young children stay for long periods in placements where they are not liked and are unhappy. We think they should move but this will have a bad effect on the movement indicators.

5    See Appendix II. The lack of correlations between indicators is evidence against the existence of a single dimension of 'organisational excellence' that the different indicators tap. The lack of strong correlations between the overall measure of 'organisational performance' and individual indicators suggests that no one performance indicator is a particularly strong indicator of organisational strength.

# References

Aldgate, J. and Bradley, M. (1999) *Supporting Families Through Short Term Fostering*. London: The Stationery Office.

Archer, L., Hicks, L. and Little, M. (1998) *Caring for Children Away from Home: Messages from Research*. Chichester: Wiley.

Baker, C. (2006) 'Disabled children's experience of permanency in the looked after system.' *British Journal of Social Work, 37*, 7, 1173–1188.

Berridge, D. and Brodie, I. (1998) *Children's Homes Revisited*. London: Jessica Kingsley Publishers.

Biehal, N. (2005) *Working with Adolescents: Supporting Families, Preventing Breakdown*. London: British Agencies for Adoption and Fostering.

Biehal, N. (2006) *Reuniting Looked After Children With Their Families. A Review of the Research*. London: National Children's Bureau/Joseph Rowntree Foundation.

Biehal, N., Clayden, J., Stein, M. and Wade, J. (1995) *Moving On: Young People and Leaving Care Schemes*. London: HMSO.

Bowlby, J. (1979) *The Making and Breaking of Affectional Bonds*. London: Tavistock.

Broad, B. (1998) *Young People Leaving Care: Life After the Children Act*. London: Jessica Kingsley Publishers.

Bullock, R., Little, M. and Milham, S. (1993) *Going Home: The Return of Children Separated from their Families*. London: Dartmouth.

Bullock, R., Good, D. and Little, M. (1998) *Children Going Home: the Reunification of Families*. Aldershot: Ashgate.

Chamberlain, P. (1998) *Family Connections: A Treatment Foster Care Model for Adolescents with Delinquency*. Eugene, Oregon: Castalia Publishing Company.

Clegg, S., Kornberger, M. and Pitsis, T. (2005) *Managing and Organisations: An Introduction to Theory and Practice*. London: Sage.

Colton, M. (1988) *Dimensions of Substitute Care: A Comparative Study of Foster and Residential Care Practice*. Aldershot: Avebury.

Commission for Social Care Inspection (2004) *Social Services Performance Assessment Framework Indicators 2003–2004*. London: CSCI.

Dando, I. and Minty, B. (1987) 'What makes good foster parents?' *British Journal of Social Work 17*, 388–400.

Department for Education and Skills (2001) 'Health Minister announces major review of fostering and placement services.' Press release. Available at www.dfes.gov.uk/qualityprotects/doc/190302.doc (accessed on 9 November 2007)

Department for Education and Skills (2003) *Every Child Matters*. (Cm 5860). London: The Stationery Office.

Department for Education and Skills (2006) *Care Matters: Transforming the Lives of Children and Young People in Care*. (Cm 6932). London: The Stationery Office.

Dixon, J. and Stein, M. (2005) *Leaving Care: Throughcare and Aftercare in Scotland*. London: Jessica Kingsley Publishers.

Farmer, E. and Parker, R. (1991) *Trials and Tribulations*. London: HMSO.

Farmer, E., Lipscombe, J. and Moyers, S. (2005) 'Foster carer strain and its impact on parenting and placement outcomes for adolescents.' *British Journal of Social Work 35*, 237–53.

Farmer E. and Moyers S. (forthcoming) *Kinship Care: Fostering Effective Family and Friends Placements*. London: Jessica Kingsley Publishers.

Farmer E., Sturgess W. and O'Neill T. (forthcoming) *The Reunification of Looked After Children with Their Parents: Patterns, Interventions and Outcomes*. Report to the Department for Education and Skills, School for Policy Studies, University of Bristol.

Gibbs, I. and Sinclair, I. (1998) 'Private and local authority children's homes: a comparison.' *Journal of Adolescence 21*, 517–27.

Gibbs, I. and Sinclair, I. (2000) 'Bullying, sexual harassment and happiness in residential children's homes.' *Child Abuse Review 9*, 247–56.

Glaser, B. and Strauss, A. (1967) *The Discovery of Grounded Theory: Strategies for Qualitative Research.* London: Weidenfeld and Nicholson.

Hensey, D., Williams, J. and Rosenbloom, L. (1983) 'Intervention in child abuse: Experience in Liverpool.' *Developmental Medicine and Child Neurology 25*, 606–11.

Hicks, L., Gibbs, I., Weatherly, H. and Byford, S. (2007) *Managing Children's Homes: Developing Effective Leadership in Small Organisations.* London: Jessica Kingsley Publishers.

Howe, D. (1997) *Patterns of Adoption.* London: Blackwell Science.

Hunt, J., Waterhouse, S. and Lutman, E. (2007) *Keeping Them in the Family: Outcomes for Abused and Neglected Children Placed With Family or Friends Carers Through Care Proceedings.* Draft report to the Department for Education and Skills. Department of Applied Social Studies, University of Oxford.

King, J. and Taitz, L. (1985) 'Catch-up growth following abuse.' *Archives of Disease in Childhood 60*, 1152–4.

Milham, S., Bullock, R., Hosie, K. and Haak, M. (1986) *Lost in Care.* Aldershot: Gower.

Office of the Children's Rights Director (OCRD) (2007) *Rights 4 Me.* London: Office of the Children's Rights Director.

Office of the Deputy Prime Minister (2005) *The English Indices of Deprivation 2004 – Summary (Revised).* Available at www.communities.gov.uk/documents/communities/pdf/131206 (accessed on 9 November 2007).

Packman, J. and Hall, C. (1998) *From Care to Accommodation: the Implementation of Section 20 of the Children Act 1989.* London: Stationery Office.

Packman, J., Randall, J. and Jacques, N. (1986) *Who Needs Care? Social Work Decisions About Children.* Oxford: Blackwell.

Paton, R. (2003) *Managing and Measuring Social Enterprises.* London: Sage.

Quinton, D., Rushton, A., Dance, C. and Mayes, D. (1998) *Joining New Families: A Study of Adoption and Fostering In Middle Childhood.* Chichester: Wiley.

Rowe, J., Hundleby, M. and Garnett, L. (1989) *Child Care Now: A Survey of Placement Patterns* (Research Series 6). London: British Agencies for Adoption and Fostering.

Rutter, M. (1995) 'Clinical implications of attachment concepts – retrospect and prospect.' *Journal of Clinical Psychology and Psychiatry 36*, 549–72.

Schofield, G. (2002) 'The significance of a secure base: a psychosocial model of long-term foster care'. *Child and Family Social Work 7*, 4, 259–72.

Schofield, G. (2003) *Part of the Family: Pathways Through Foster Care.* London: British Agencies for Adoption and Fostering.

Selwyn, J., Frazer, L. and Quinton, D. (2006) 'Paved with good intentions: The pathway to adoption and the costs of delay.' *British Journal of Social Work 36*, 4, 561–76.

Sinclair, I. (1971) *Hostels for Probationers.* London: HMSO.

Sinclair, I. (1975) 'The Influence of Wardens and Matrons on Probation Hostels: A Study of a Quasi Family Institution.' In J. Tizard, I. Sinclair and R. Clarke (eds) *Varieties of Residential Experience.* London: Routledge.

Sinclair, I. (2005) *Fostering Now: Messages from Research.* London: Jessica Kingsley Publishers.

Sinclair, I. (2006) 'Residential Care in the UK.' In C. McAuley, P. Pecora and W. Rose (eds) *Enhancing the Well-being of Children and Families Through Effective Interventions: International Evidence for Practice.* London: Jessica Kingsley Publishers.

Sinclair, I., Baker, C., Wilson, K. and Gibbs, I. (2005b) *Foster Children: Where They Go and How They Get On.* London: Jessica Kingsley Publishers.

Sinclair, I. and Gibbs, I. (1998) *Children's Homes: A Study in Diversity.* Chichester: Wiley.

Sinclair, I., Gibbs, I. and Wilson, K. (2004) *Foster Carers: Why They Stay and Why They Leave.* London: Jessica Kingsley Publishers.

Sinclair, I. and Wilson, K. (2003). 'Matches and mismatches: the contribution of carers and children to fostering success.' *British Journal of Social Work 33*, 871–84.

Sinclair, I., Wilson, K. and Gibbs, I. (2005a) *Foster Placements: Why They Succeed and Why They Fail.* London: Jessica Kingsley Publishers.

Smith P. (1995) 'On the unintended consequences of publishing performance data in the public sector.' *International Journal of Public Administration 18*, 2–3, 277–310.

Stein, M. (2004) *What Works for Young People Leaving Care?* Barkingside: Barnardo's.

Stein, M. and Carey, K. (1986) *Leaving Care.* Oxford: Blackwell.

Stein, M. and Wade, J. (2000) *Helping Care Leavers: Problems and Strategic Responses.* London: Department of Health.

Strathern, M. (2000) *Audit Cultures.* London: Routledge.

Taussig, H., Clyman, R. and Landsverk, J. (2001) 'Children who return home from foster care: a 6 year prospective study of behavioral health outcomes in adolescence.' *Pediatrics 108*, 1, p.e10.

Thoburn, J., Norford, L. and Rashid, S. (2000) *Permanent Family Placement for Children of Minority Ethnic Origin.* London: Jessica Kingsley Publishers.

Tizard, B. (1975) 'Varieties of Residential Nursery Experience.' In J. Tizard, I. Sinclair and R. Clarke (eds) *Varieties of Residential Experience.* London: Routledge.

Wade, J. and Dixon, J. (2006) 'Making a home, finding a job: investigating early housing and employment outcomes for young people leaving care.' *Child and Family Social Work 11*, 3, 199–208.

Wade, J., Mitchell, F. and Baylis, G. (2005) *Unaccompanied Asylum Seeking Children: The Response of Social Work Services.* London: British Agencies for Adoption and Fostering.

Walker, M., Hill, M. and Triseliotis, J. (2002) *Testing the Limits of Foster Care: Fostering as an Alternative to Secure Accommodation.* London: British Association for Adoption and Fostering.

Wilson, K., Sinclair, I., Taylor, C. and Pithouse, A. (2004) *Fostering Success: An Exploration of the Research Literature on Foster Care.* London: Social Care Institute of Excellence.

Zimmerman, R. (1982) 'Foster care in retrospect.' *Tulane Studies in Social Welfare 14*, 1–119.

# Subject Index

A1 ('three placements') measure
  analysis of national data  283–5, 290, 293, 297,
    301, 303
  carers, homes and outcomes  226
  children and outcomes  198–201, 205
  councils and outcomes  254–5, 257, 258
  monitoring and quality assurance  306
  overview  270, 273
  placements and outcomes  214, 215, 216
  study samples  279
abuse
  chance of permanence  71
  children based in care  181
  children's characteristics  37, 38, 39, 40
  children's families, wishes and behaviour  44–5, 47,
    52, 57–61
  different paths in care  104, 107, 111
  'doing-well' score  204
  going home and leaving care  121, 264
  how placements are used  141, 144, 145, 152, 272
abused adolescents  66–71, 76–7, 153, 172, 263
ADHD (attention deficit hyperactivity disorder)  51, 54,
  61, 62, 108
admissions
  decision  86–7
  length of stay  90–3
  overview  85–6, 99–102
adolescent entrants
  chance of permanence  66–71, 77–9, 82, 83
  definition  263
  placements  153, 172
adolescent graduates
  admissions and discharges  99, 101
  chance of permanence  66–71, 73–6, 82
  family difficulties  45
  placements  153, 172
  research study  263, 267, 269
adoption
  admissions and discharges  90, 94, 95, 96, 101
  analysis of national data  286–90, 293, 298, 301,
    302
  chance of permanence  71, 73
  children and outcomes  202
  children's characteristics  32, 35
  councils and outcomes  253
  different paths in care  108–9, 110, 112
  ethnicity  49
  how one placement leads to another  161, 175, 176,
    177
  how placements are used  136, 145, 152, 153, 154

monitoring and quality assurance  305
movements  15, 16, 261, 262
placement and outcomes  211
research study  264, 267–8, 275
teams and outcomes  241, 243–6, 248
African children  34
agency foster care  208, 253, 254
age of child
  admissions and discharges  89–90, 92, 93, 95, 96,
    99
  carers, homes and outcomes  224, 226–7
  chance of permanence  82
  children and outcomes  198, 199, 201, 202, 205
  children's characteristics  30–2, 33–5, 37–40
  children's families, wishes and behaviour  44–7,
    48–55, 57–60
  different paths in care  104, 108
  how one placement leads to another  168, 169
  how placements are used  136, 138–40, 144–5,
    147, 149, 151, 153
  placement and outcomes  215, 216, 219
  research study  264
  teams and outcomes  240ù1
asylum seekers
  admissions and discharges  92, 93
  carers, homes and outcomes  230, 231
  chance of permanence  66–71, 79–80, 83
  children's characteristics  34, 35–7, 39, 40
  children's families, wishes and behaviour  49–51,
    53, 56, 58, 60, 62
  councils and outcomes  253
  different paths in care  104, 107, 112
  how one placement leads to another  169, 171, 172,
    176, 178
  how placements are used  148, 149, 150, 153, 154
  research study  263, 267
authoritative parenting  222

babies  138, 159, 199
birth parents
  chance of permanence  76
  children based in care  186, 188, 189
  earlier research  22
  going home and leaving care  119, 120, 121, 124,
    130
  how placements are used  136, 152
  placement and outcomes  214, 271
black children
  children's characteristics  33, 34, 35, 36, 37

black children *cont.*
    children's families, wishes and behaviour  49, 50
    how one placement leads to another  175, 178
    how placements are used  147, 155
    research study  268, 269
British citizenship  80
bullying  230

CAMHS *see* Child and Adolescent Mental Health
    Service
care acceptance
    chance of permanence  68, 70
    children and outcomes  202
    children's families, wishes and behaviour  44, 54–8,
        59, 60, 61
    going home and leaving care  130
care careers
    admissions and discharges  91, 92
    chance of permanence  69
    children and outcomes  204, 205
    children's characteristics  32, 39
    policy background  15, 17
    teams and outcomes  246–7
*Care Matters*  17
care orders
    chance of permanence  72
    children based in care  187, 188
    children's characteristics  37–9
    children's families, wishes and behaviour  54, 61
    how one placement leads to another  177
    how placements are used  152, 155, 271
carers
    carers, homes and outcomes  221–3, 224–7, 232
    children based in care  187, 194
    councils and outcomes  252, 256, 257
    how placements are used  143
    leaving care  128, 130
    research study  266, 275, 307
    teams and outcomes  248
Care Standards Act (2004)  27
care system
    admissions and discharges  85–102
        admission  86–7
        destination on discharge  93–9
        leaving care curve  88–90
        length of stay  90–3
        overview  85–6
    children based in care  181–96
        care as a strong base  182–4
        care as a weak base  184–6
        family and friends care  186–9
        no place to be  189–93
        notes  196
        overview  181–2, 193–5
    councils and outcomes  58–9, 252
    earlier research  15–16, 18–23
    outcomes of care  11, 12
    research study  23–4, 261ù76
    *see also* placements
caseloads  239, 244, 246, 248

case studies
    chance of permanence  72–7, 78–81
    children based in care  183, 185–8, 189–93
    going home and leaving care  115–19, 121, 123–8
challenging behaviour
    carers, homes and outcomes  231
    chance of permanence  68, 69
    children and outcomes  199–203, 205
    children based in care  194
    children's families, wishes and behaviour  44–6,
        48–51, 53, 56, 60, 62
    different paths in care  107
    going home and leaving care  120, 129, 130
    how one placement leads to another  169, 170, 178
    how placements are used  140, 147
    research study  264, 268, 269
Child and Adolescent Mental Health Service (CAMHS)
    242, 243, 244
child protection register  117
children
    admissions and discharges  85–102
        admission  86–7
        destination on discharge  93–9
        leaving care curve  88–90
        length of stay  90–3
        overview  85–6, 99–102
    chance of permanence  65–84
        abused adolescents  76–7
        adolescent entrants  77–9
        adolescent graduates  73–6
        asylum seekers  79–80
        disabled children  81–2
        method  66
        overview  65, 82–4
        statistical differences  68–71
        trial typology  66–7
        young entrants  71–3
    children based in care  181–96
        care as a strong base  182–4
        care as a weak base  184–6
        family and friends care  186–9
        no place to be  189–93
        notes  196
        overview  181–2, 193–5
    children's characteristics  29–41
        age and age at entry  30–2
        asylum seekers  35–7
        care orders  37–9
        method  29–30
        need codes  37
        notes  40–1
        overview  29, 39–40
        sex and ethnicity  32–5
    children's families, wishes and behaviour  43–63
        age  44–7
        asylum seekers  50–1
        care acceptance  54–8
        differences between councils  58–9
        disabled children  51–4
        ethnicity  49–50
        method  44

need codes 47–8
notes 62–3
overview 43–4, 59–62
sex 49
different paths in care 103–13
outcomes of care 197–206
'doing-well' score 203–4
method 197–8
notes 205–6
overview 197, 205
stability 198–203
Children Act (1989) 21
Children Act (2004) 27
Children and Families teams 235, 236
Children (Leaving Care) Act (2000) 27
children's homes
carers, homes and outcomes 228
children based in care 189, 191, 192
councils and outcomes 252
how one placement leads to another 167
how placements are used 136, 149, 154
placements and outcomes 208, 211, 213
Children's Rights Director 21
*Choice Protects* 17, 27
councils
analysis of national data 292–3, 295, 296–9, 300, 303
carers, homes and outcomes 222, 228–9
chance of permanence 67
children and outcomes 205
children based in care 192
children's families, wishes and behaviour 58–9, 62
councils and outcomes 251–9
different paths in care 103, 105, 107, 109, 110, 112
how placements are used 141, 143, 145–9, 150–1, 154–5
leaving care 131
monitoring and quality assurance 305, 306, 307, 308
placements and outcomes 208, 210, 218
research study 262, 264, 267, 272–5
study samples 277–9
teams and outcomes 235, 236, 242, 244, 245, 248
crime 230
culture 184

D35 ('long-term stability') indicator
analysis of national data 283, 287, 290, 298–9, 301–3
children and outcomes 198, 201–2, 205, 256, 257–8
councils and outcomes 273
how one placement leads to another 172, 173, 174
measuring success 270
monitoring and quality assurance 307
placements and outcomes 208, 214, 215
study samples 279, 281
teams and outcomes 247
Department for Education and Skills (DfES) 21, 30, 172

Department of Health 21, 33
disabled children
carers, homes and outcomes 230
chance of permanence 66–71, 81–2, 83
children's families, wishes and behaviour 51–4, 60–1, 62
different paths in care 104, 107, 108, 111, 112, 113
how one placement leads to another 172, 178
how placements are used 140, 145, 147, 149, 150, 152–5
research study 263, 264, 265, 266, 268
teams and outcomes 236, 245
discharges
destinations on discharge 93–9
leaving care curve 88–90
overview 85, 101
'doing-well' score
carers, homes and outcomes 225, 226, 227, 231
children and outcomes 203–4
councils and outcomes 256–7, 258
placements and outcomes 208, 217–18
research study 270, 272, 307
teams and outcomes 247
domestic violence 44, 45, 60, 107, 204, 264

early care leavers 110, 111, 112
education
analysis of national data 288–90, 292, 298–9
carers, homes and outcomes 230
children based in care 191, 195
councils and outcomes 253
how placements are used 148, 151, 274
emergency placements 138, 176, 241, 247
employment 289, 290, 299
ethnicity
chance of permanence 80
children based in care 184
children's characteristics 33–5, 36, 37, 41
children's families, wishes and behaviour 49–50
placements 151, 171
*Every Child Matters* 17

family difficulties
chance of permanence 68
children and outcomes 204
children's families, wishes and behaviour 44–7, 49
different paths in care 104, 107
leaving care 130
field resources 243, 244, 246, 248
foster care
admissions and discharges 101
analysis of national data 286, 287, 290, 301
carers, homes and outcomes 221–3, 224–7, 232
chance of permanence 83
children and outcomes 201, 202
children based in care 182, 183, 188, 190, 192, 195
councils and outcomes 252, 256, 257, 258
earlier research 21, 22

foster care *cont.*
   going home and leaving care 121, 125, 127, 130
   monitoring and quality assurance 306, 307
   policy background 17
   research study 262, 263, 266, 268, 271–2, 275
   teams and outcomes 244
   *see also* placements
fostering quality score 222–7
friends care 186–9, 271, 272

gender 32, 37, 49, 53
government 274–5

homes *see* children's homes; residential care
hostels 27, 80, 132, 149, 171, 230

independent living 94, 99, 101, 126, 129, 153
independent placements
   councils and outcomes 252
   how placements are used 145–7, 151, 154, 155, 178
   placements and outcomes 211, 214, 271

kin care *see* relatives care

learning difficulties 51, 54, 62, 81, 127, 183
leaving care 115–32
   admissions and discharges 88–90, 94, 96–9, 101
   brief care leading to permanent admission 119–22
   brief care leading to return home 116–19
   care as a launch pad 126–9
   different paths in care 106–7, 110–11
   earlier research 21
   leaving care curve 101
   method 115–16
   overview 129–31
   repeated care or late returns 122–6
   teams and outcomes 236
   treatment foster care 266
length of placement
   admissions and discharges 90–3
   carers, homes and outcomes 225, 229–32
   chance of permanence 69–72, 74, 77, 79, 80, 82
   how one placement leads to another 160–2, 163–5
   how placements are used 136–8, 152, 153
lodgings 76, 78, 171, 177, 189
London councils 146, 147, 151, 154, 237

minority ethnic groups
   children's characteristics 34
   children's families, wishes and behaviour 49, 50
   how one placement leads to another 175, 178
   how placements are used 147, 155
   research study 268, 269
monitoring 305–8
movement of children in care
   carers, homes and outcomes 232
   children and outcomes 198, 199, 201, 205

   children based in care 192
   children's characteristics 30, 40
   earlier research 19, 20
   how one placement leads to another 165–6, 176, 177–8
   placements and outcomes 214, 216, 219
   research study 261, 268–9, 270, 273, 297, 305
   teams and outcomes 239, 240, 248

need codes
   children and outcomes 198
   children's characteristics 37, 38, 39, 41
   children's families, wishes and behaviour 47–8, 52, 53
   different paths in care 104, 108, 111
   how one placement leads to another 168
   how placements are used 140, 141, 144, 145, 147
neglect
   chance of permanence 71, 74
   children's characteristics 37, 38, 39, 40
   children's families, wishes and behaviour 43, 47, 52, 59, 60, 61
   research study 264
New Public Management 19

OFSTED (Office for Standards in Education, Children's Services and Skills) 18
outcomes of care
   carers, homes and outcomes 221–34
      fostering quality score 221–3
      length of placement 229–32
      multi-level model of foster care 224–7
      overview 221, 232–3
      residential units 227–9
   children and outcomes 197–206
      'doing-well' score 203–4
      method 197–8
      notes 205–6
      overview 197, 205
      stability 198–203
   councils and outcomes 251–9
   placements and outcomes 207–20
      doing-well measures 217–18
      overview 207, 218–19
      placement quality 210–14
      stability outcome measures 214–16
      type of placement 207–10
   research study 16, 271–3, 307
   teams and outcomes 235–49
      care careers 246–7
      caseloads 239
      councils 242
      'doing-well' measures 247
      kinds of team 235–6
      overview 235, 248
      placement choice 244–6
      resources and work pressure 242–4
      resources available 239–42
      social workers 237–8
      stability 247

out of county placements
    children based in care  192
    how one placement leads to another  176, 178
    how placements are used  151, 154, 155
    placements and outcomes  213, 214, 218
    research study  268, 272

parents (placement with)
    children based in care  188
    how placements are used  136, 152, 153, 154
    placements and outcomes  208, 211
    research study  271, 272
    teams and outcomes  244
Performance Assessment Framework (PAF)  172, 293,
    294–5, 296
performance indicators
    analysis of national data  283–4, 285–90, 291–6,
        302–3
    contribution of research  19–20
    councils and outcomes  251
    monitoring and quality assurance  305–6, 307
    research study  274
placement panels  252–3, 273
placements
    admissions and discharges  85–6, 87
    carers, homes and outcomes  222–7, 232
    chance of permanence  69, 71, 73
    children and outcomes  198–201, 204, 205
    children based in care  184–7, 190, 192, 194, 195
    councils and outcomes  252–3, 254–5
    earlier research  19, 20–1, 22
    going home and leaving care  120, 121
    how one placement leads to another  159–79
        average placement length  163–5
        length and purpose  160–2
        notes  178–9
        overview  159–60, 175–8
        placement success and policy groups  172
        placement success and stability  172–5
        successful sequence of placements  165–8
        variables associated with placement success
            168–72
    how placements are used  133–57
        children placed with their parents  152
        duration and frequency  136–9
        foster care  140–3
        foster care in independent sector  145–7
        method  133–5
        overview  133, 153–5
        placements outside the council  150–1
        policy groups  152–3
        relative foster care  143–5
        residential care  148–50
    monitoring and quality assurance  305, 307, 308
    movement of children in care  15, 16, 261, 262
    placements and outcomes  207–20
        'doing-well' measures  217–18
        overview  207, 218–19
        placement quality  210–14
        stability  214–16
        type of placement  207–10

policy background  17
    research study  268–9, 271–2, 273–4
    teams and outcomes  244–6
placement success
    carers, homes and outcomes  227
    how one placement leads to another  166–8,
        169–71, 172–5
    measuring success  270
    placements and outcomes  208, 209, 210
policy  17–18, 252, 253, 273
policy groups  66–71, 152–3, 172
prison  154
probation hostels  27, 132
PSA (Public Service Agreement) target indicator
    analysis of national data  288, 290, 297, 301, 303
    children and outcomes  198, 202–3, 205
    councils and outcomes  255–6, 257, 258
    how one placement leads to another  172
    placements and outcomes  208, 214
    research study  270, 273
    study samples  281
    teams and outcomes  247

quality assurance  274, 275, 305–8
quality of care  214–18, 227–32, 272, 273–4
*Quality Protects*  17, 18, 27, 274, 275, 305

relatives care
    carers, homes and outcomes  226, 232
    children based in care  186–9, 194
    children's families, wishes and behaviour  43–63
    how placements are used  143–5, 154
    placements and outcomes  209–11, 213, 214, 218
    research study  271, 272
    teams and outcomes  244, 245, 246
religion  184
remand care  140, 141, 155, 231
repeat admissions
    chance of permanence  69
    children and outcomes  201, 202, 203
    councils and outcomes  253
    different paths in care  104–6, 107–10, 112, 113
    going home and leaving care  122
    how placements are used  168
    research study  264, 265
    teams and outcomes  246
research study
    analysis of national data  283–303
        method  284–5
        overview  283–4, 302–3
        performance indicators  285–90
        relationship of scores  290–6
        social and other factors  300–1
        stability and councils  296–9
    monitoring and quality assurance  305–8
    overview  18–26, 261–76
    study samples  277–82
residence orders  96
residential care
    carers, homes and outcomes  227–9, 230
    chance of permanence  71, 77, 80–3

residential care *cont.*
   children based in care 190–2
   councils and outcomes 252
   earlier research 21, 22
   how one placement leads to another 175, 178
   how placements are used 135, 136, 138, 139,
      148–50, 153–5
   monitoring and quality assurance 307
   placements and outcomes 208, 218, 219
   research study 265–6, 268, 271–3, 275
   teams and outcomes 244, 246
residential schools 136, 149, 150, 154, 211, 230
resources
   councils and outcomes 252, 253
   teams and outcomes 239–44, 246, 248
respite care 81
return home 115–32
   admissions and discharges 86–8, 94, 95, 99, 101
   brief care leading to permanent admission 119–22
   brief care leading to return home 116–19
   care as a launch pad 126–9
   chance of permanence 69, 72, 83
   children based in care 190
   children's families, wishes and behaviour 58
   different paths in care 106–7, 109–11
   earlier research 21
   how one placement leads to another 176, 177
   how placements are used 152, 154
   method 115–16
   overview 129–31
   repeated care or late returns 122–6
   research study 264–6, 272–3
   teams and outcomes 245, 248

school performance
   analysis of national data 301
   carers, homes and outcomes 231, 232
   children and outcomes 201, 202, 203, 205
   children's families, wishes and behaviour 44,
      46–51, 53, 56, 60–2
   leaving care 129
school support
   children based in care 184, 195
   how placements are used 151
   research study 265, 269
   teams and outcomes 242, 243, 247, 248
secure accommodation 151, 167, 191, 209
sex 32, 34, 37, 49, 53
shared care 124–5, 130, 265–6
siblings
   children based in care 184, 187, 194
   different paths in care 105, 108
   going home and leaving care 117, 118, 119
   how one placement leads to another 175, 179
   research study 265, 269
Smith, Jacqui 17
social conditions 296–9, 300, 301, 302
social workers
   chance of permanence 75, 78
   children based in care 192–3
   councils and outcomes 252, 253

   research study 265
   teams and outcomes 237–8, 239, 243, 244
stability
   analysis of national data 290, 291, 292, 296–9
   carers, homes and outcomes 226, 232
   children and outcomes 198–203, 258
   monitoring and quality assurance 305
   placements and outcomes 214–16, 270
   teams and outcomes 247, 248
substance abuse
   children and outcomes 204
   children's families, wishes and behaviour 44, 45, 60
   different paths in care 107
   going home and leaving care 117, 118, 119, 264
survival curve 89

teams and outcomes 235–49
   care careers 246–7
   caseloads 239
   councils 242, 273
   'doing-well' measures 247
   kinds of team 235–6
   overview 235, 248
   placement choice 244–6
   resources and work pressure 242–4
   resources available 239–42
   social workers 237–8
   stability 247
training 289, 290, 293, 299
treatment foster care
   children based in care 194
   how one placement leads to another 161, 167, 176
   how placements are used 140, 141, 154, 155
   role for 266–7

vacancy rates (social workers) 237, 238, 244
voluntary accommodation
   children's characteristics 37, 38, 39
   children's families, wishes and behaviour 55
   how one placement leads to another 169, 170, 171,
      176, 178

white children
   children's characteristics 33, 34, 35, 36, 37
   children's families, wishes and behaviour 49
   different paths in care 108
   how placements are used 147
work pressure score 242, 243, 244, 245

young entrants
   admissions and discharges 101
   chance of permanence 66–70, 71–3, 82
   different paths in care 112
   how one placement leads to another 172
   how placements are used 152, 153
   research study 262, 263, 267
young offender institutions 136, 149, 189, 190

# Author Index

Archer, L. 21, 219

Baker, C. 21, 22, 27, 52, 108, 130, 154, 219, 267, 276
Baylis, G. 267
Berridge, D. 21, 219
Biehal, N. 21, 265, 267, 270
Bowlby, J. 275
Broad, B. 267
Brodie, I. 21, 219
Bullock, R. 21
Byford, S. 21, 22, 27, 211, 219, 228, 230, 234

Carey, K. 21
Chamberlain, P. 276
Clayden, J. 21, 267
Clegg, S. 22
Clyman, R. 22
Colton, M. 22
Commission for Social Care Inspection 278, 303

Dance, C. 21
Dando, I. 22
Department for Education and Skills (DfES) 17
Dixon, J. 21, 267

Farmer, E. 21, 27, 186, 219, 265, 271
Frazer, L. 95, 108, 276

Garnett, L. 20, 21, 22, 71, 88, 101, 133, 136, 154, 166, 179, 276
Gibbs, I. 21, 22, 27, 130, 186, 189, 211, 219, 228, 230, 233, 234, 267, 276
Glaser, B. 132
Good, D. 21

Haak, M. 21
Hall, C. 21
Hensey, D. 22
Hicks, L. 21, 22, 27, 211, 219, 228, 230, 234
Hill, M. 157, 195
Hosie, K. 21
Howe, D. 276
Hundleby, M. 20, 21, 22, 71, 88, 101, 133, 136, 154, 166, 179, 276
Hunt, J. 27, 186, 271

Jacques, N. 21

King, J. 22
Kornberger, M. 22

Landsverk, J. 22
Lipscombe, J. 21, 186, 219
Little, M. 21, 219
Lutman, E. 186, 271

Mayes, D. 21
Milham, S. 21
Minty, B. 22
Mitchell, F. 267
Moyers, S. 21, 186, 219, 271

Office of the ChildrenÆs Rights Director (OCRD) 21
Office of the Deputy Prime Minister 284
OÆNeill, T. 265

Packman, J. 21
Parker, R. 21
Paton, R. 19
Pitsis, T. 22

Quinton, D. 21, 95, 108, 276

Randall, J. 21
Rosenbloom, L. 22
Rowe, J. 20, 21, 22, 71, 88, 101, 133, 136, 154, 166, 179, 276
Rushton, A. 21

Schofield, G. 269
Selwyn, J. 95, 108, 276
Sinclair, I. 19, 21, 22, 27, 61, 130, 132, 154, 177, 186, 189, 207, 211, 214, 219, 222, 228, 230, 231, 233, 234, 267, 268, 271, 276
Smith, P. 19
Stein, M. 21, 267, 270
Strathern, M. 19
Strauss, A. 132
Sturgess, W. 265

Taitz, L. 22
Taussig, H. 22
Tizard, B. 22
Triseliotis, J. 157, 195

Wade, J. 21, 267, 270
Walker, M. 157, 195
Waterhouse, S. 186, 271
Weatherly, H. 21, 22, 27, 211, 219, 228, 230, 234
Williams, J. 22
Wilson, K. 21, 22, 27, 61, 130, 186, 189, 219, 233,
    267, 276

Zimmerman, R. 22